VICTOR RODRIGUEZ

I0483164

The year was 1994, there was a new gallery in a mall over Presidente Masaryk Avenue in Polanco (Mexico City's closest thing to Fifth Avenue) and Victor Rodriguez was having an opening. Showing off an obstinate photorealistic virtuosity punctuated by dazzling strokes of light and color that added dissonance to the brushstroke lyricism, he displayed outrageous still lives full of wit: sliced up tomatoes, an egg's yolk and white clinging to a hand (with a balloon attached in which it can be read: *Te voy a amar toda la vida*), a doughnut extravagantly glazed, cut by a dotted line. I still remember how Rodriguez fancied handmade catalogs of his work with photo prints, black cardboard and glitter, marker descriptions, photos of faces and objects presenting a daring redundancy, a flashy provocation that hinted at the actual nature and meaning of the paintings, at the idea and purpose of painting (as a craft and as an object), offered as an overall review of art history and its ever-changing place in our lives. In his colorful renditions of exaggerated glamour, Victor Rodriguez exists in the gap between life and style; these paintings illuminate the collusion between perception, context and education that have produced the visual delusion we inhabit.

A rather unconventional and enormous format portrait of his wife and muse Maité, titled *Gran Cabeza*, won him a prize in Arte Joven ten years ago. And as always, there is humor in Victor Rodriguez's work. The fly over Maité's cheek is, according to him, a last minute thing, a what-if that puts everything in place (the old masters have always been there) but also, a reflection on the actual event of a fly, not over the model's face but over the painting that gives us a second nature, a comment upon the object, a story foretold. Victor says he can't help it, but his excuse is, again, a reference (a dark homage) to surrealists.

The intimacies, postures and disguises of Maité as portrayed by Victor Rodriguez give us a trail of a personal story, a process of sense and sensibility that invents her beyond herself, that opens a narrative through the series of paintings.

Maité, as an image, becomes a glorification, a myth. Victor Rodriguez's last series with her as a model exposes us to a pure and exhausted portrait, graced with a nakedness that goes beyond the violent glamour he gave us a few years before, with the series of Maité sitting at the toilet, smoking a cigarette, disdainful, magically unaware of all the attention.

There have been other models, casual shots among his friends that gives them a pictorial transcendence in terms that are close to the standards of reality television. Celebrity comes in a context of exploitation in Victor's work and its narrative. Victor Rodriguez feeds upon mass media conventions to offer us the evolution of a very private reading and understanding of postmodern life. A cocktail of referential layers that include Prozac and Nouvelle Vogue (in his *Cinema Notebooks 2* we can see them both) a catalog of sentimental archeology (as in postmodern cinema). Victor Rodriguez builds his stories upon the story of painting itself as a trap that both renders and denies the sensual world.

Victor Rodriguez has found beauty in our postmodern decadence. As overwhelming and multi-referential as a *The Simpsons* episode or a Jan Vermeer, Victor Rodriguez suggests new perspectives. He dresses up art tradition as a transvestite. In the paintings that won him the Rufino Tamayo Biennale prize—big luminous portraits of himself and Maité, surrounded by meaningful paraphernalia—he presents a very smart vulgarization of symbols equivalent to those of a Jan van Eyck painting, but simultaneously equivalent to the description of the painting given through an art class broadcast through non commercial television. Michelangelo, a quatroccento's common place in a conventional understanding of western art and culture, becomes a multireferential figure that goes beyond his life and work and into pop culture. The Sistine Chapel, for example, becomes a Hollywood feature with Charlton Heston as well as an animaniacs animated short, evidence of the desacralization of our cultural standards (like kissing a Picasso). All of this can be experienced, as a process, as a document, as an object, as art, in a Victor Rodriguez (and without a video support).

There is a portrait of Maité and their child, Micaela, glancing at a drawing of Micaela pinned up on the wall—a Madonna staring at the mystery of representation. Is the miracle in the glance?

Ricardo Pohlenz
Mexico City, May 2004

This is the second edition of this book, done in a slightly different format.

In this volume are included paintings that I made in the 10 year period between 1995 and 2005, when I was 25 to 35 years old . They are arranged in chronological order, so a certain evolutive narrative can be seen. The works are grouped in series; an informal catalogue/map is included at the end of the book.

In those first 10 years of the beginning of my career many things happened, most important moving to New York from Mexico City and the birth of my daughter Micaela, to whom this book is dedicated with all my love.

I'd like to thank Jorge Pinto for believing in this project, Ramis Barquet for his unconditional support and friendship, and all my friends and people involved in the production of these works in any way.

Victor Rodriguez
Brooklyn, NY November 2006

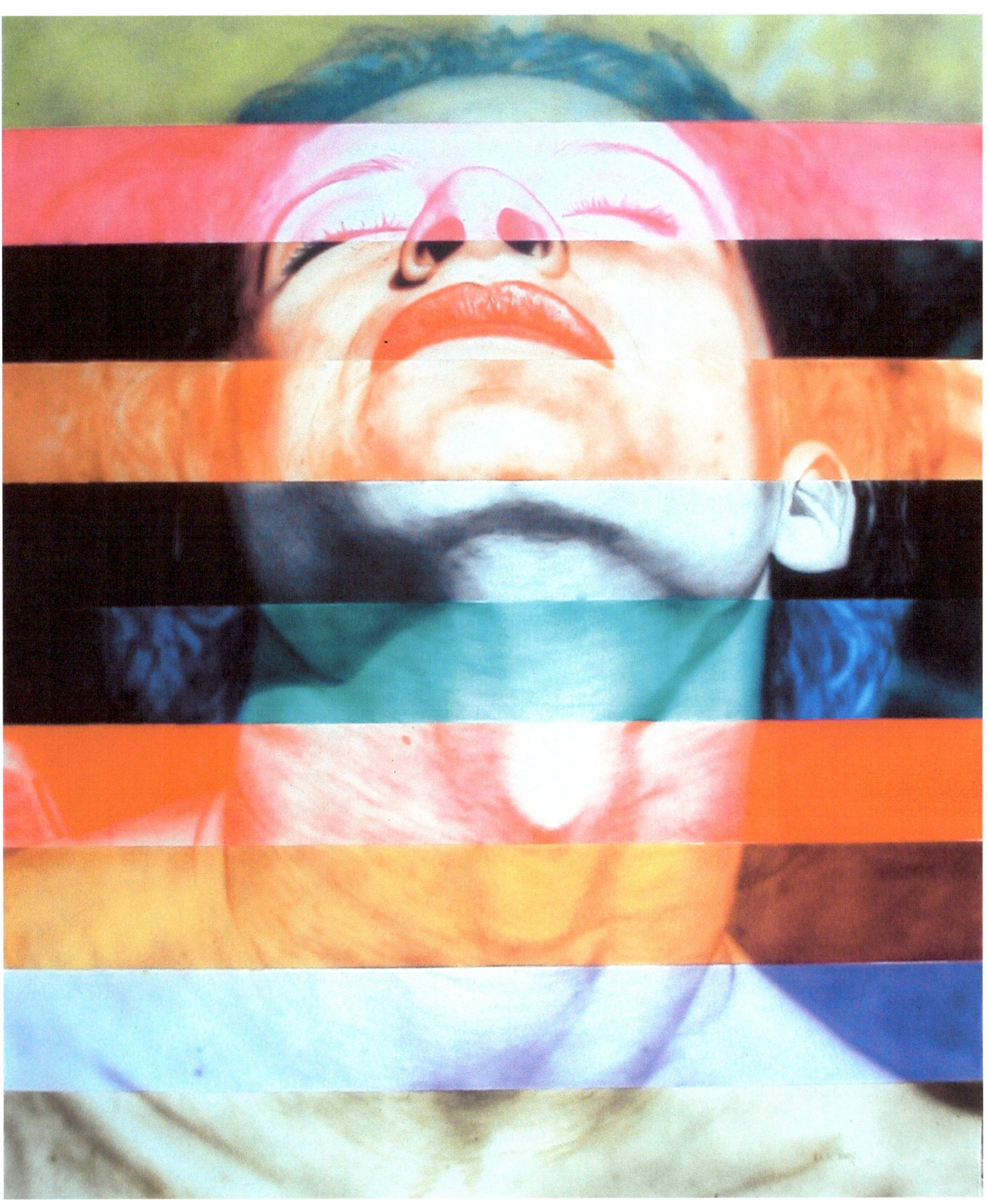

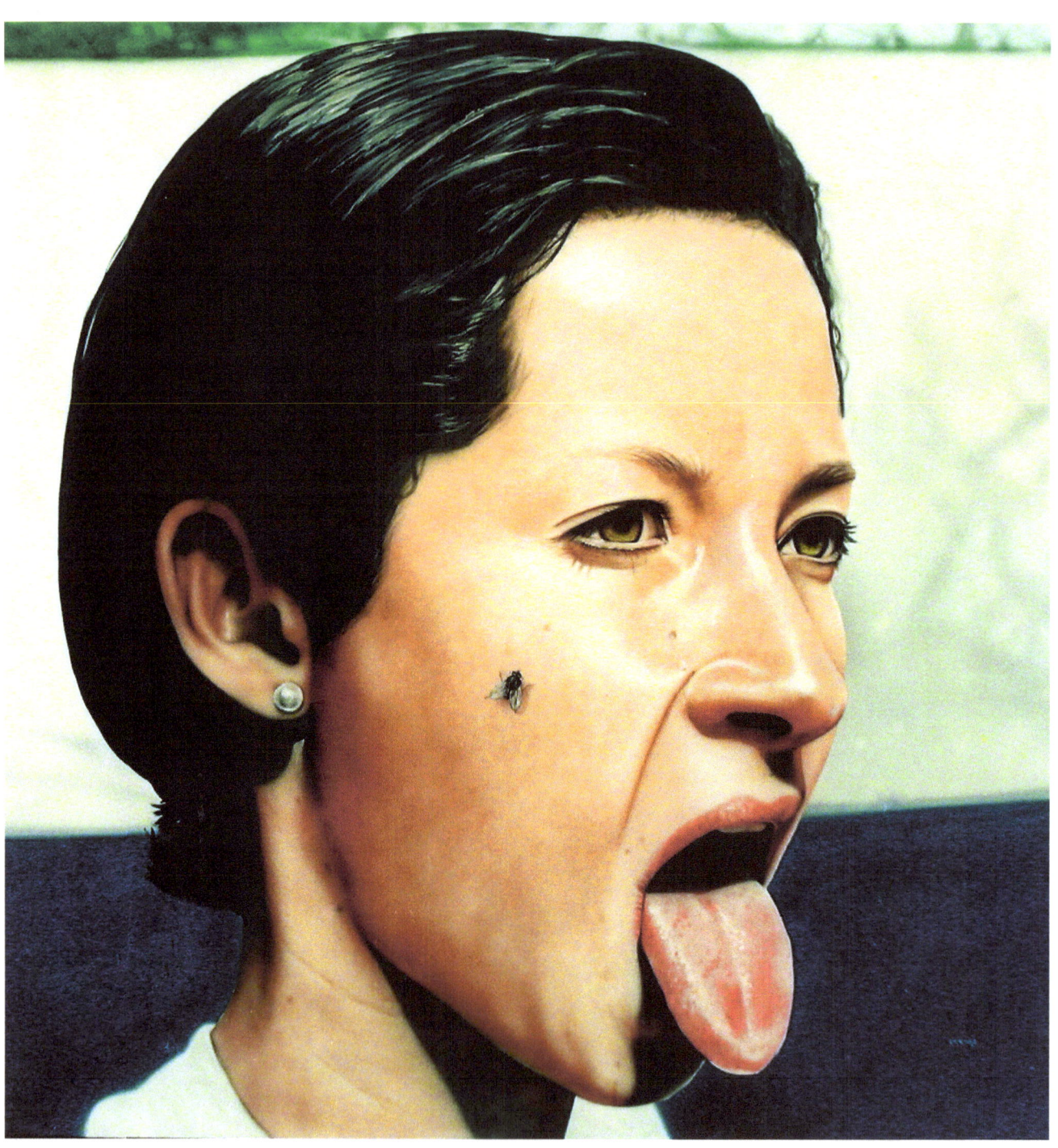

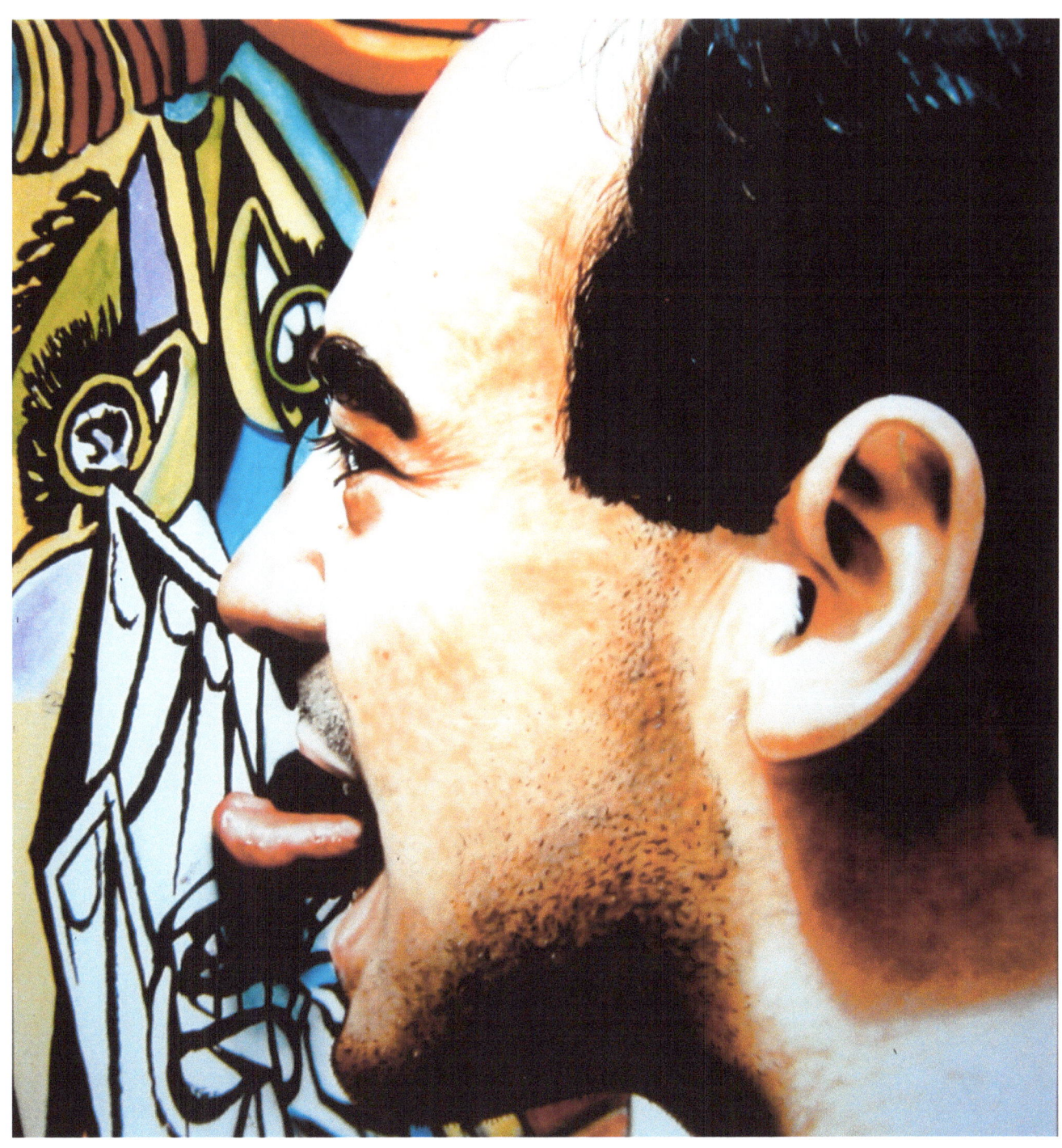

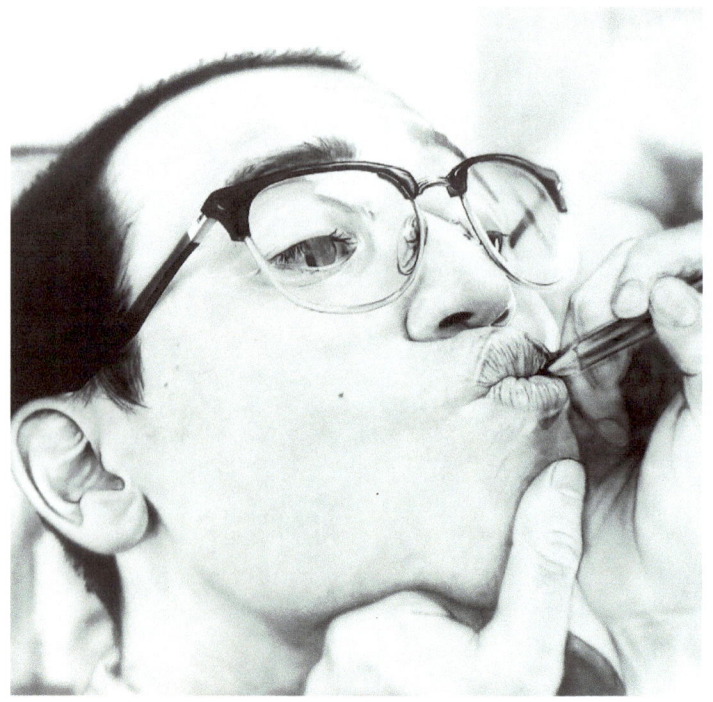

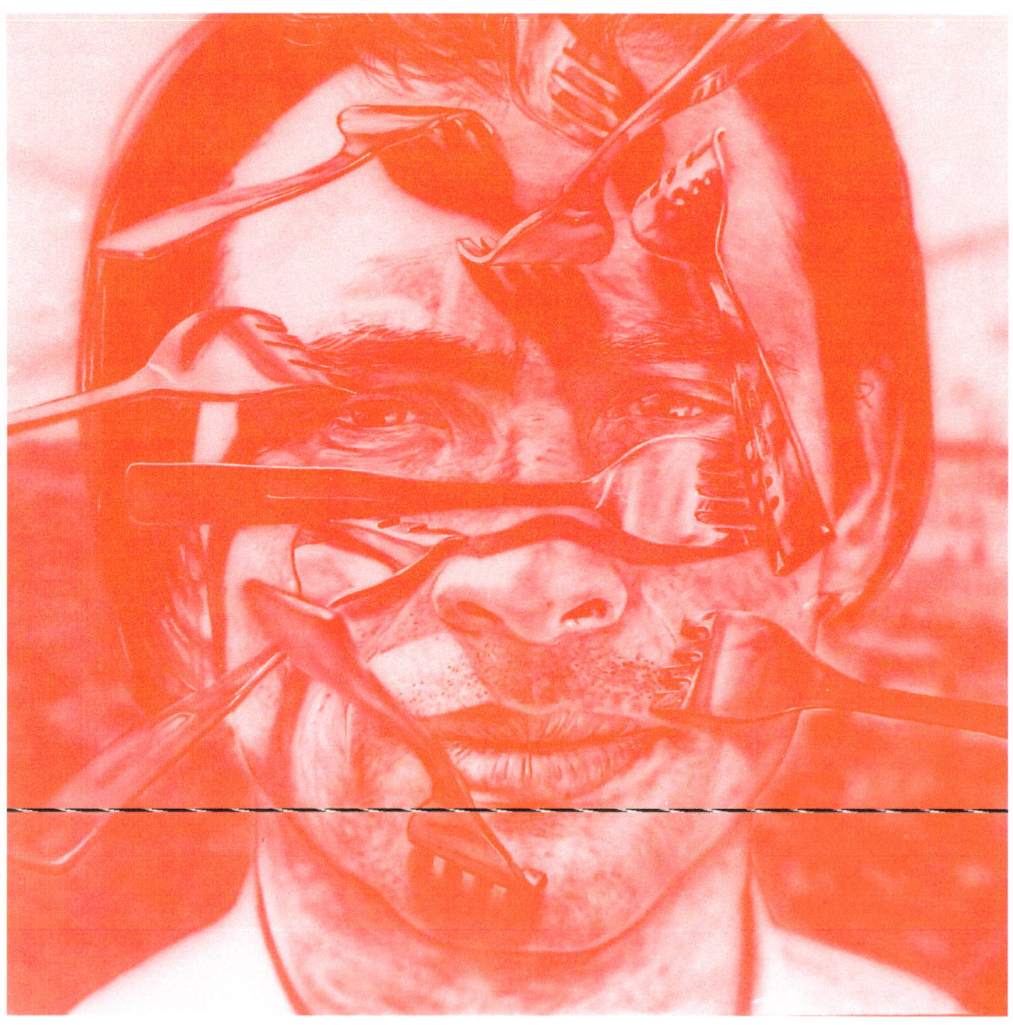

^ LIPS 150 X 150 CMS 1995   > RECORD 150 X 200 CMS 1995

^ FORKS 150 X 150 CMS 1995

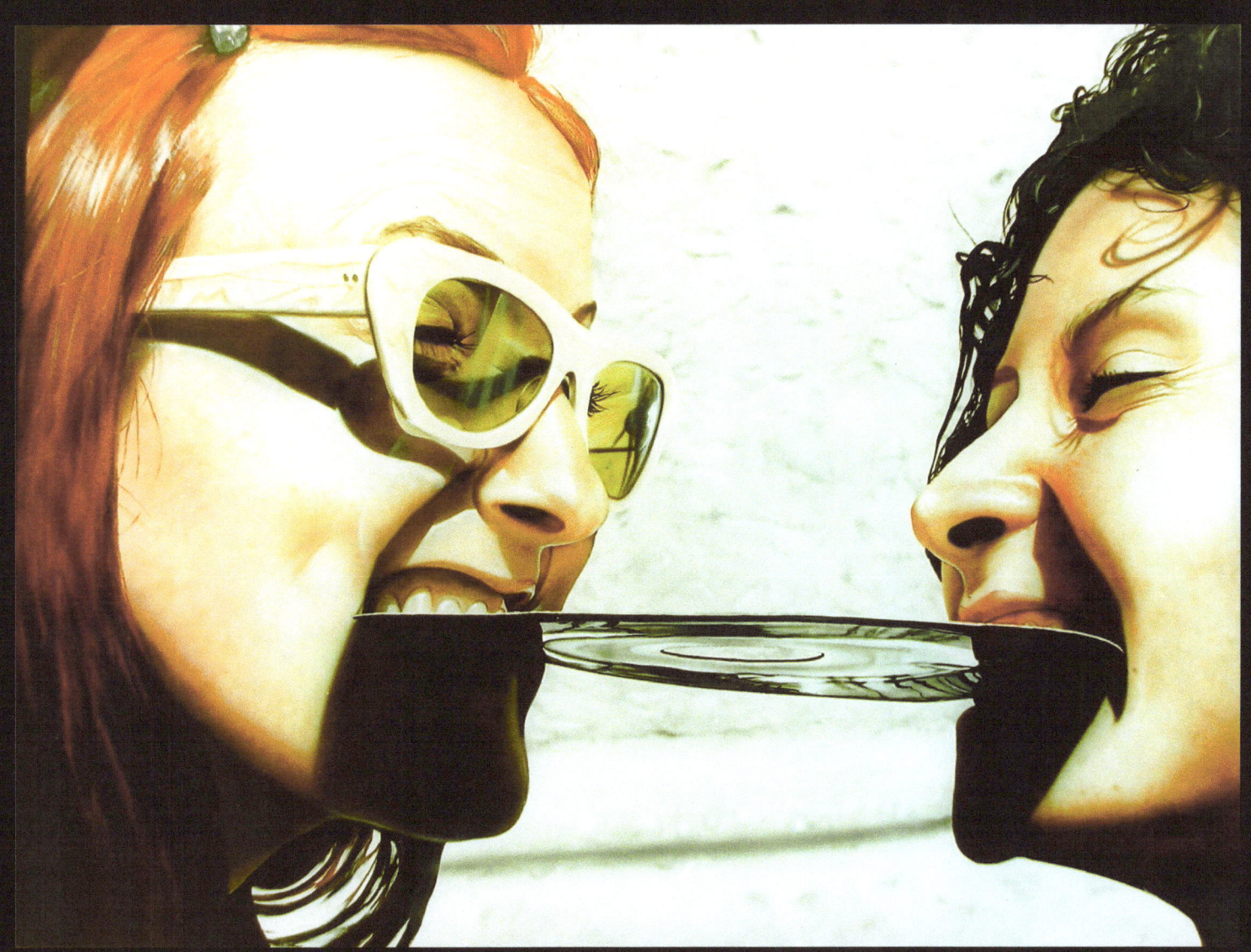

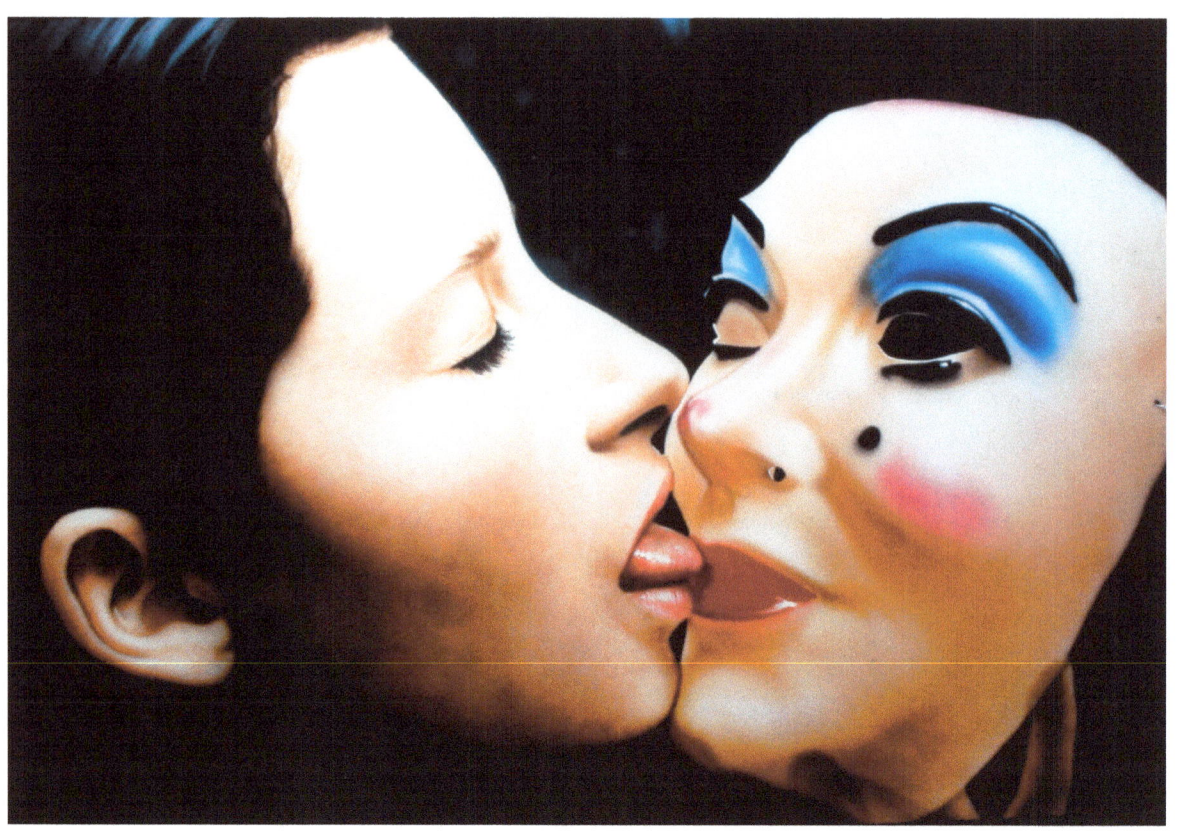

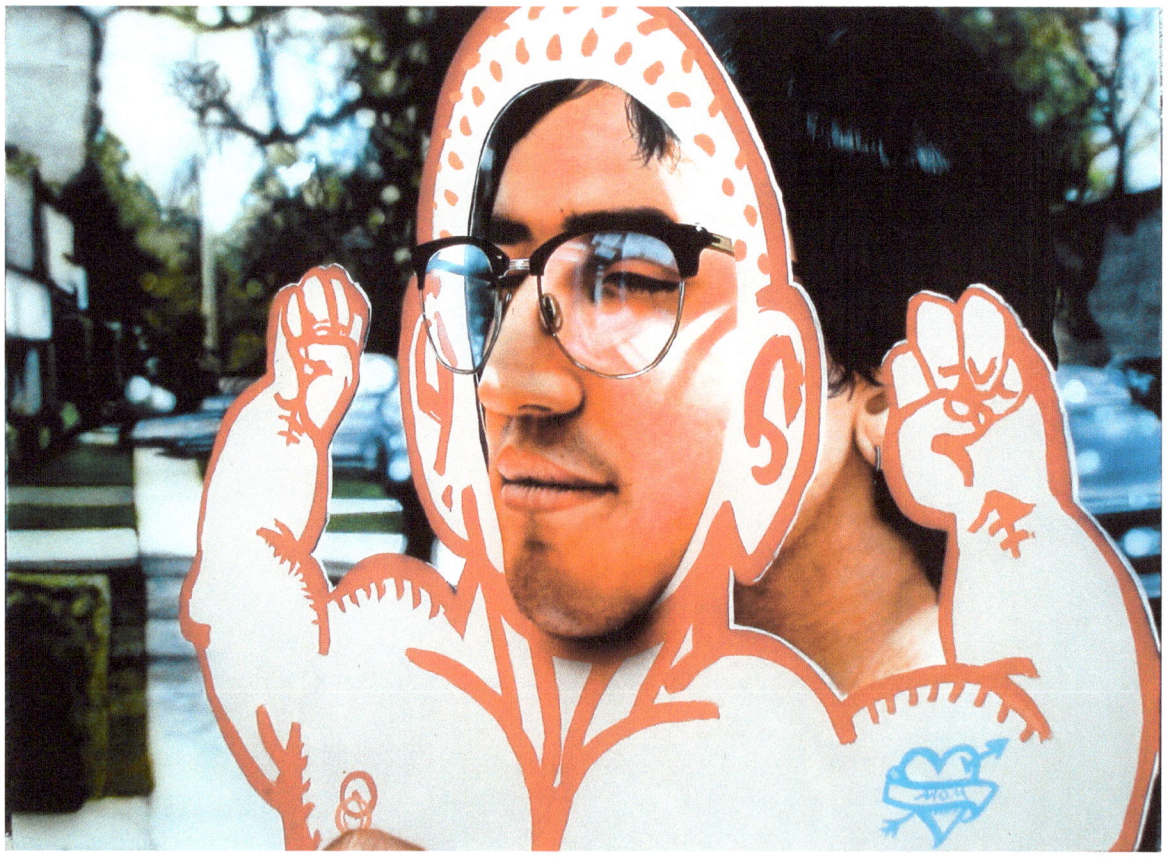

^ FRENCH KISS 150 X 200 CMS 1996   ^ STRONG MAN 150 X 200 CMS 1996

> HOLANDA 150 X 150 CMS 1996

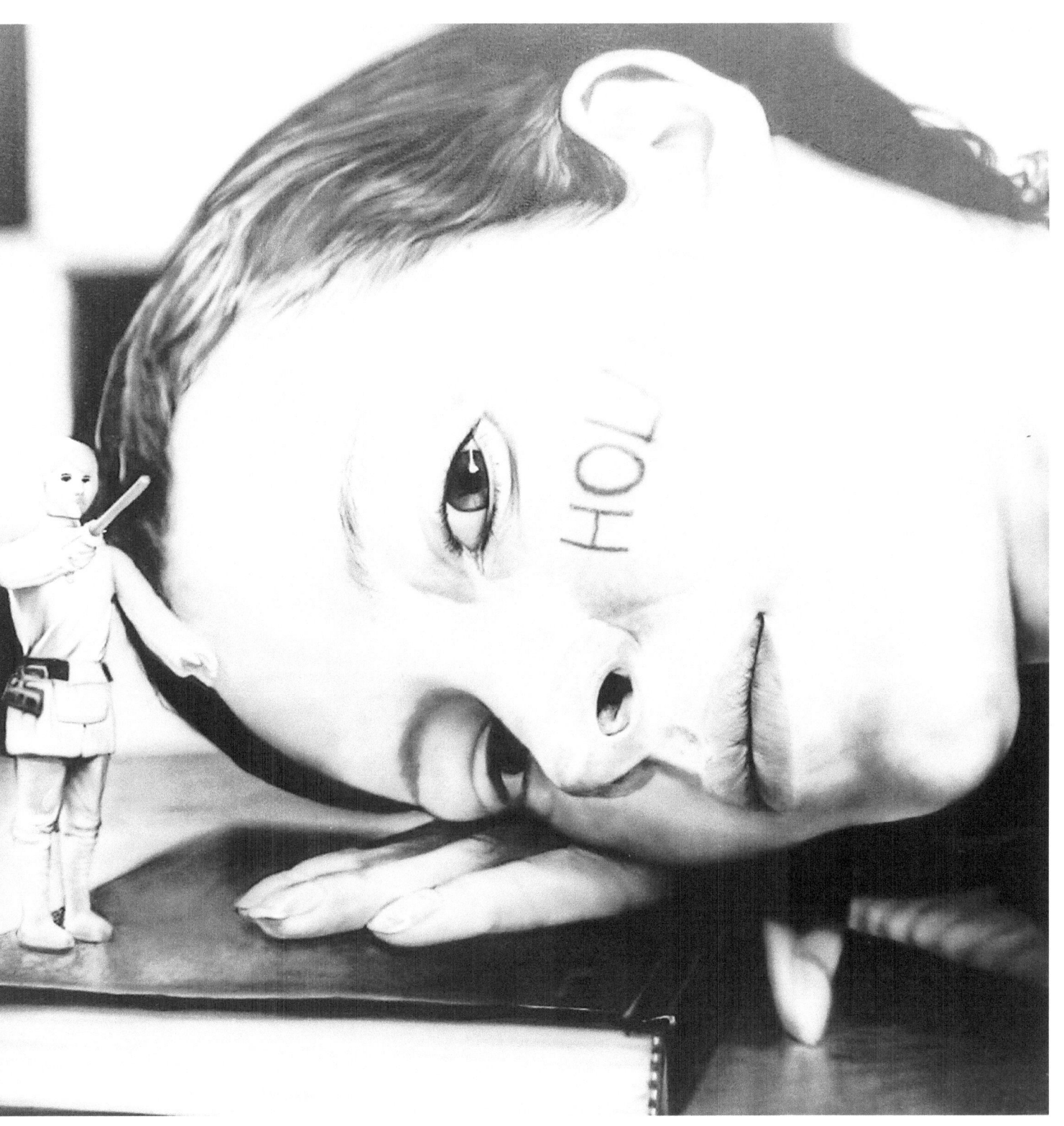

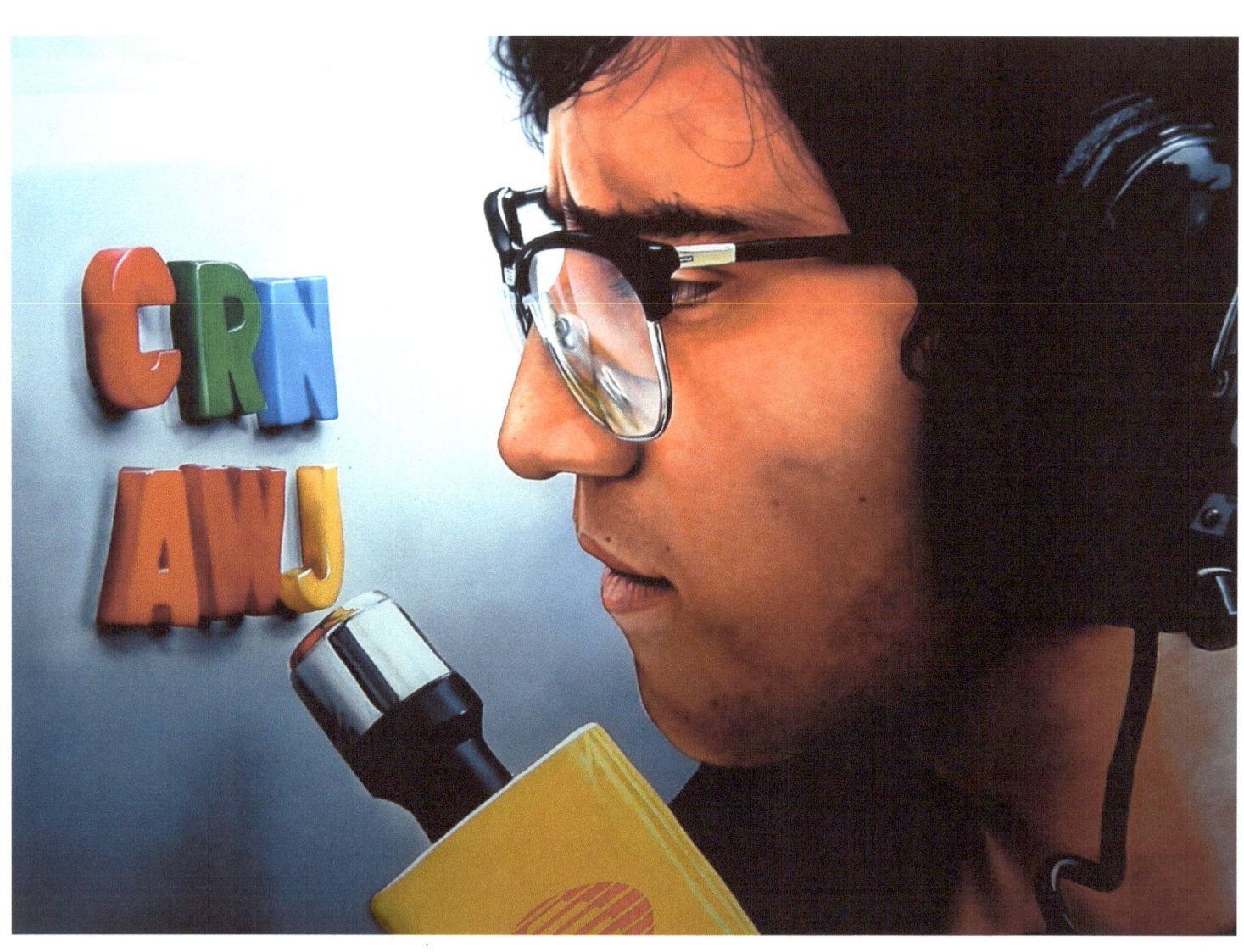

^ INTERVIEW 150 X 200 CMS 1996
> WOMEN 150 X 200 CMS 1996

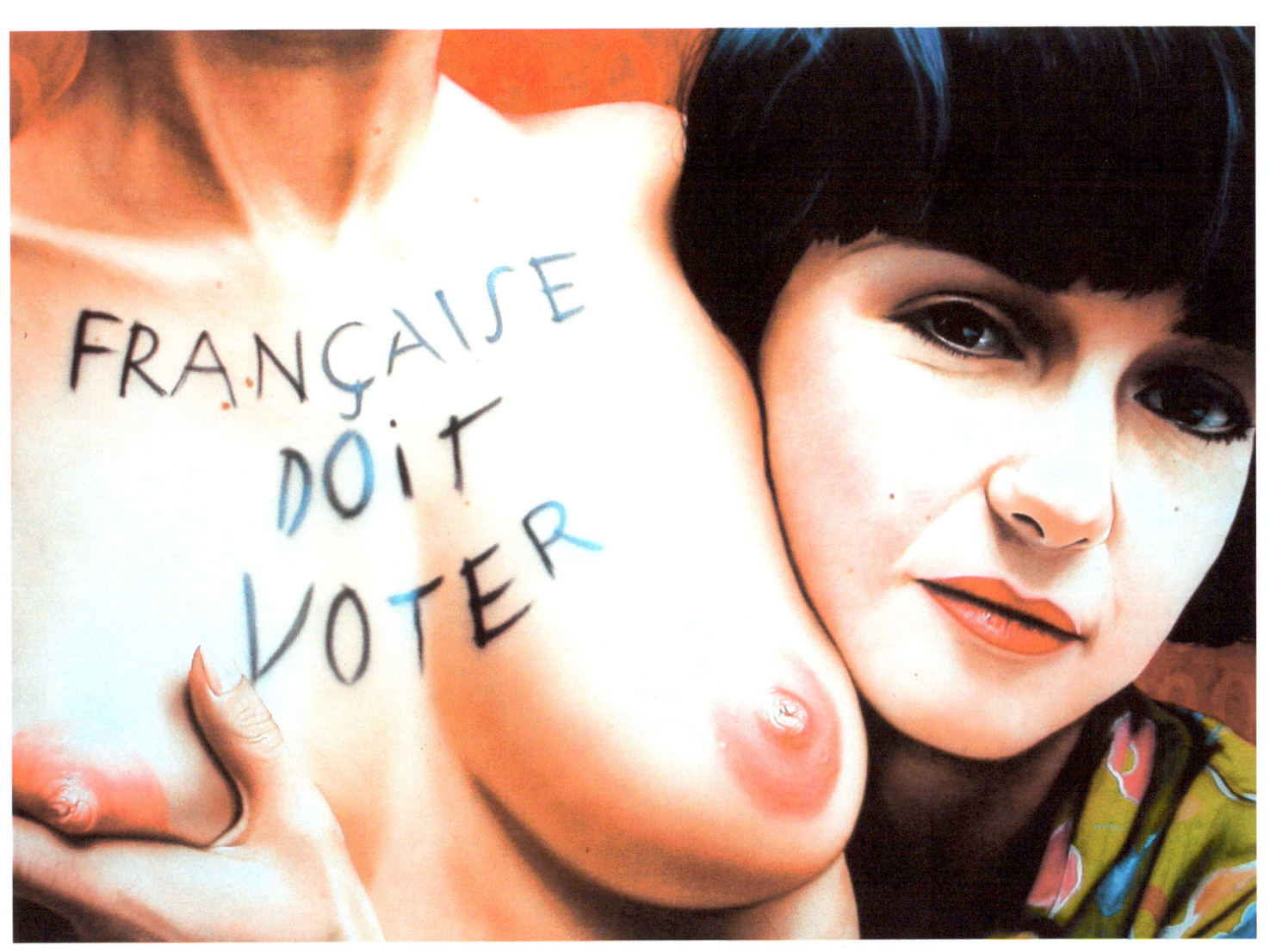

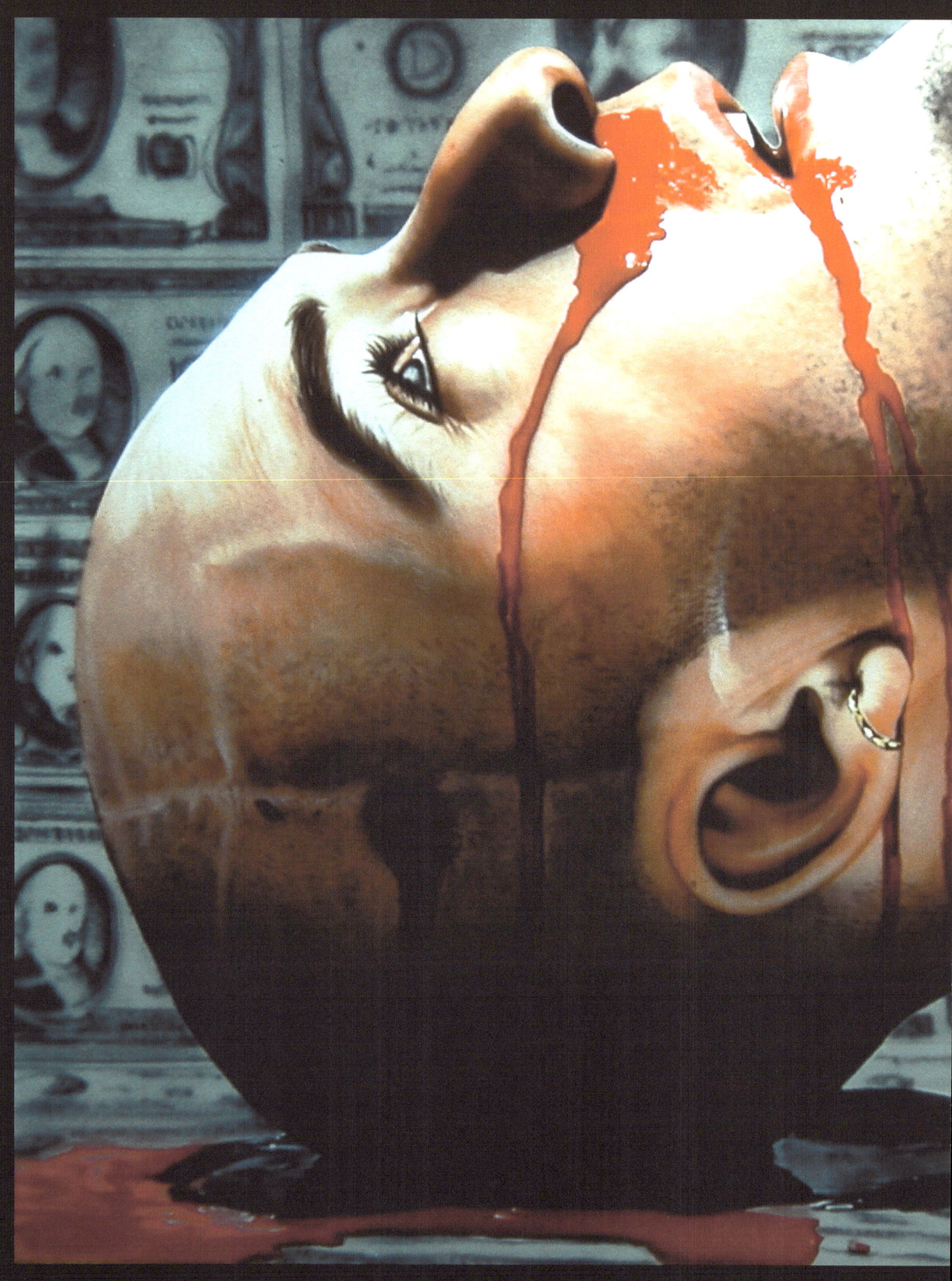

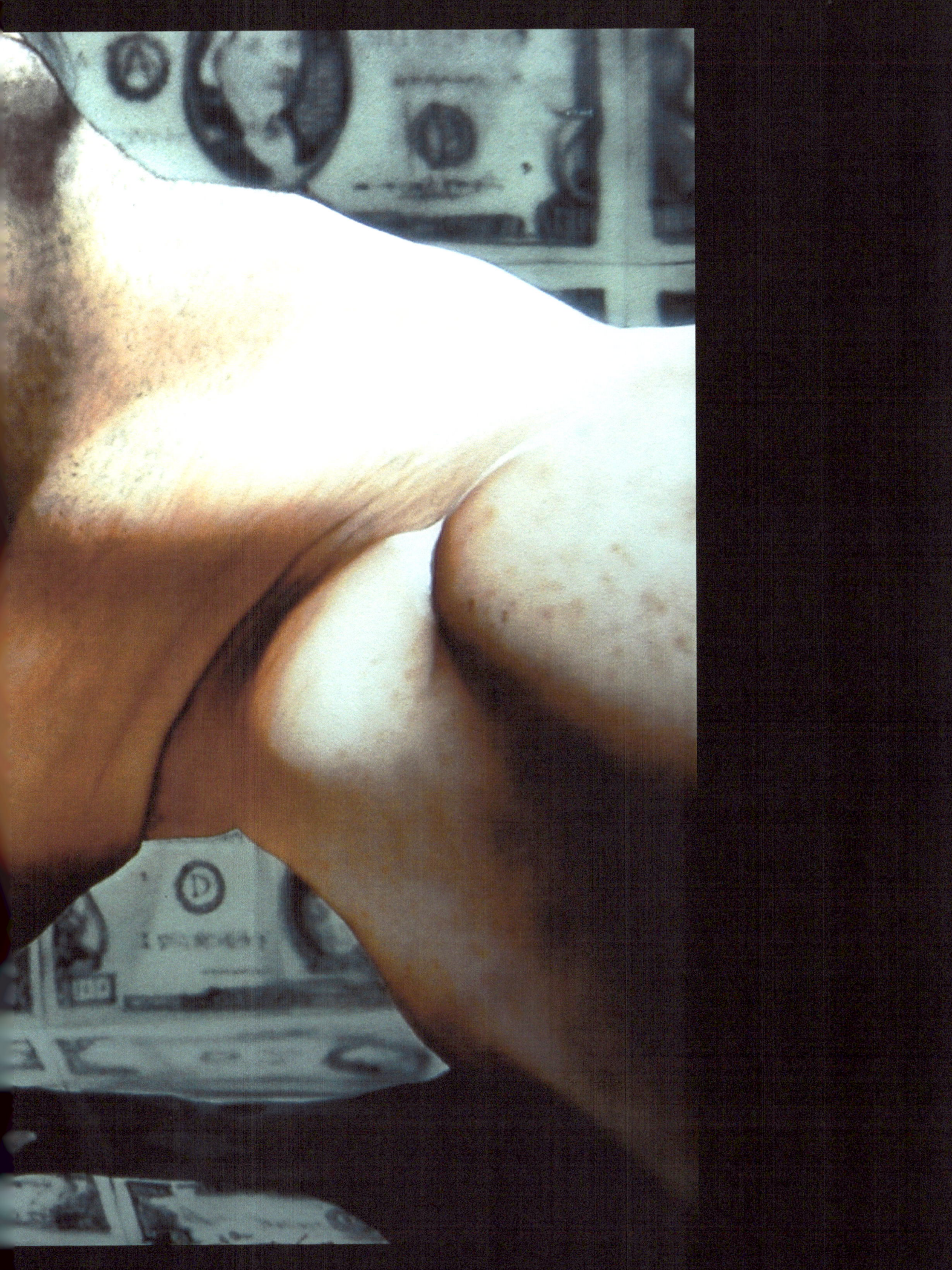

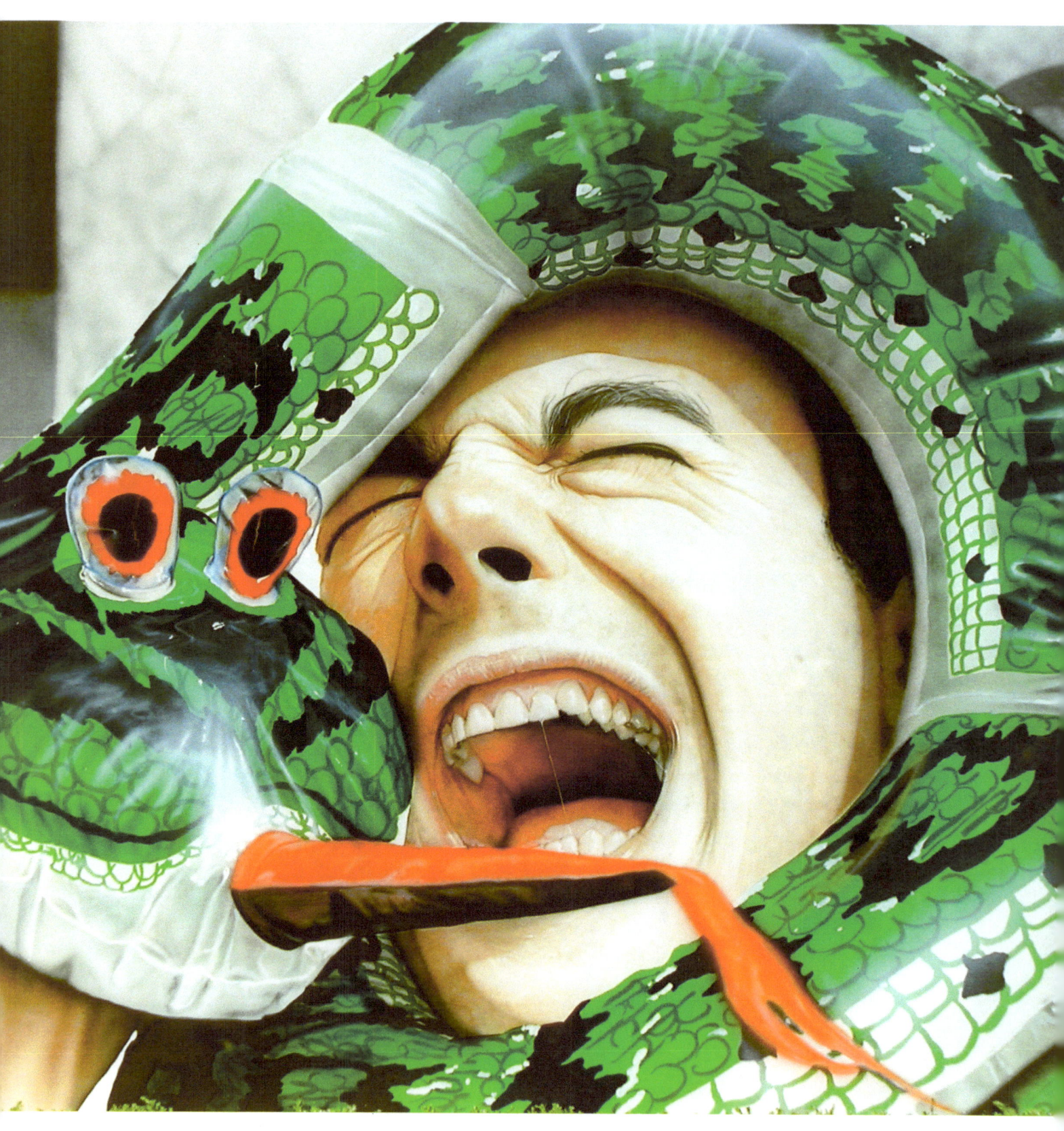

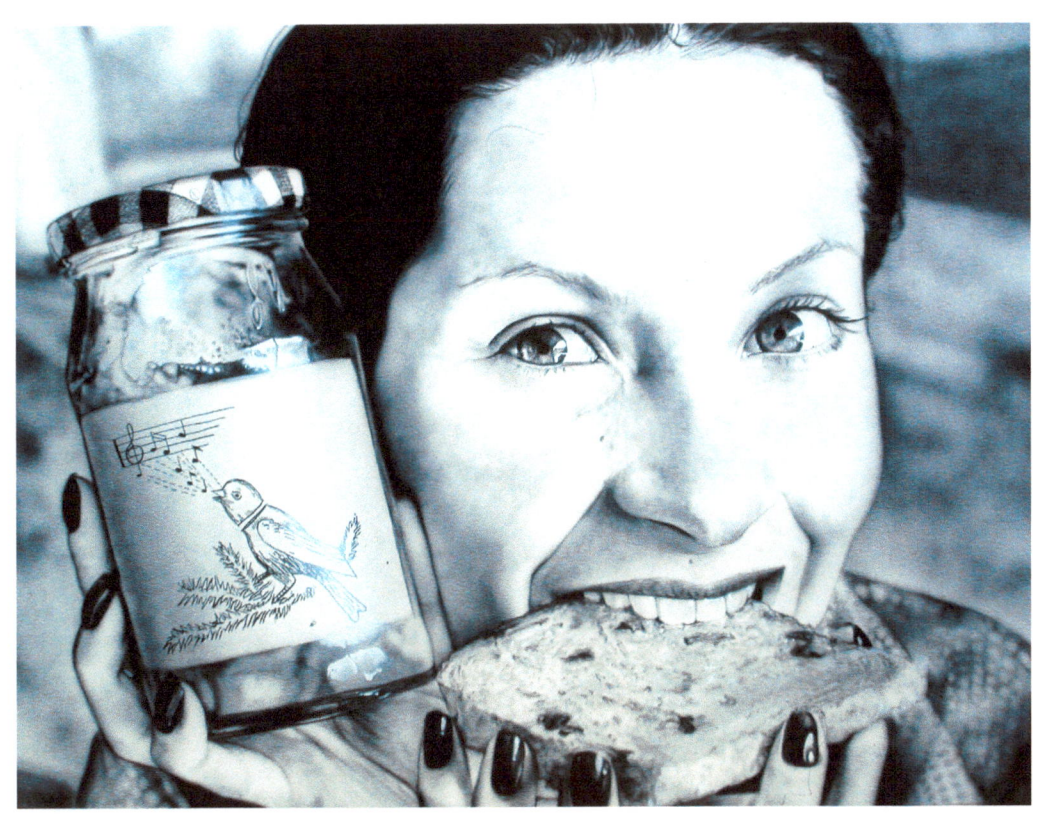

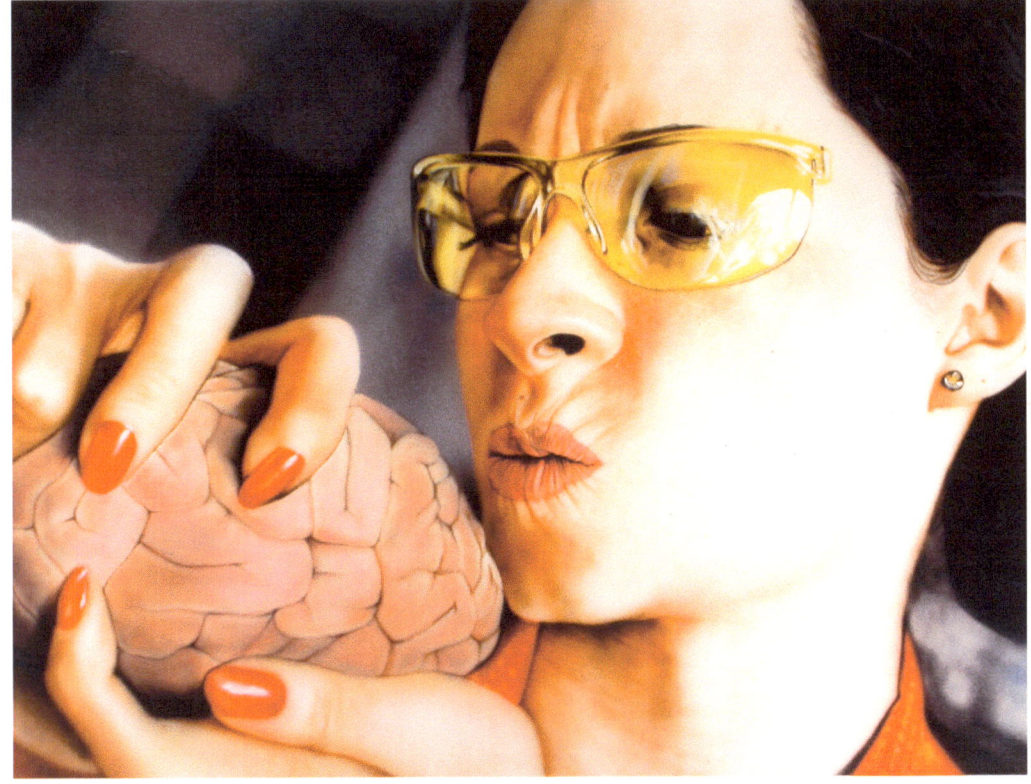

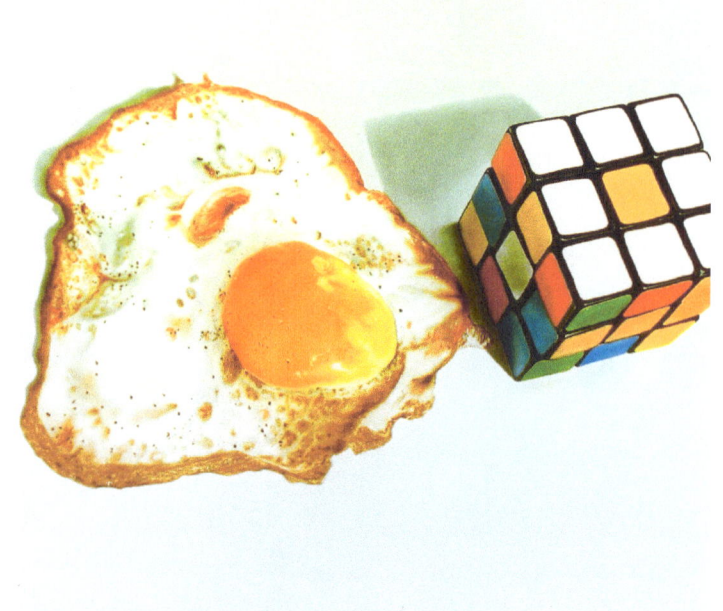

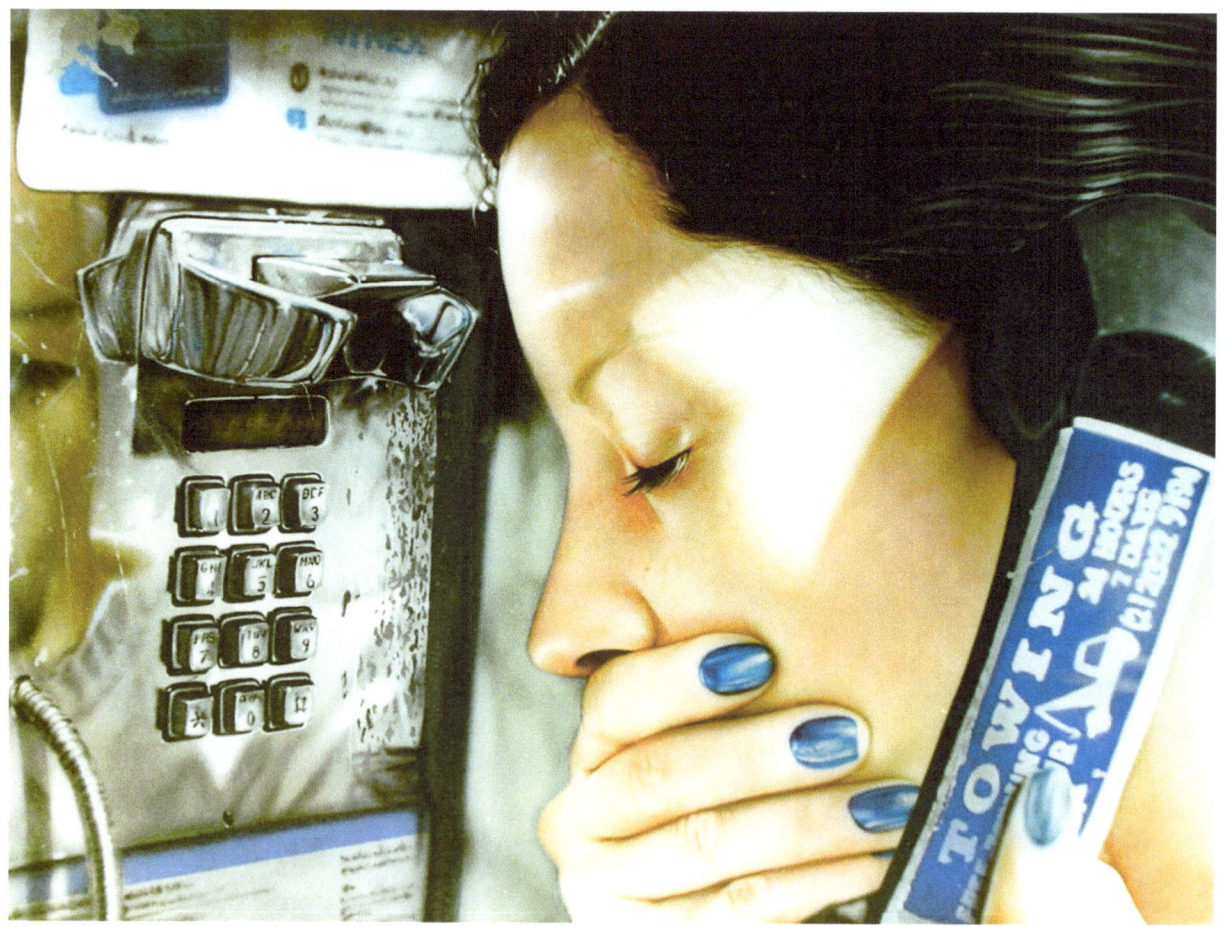

^ EGG / RUBIK 214 X 218 CMS 1997

^ BAD NEWS 148 X 198 CMS 1997   > TRICK 198 X 148 CMS 1997

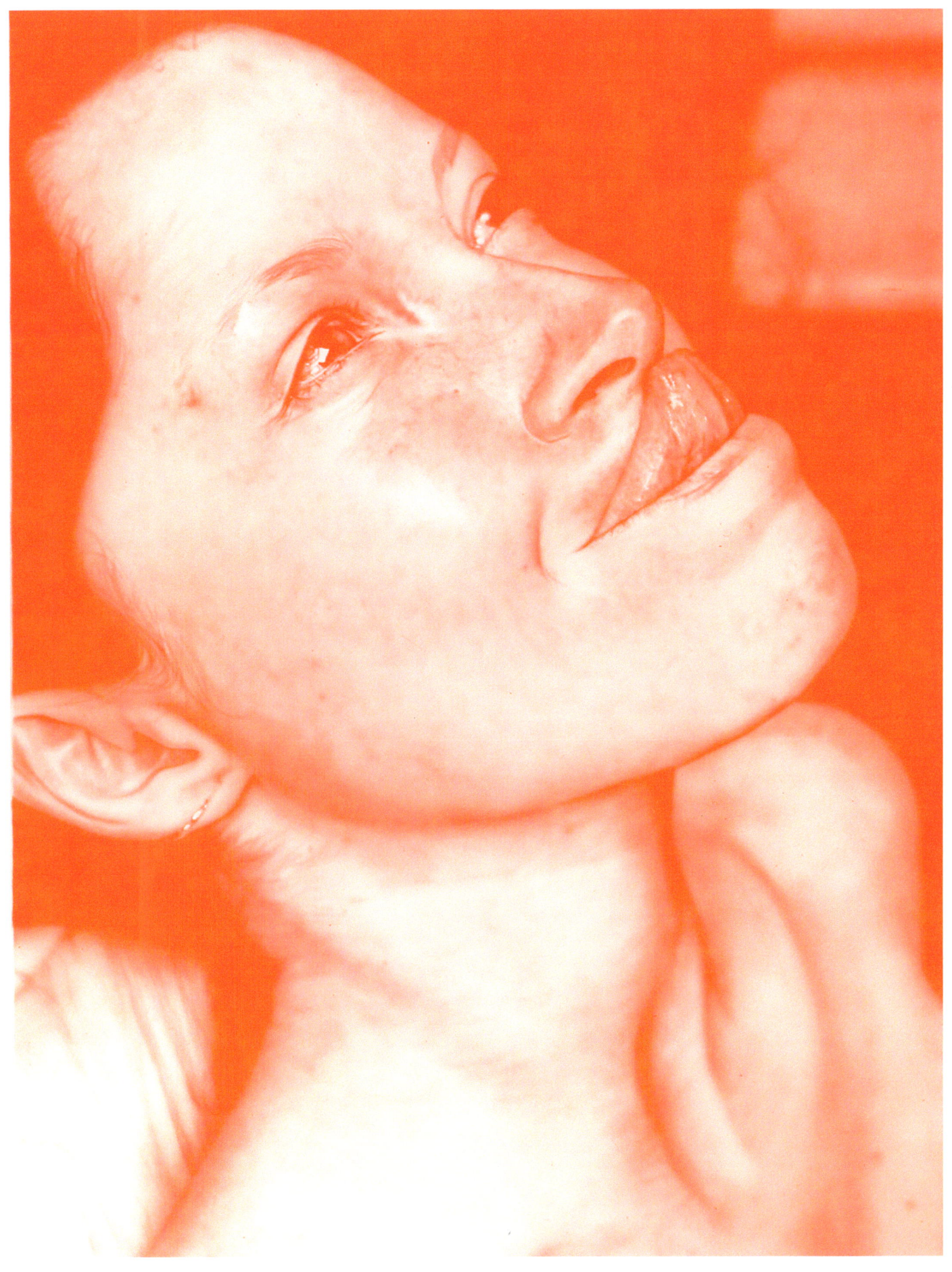

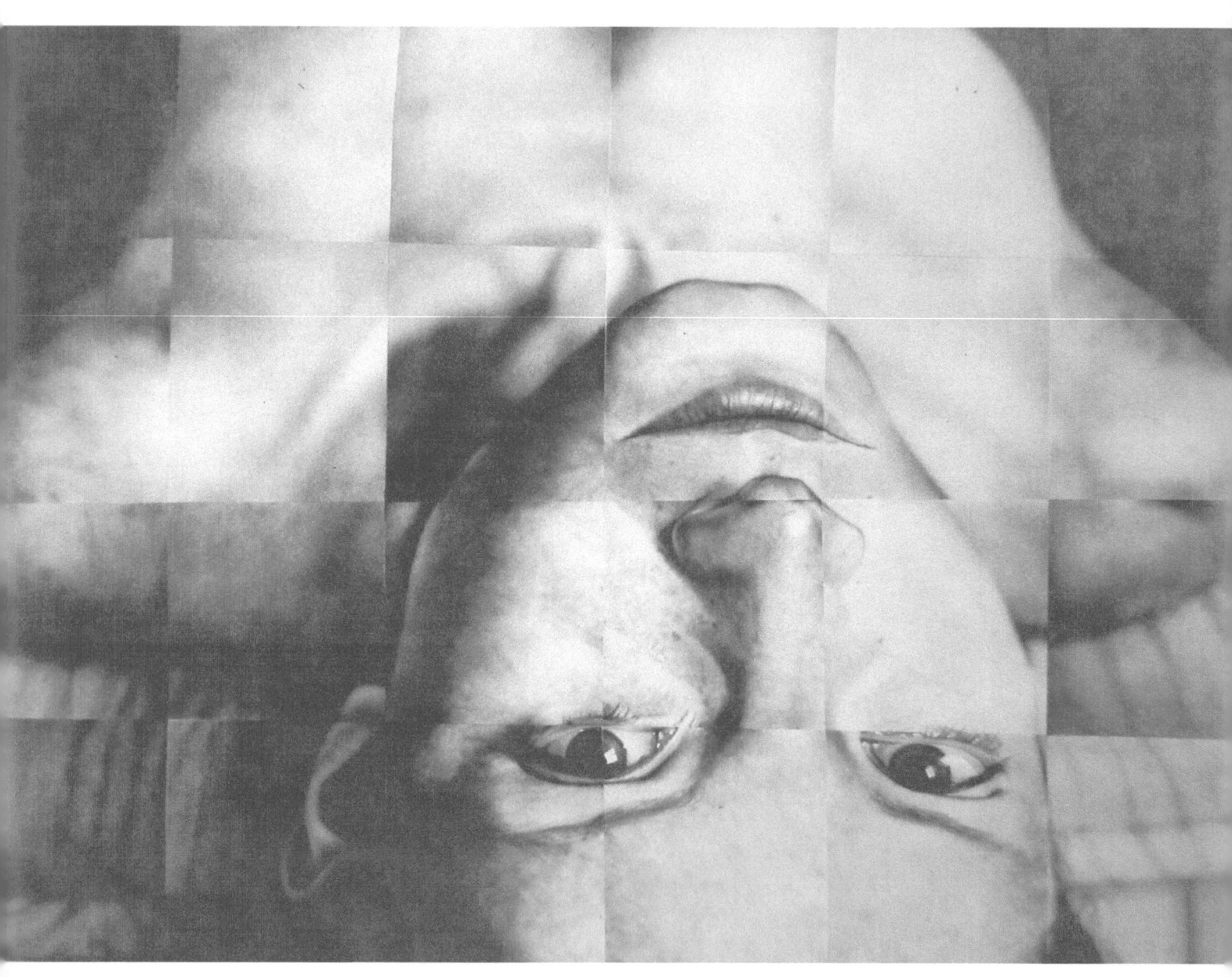

CLOSED MOUTH 148 X 198 CMS 1997

BOWL 148 X 198 CMS 1997

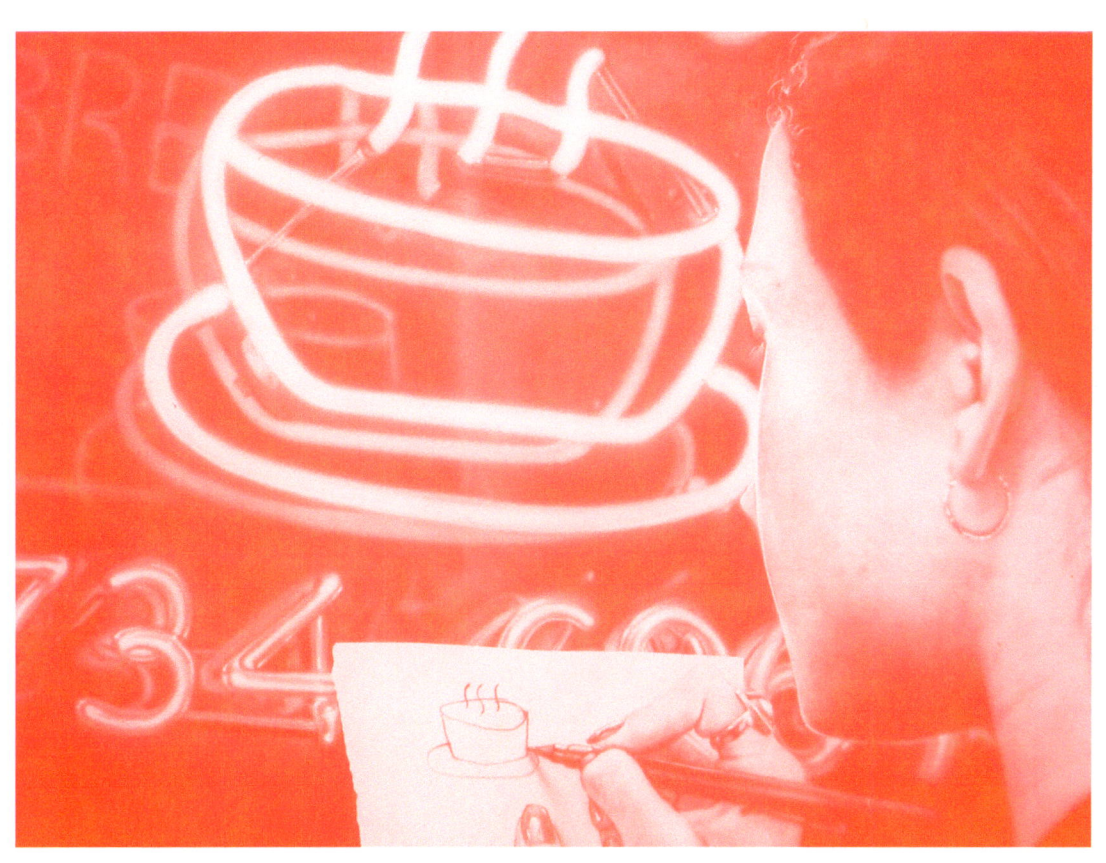

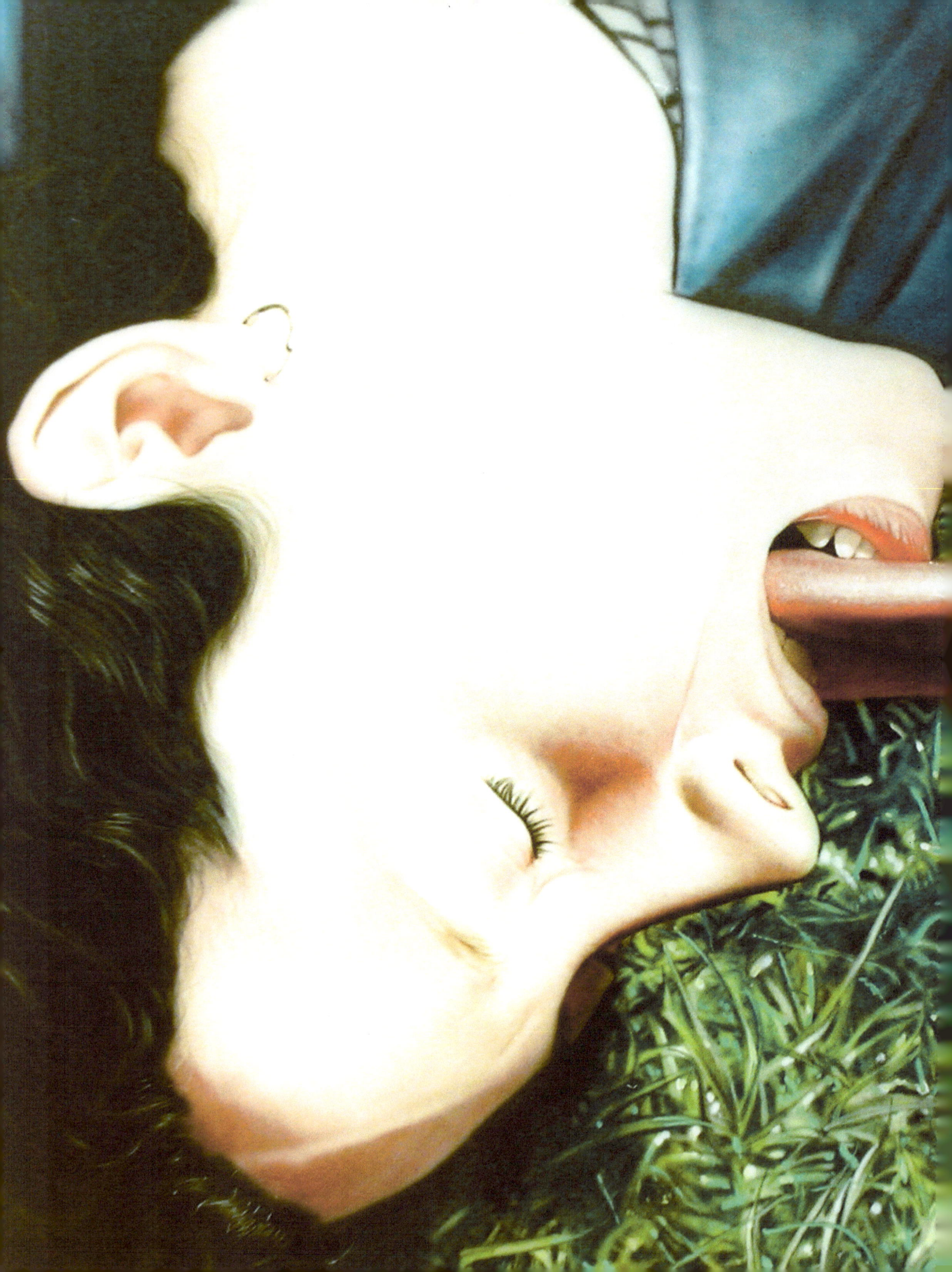

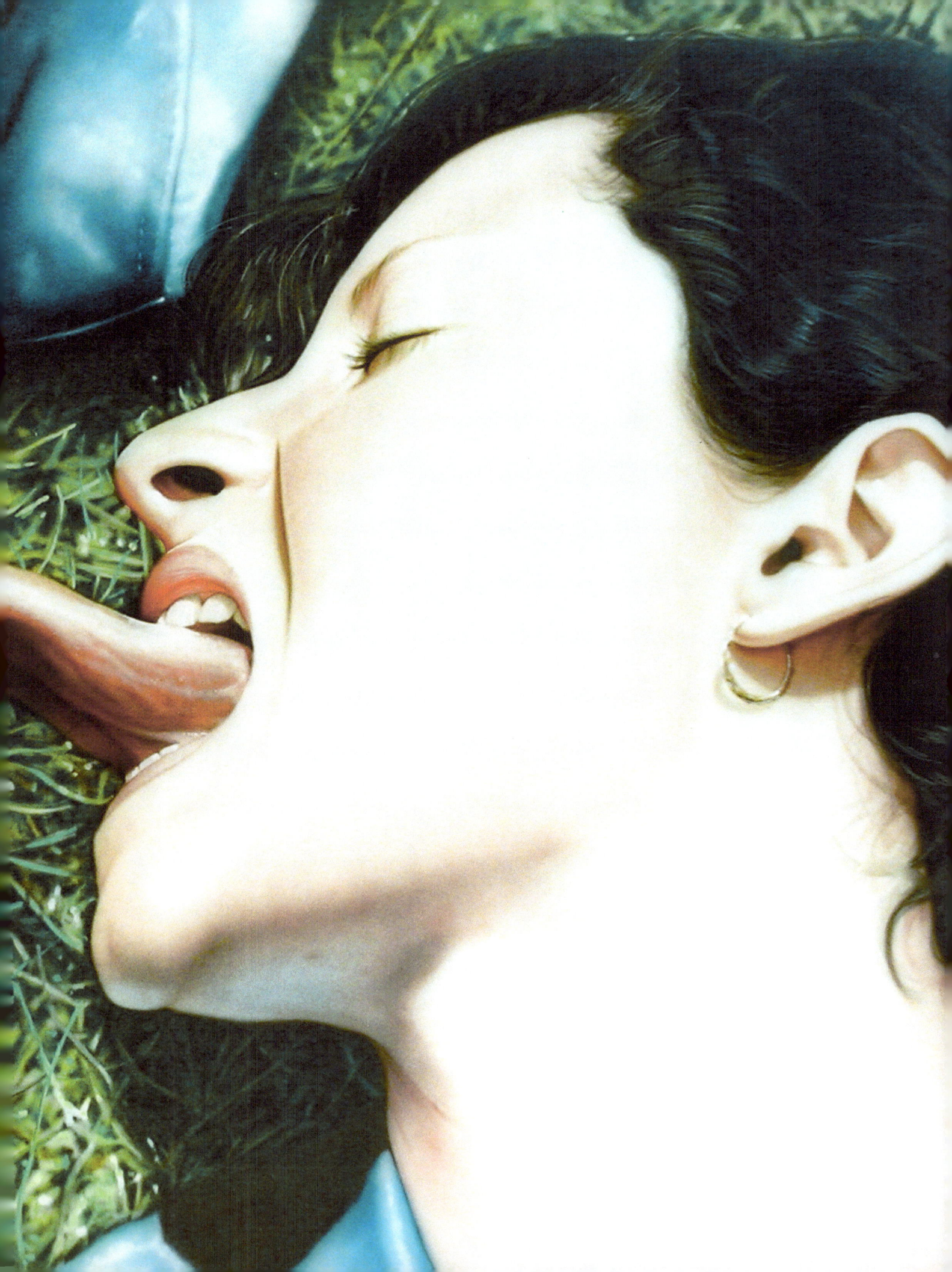

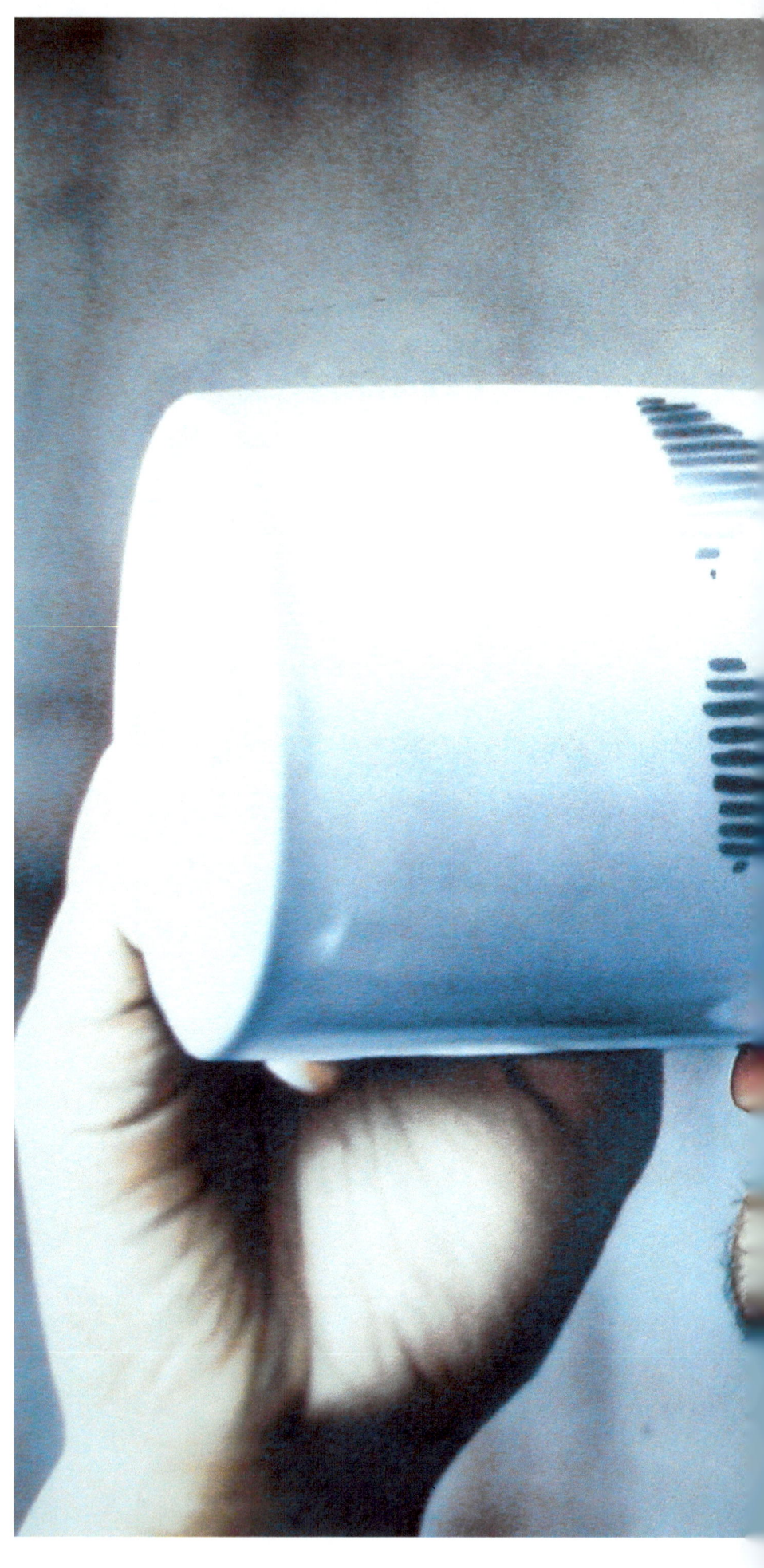

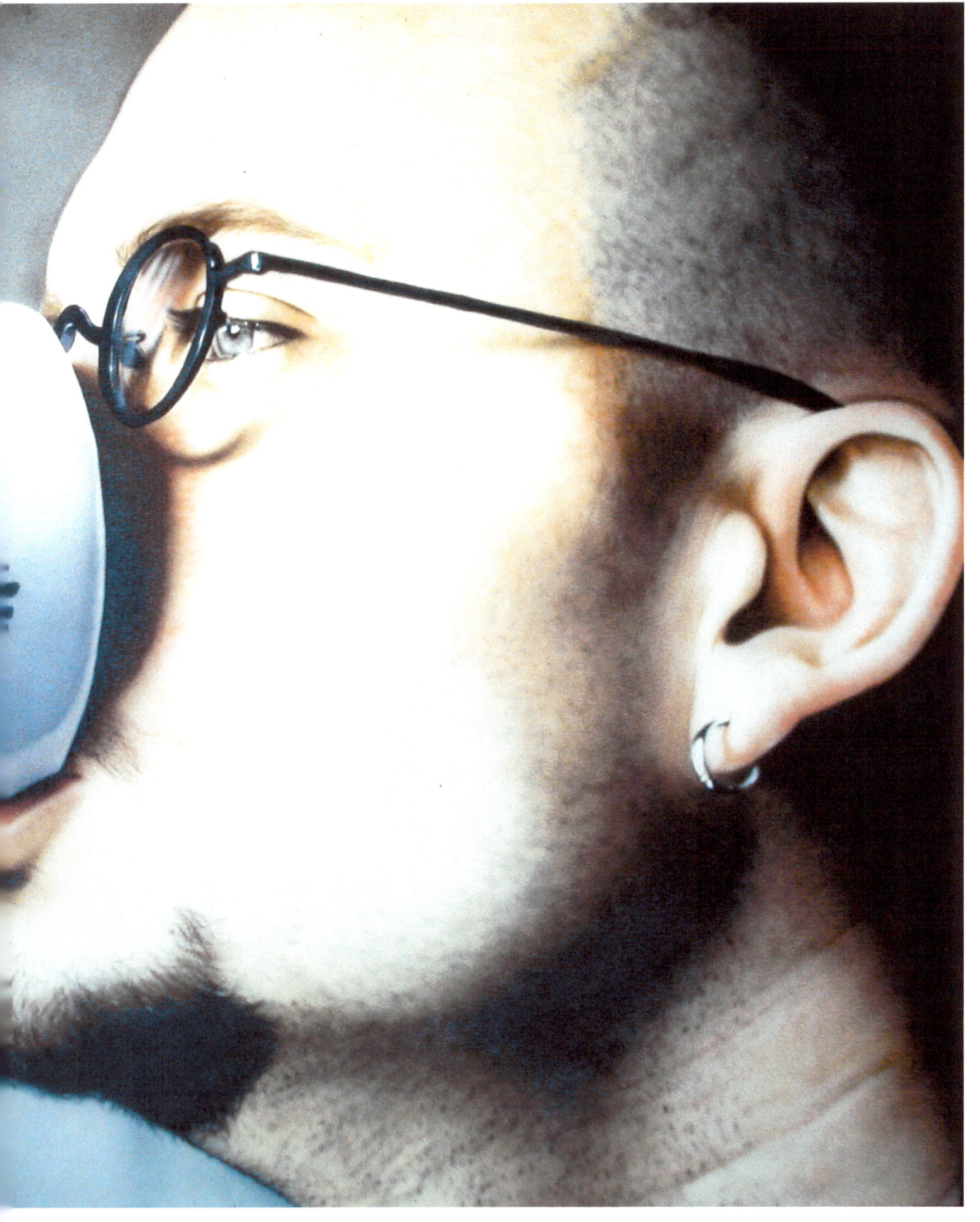

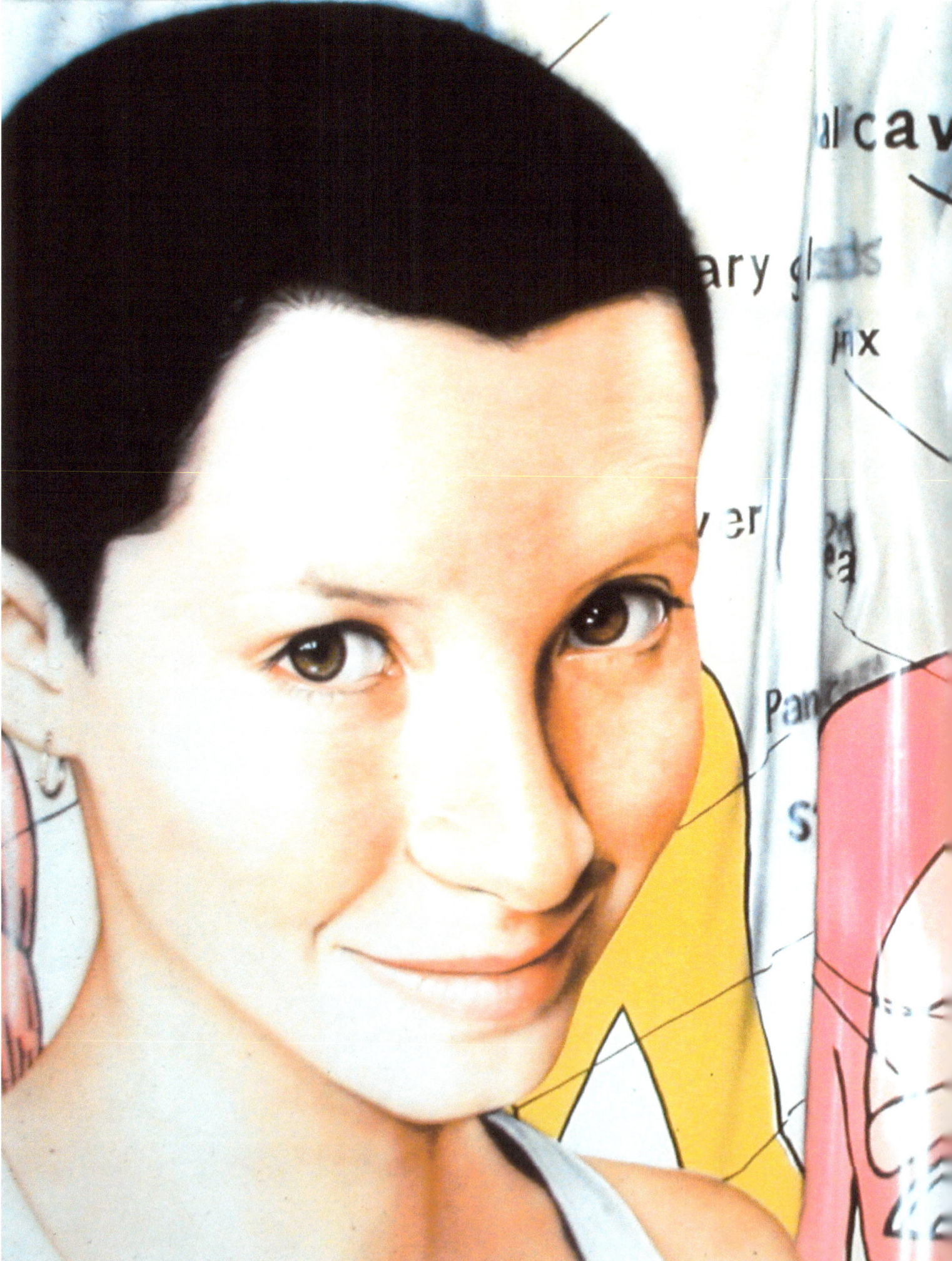

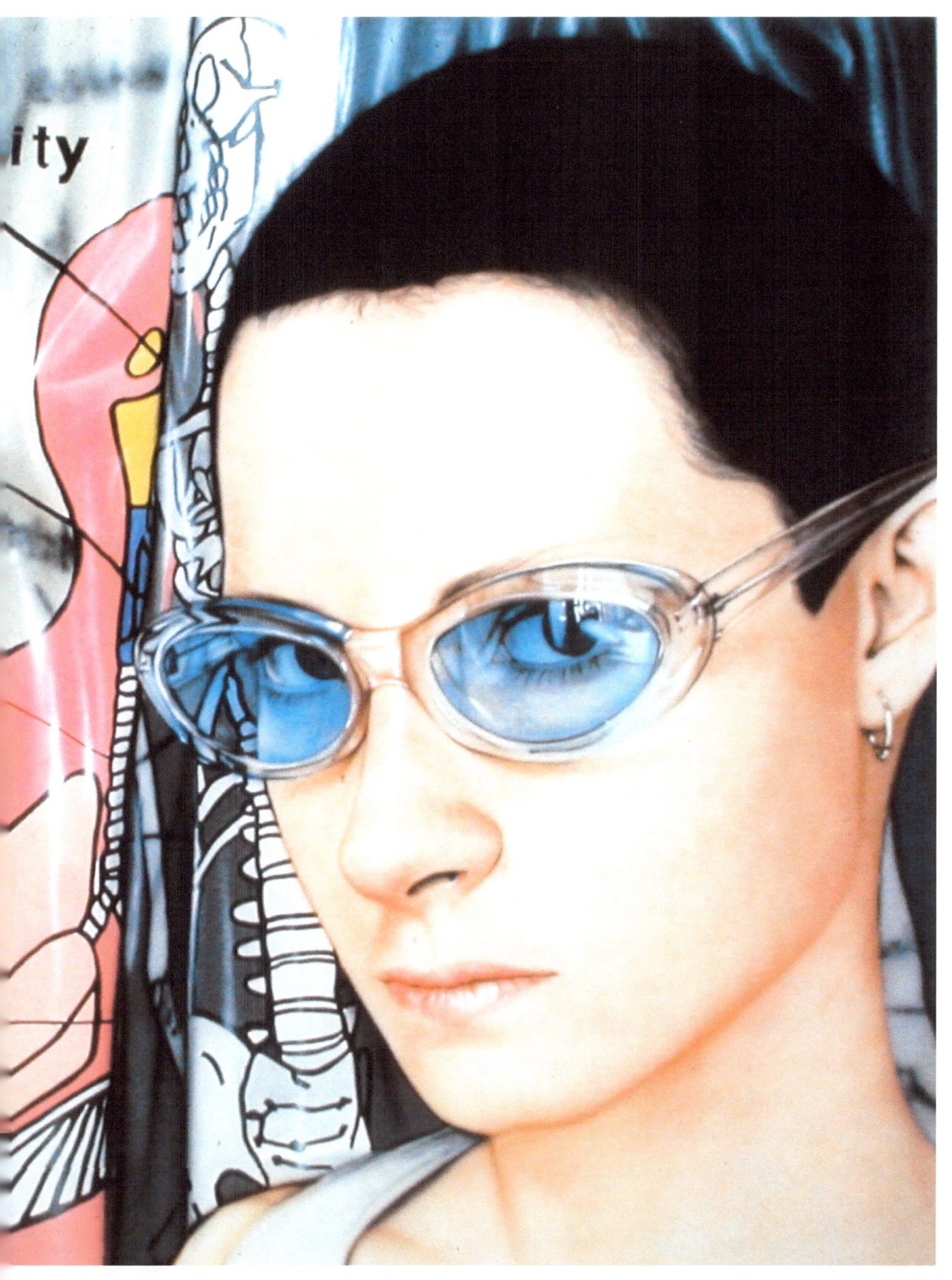

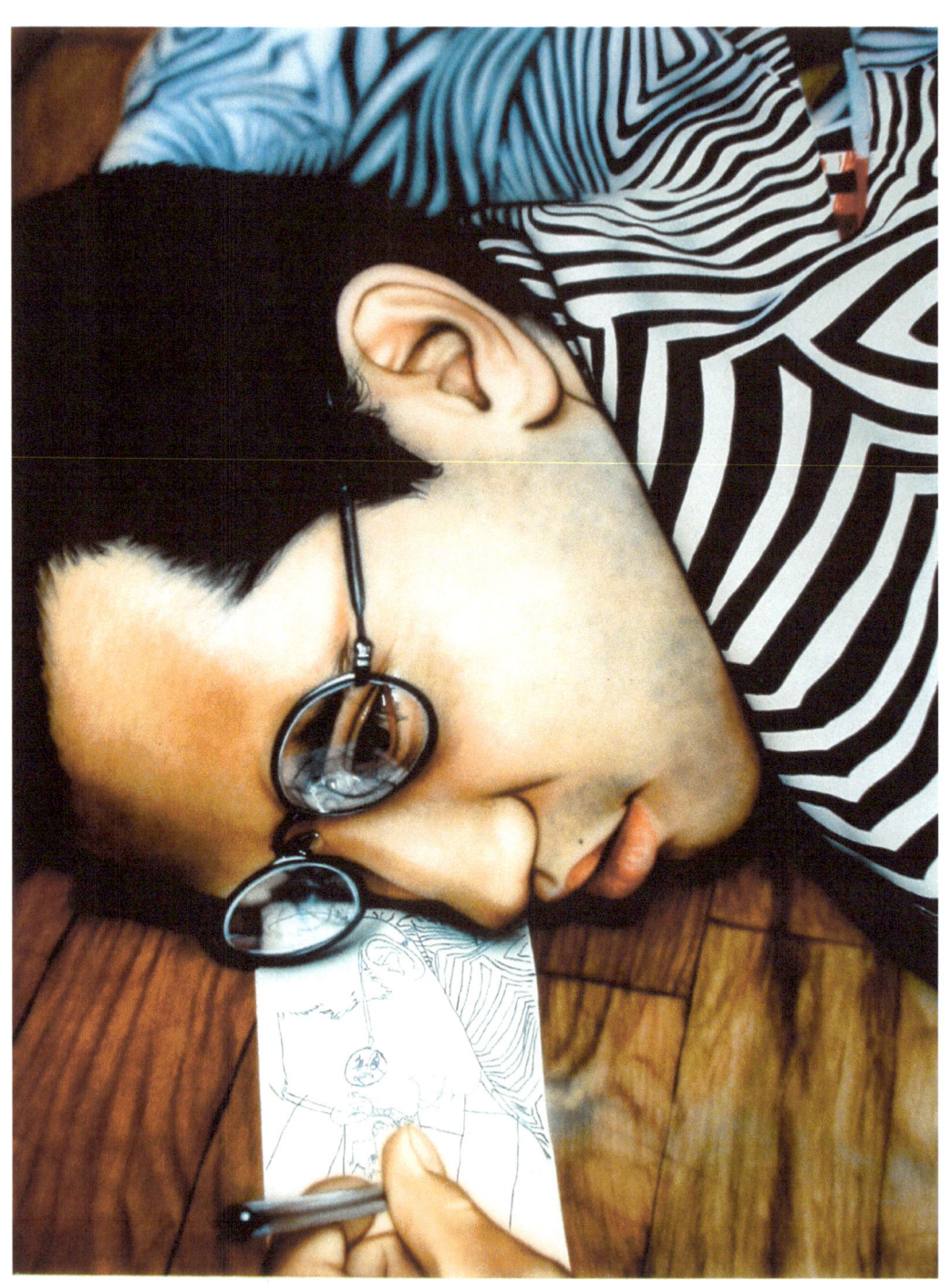

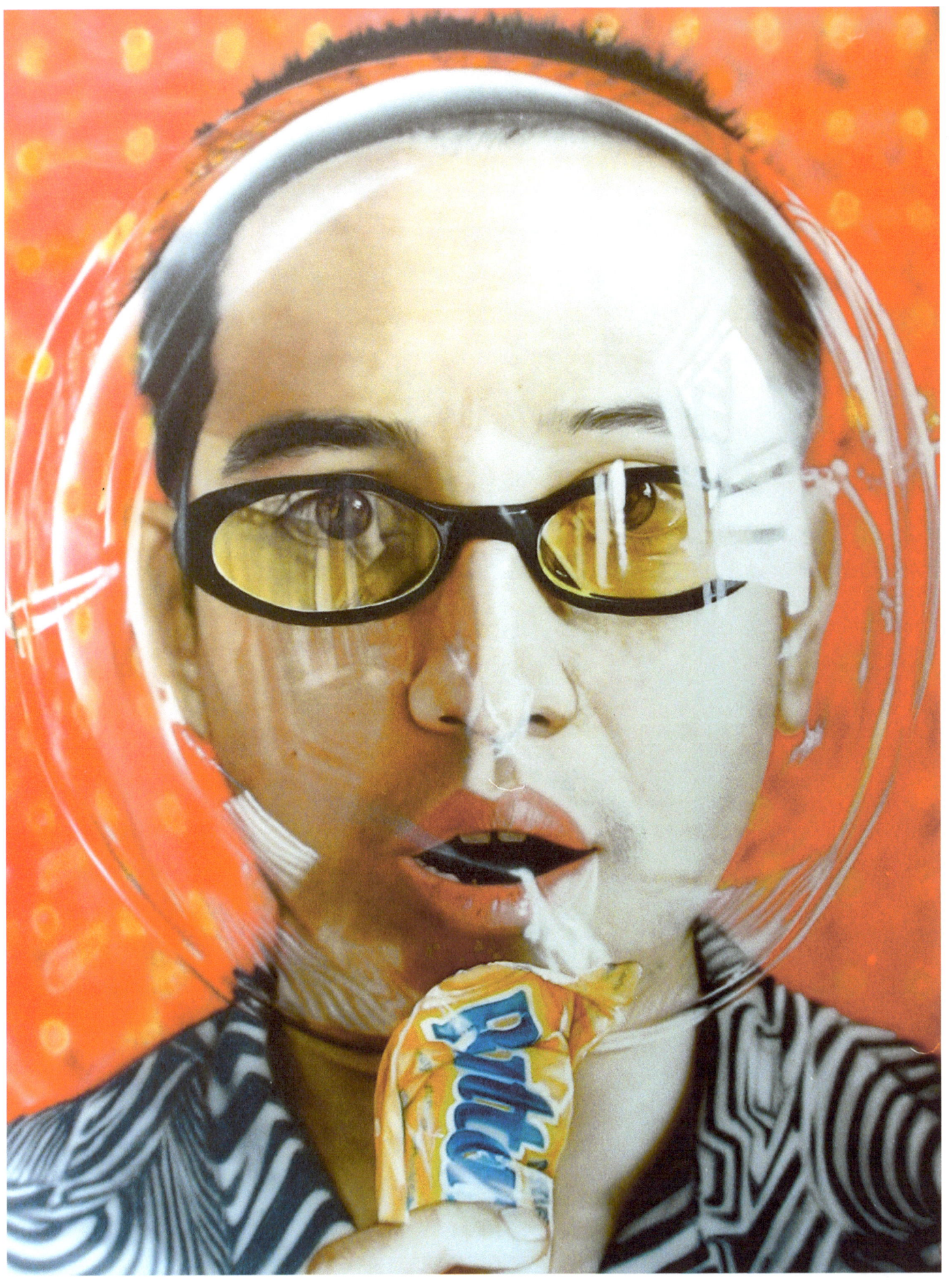

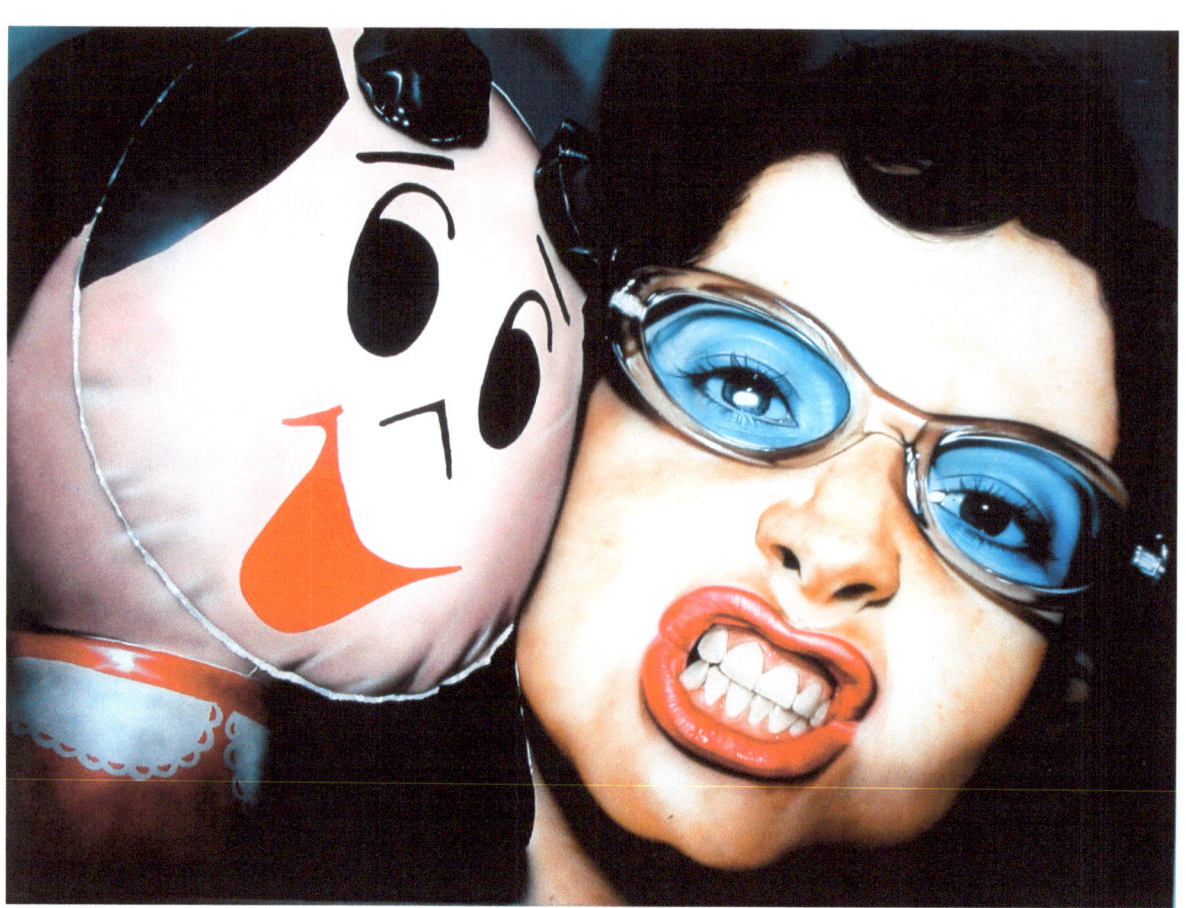

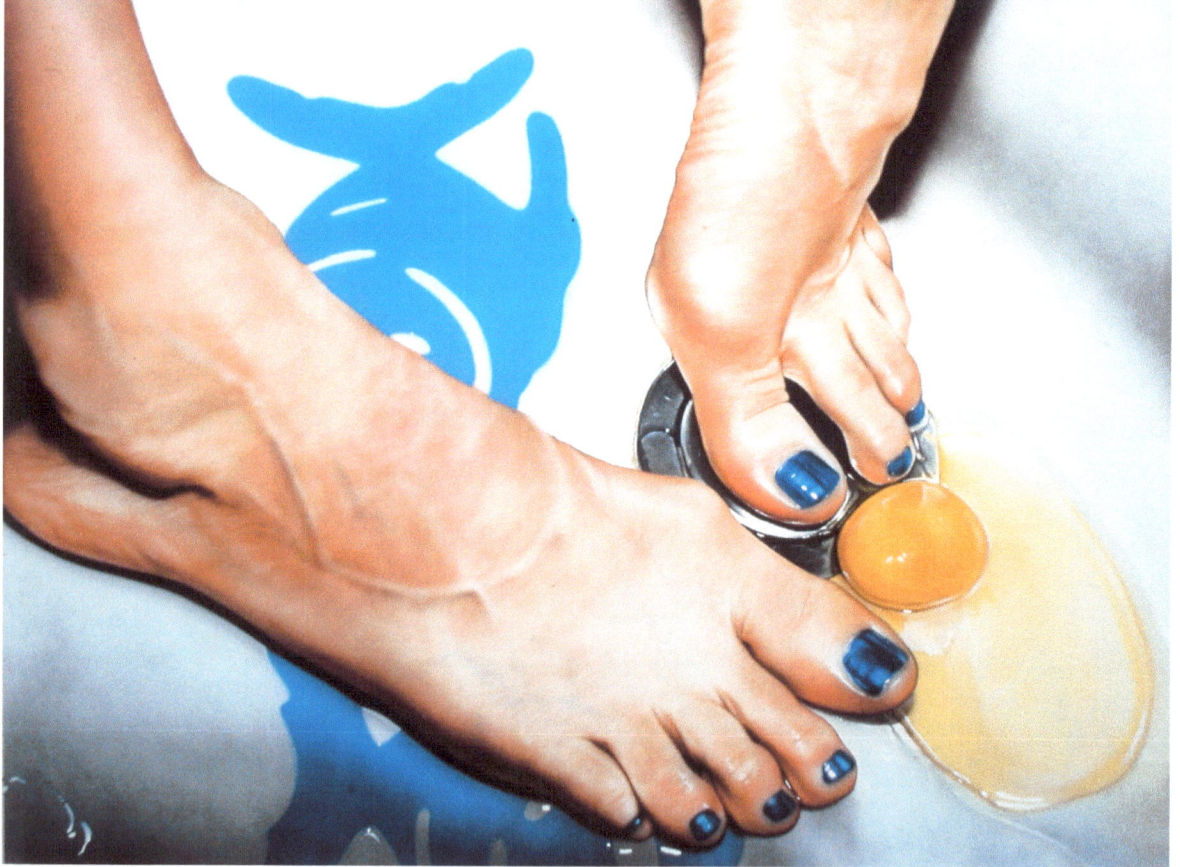

^ GIRLS 148 X 198 CMS 1998   ^ DRAIN 148 X 198 CMS 1998

> ANATOMY BOOK 180 X 150 CMS 1997

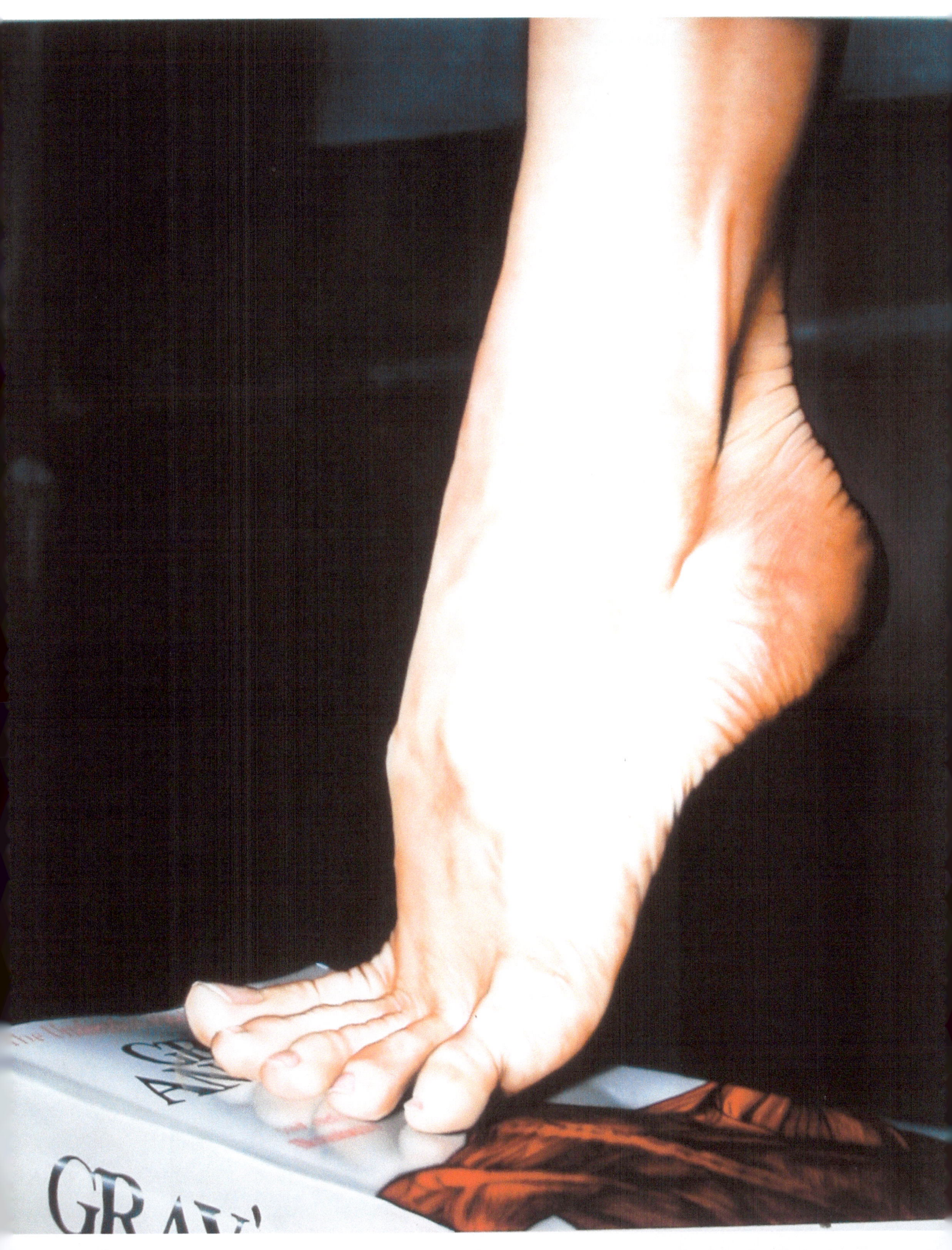

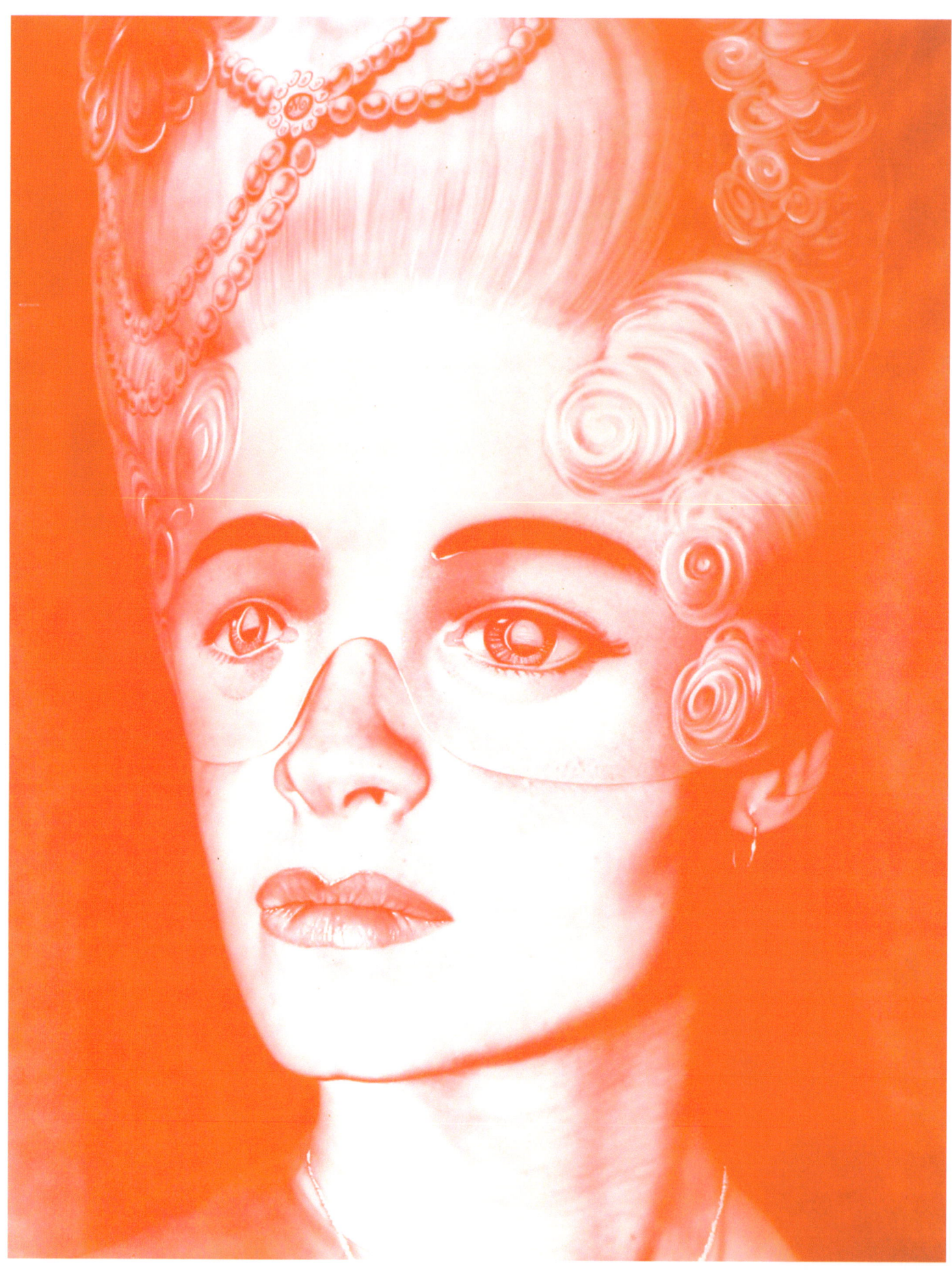

^ GRAND DAME 198 X 148 CMS 1998

> CUBE 228 X 228 CMS 1998   > TWENTY 202 X 212 CMS 1998

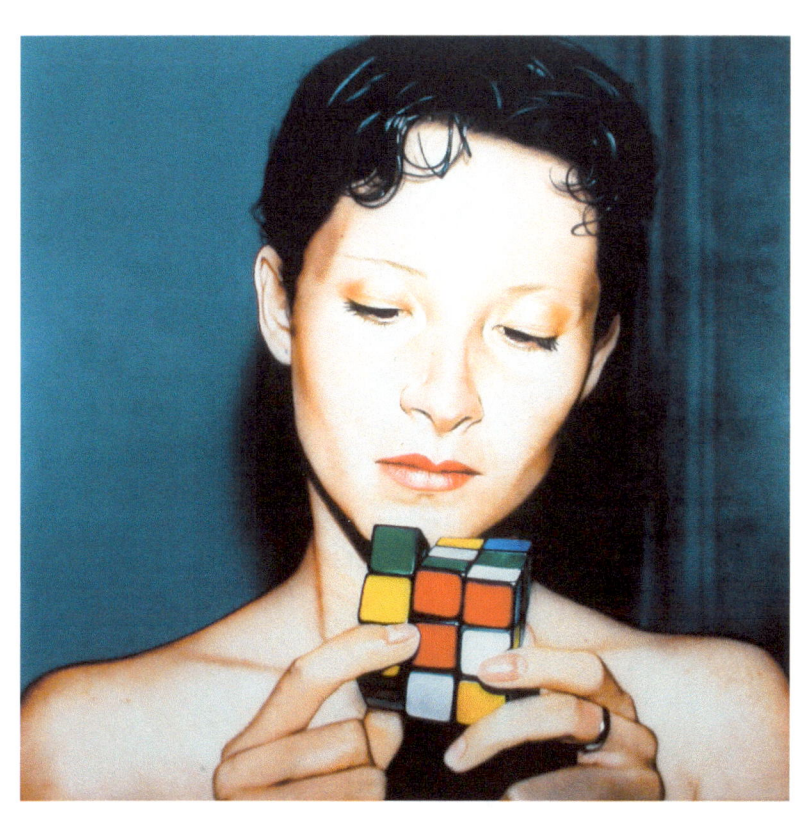

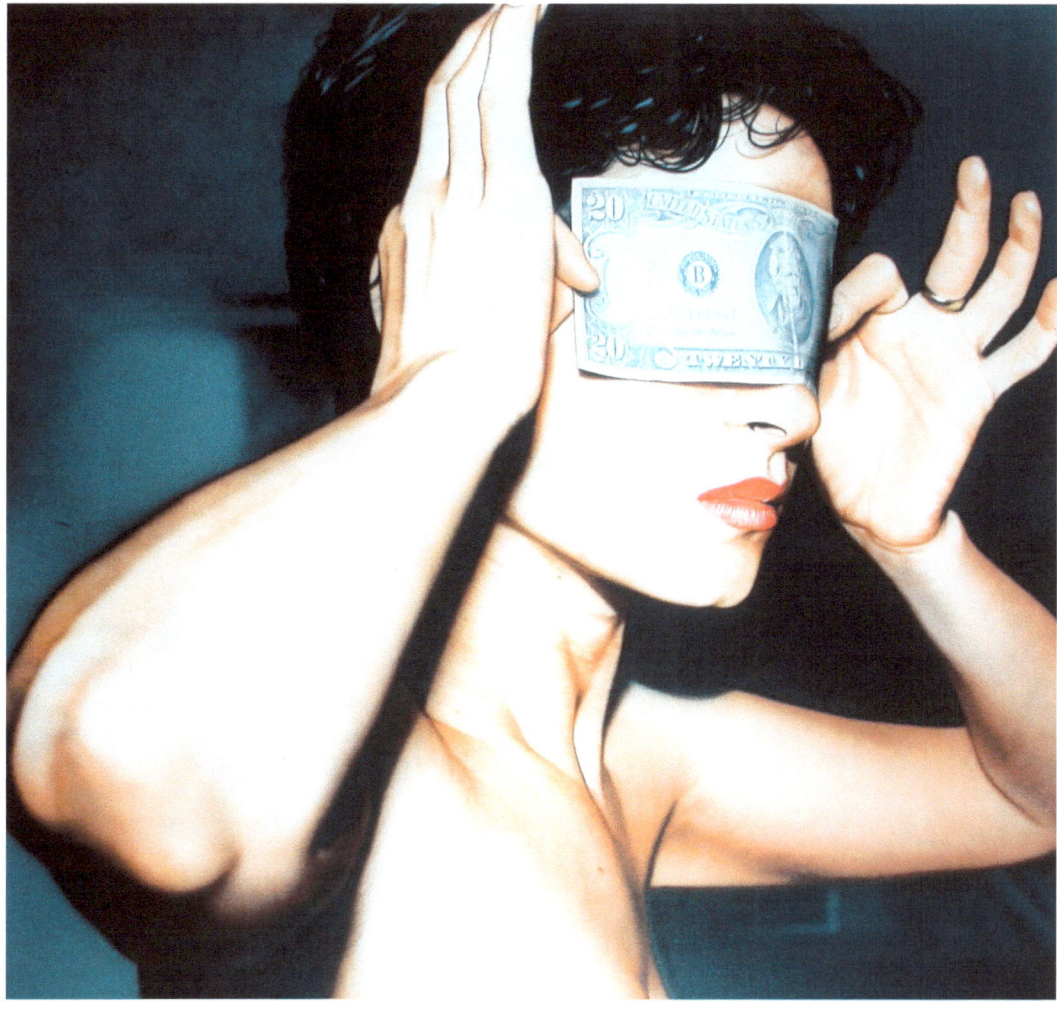

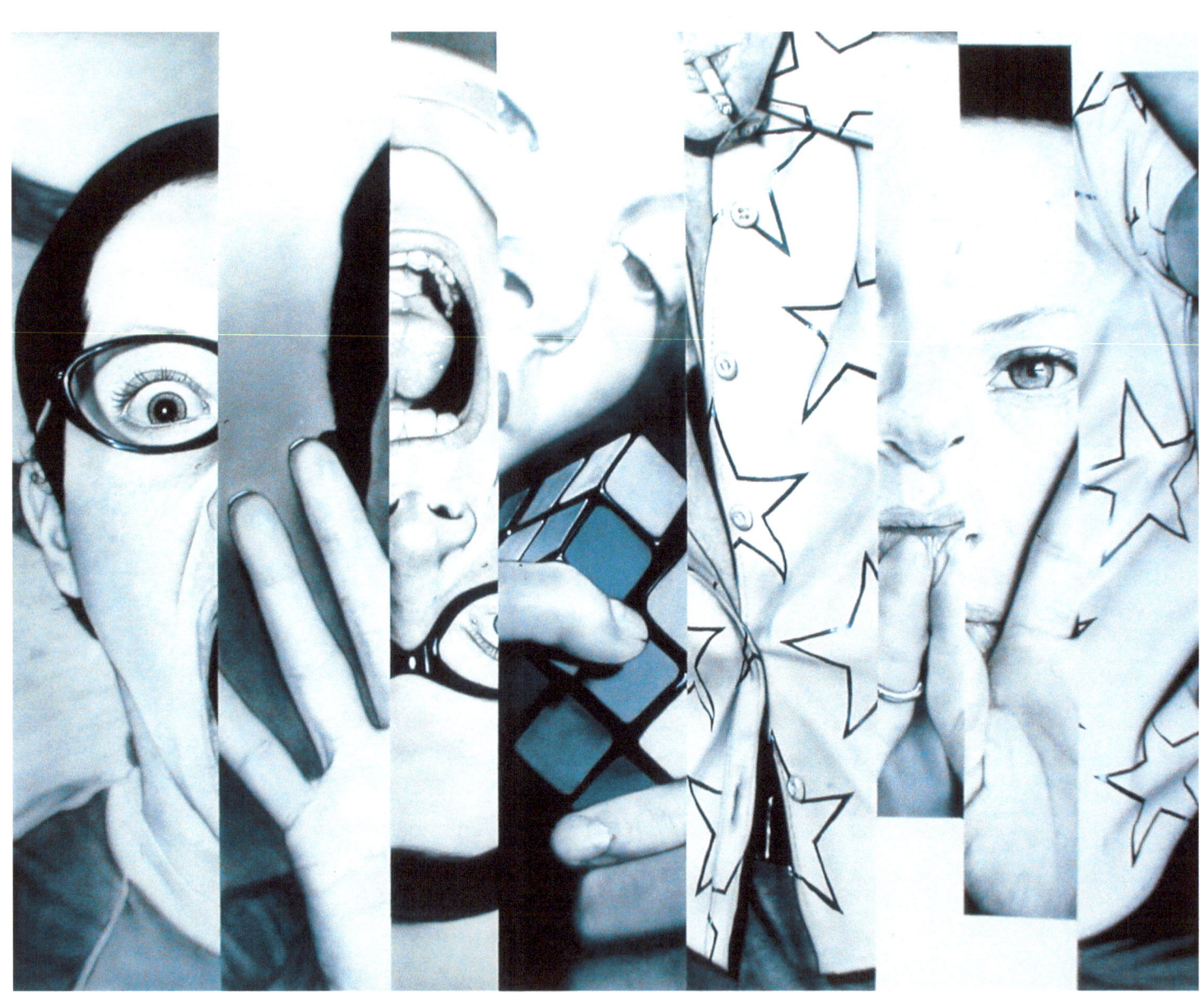

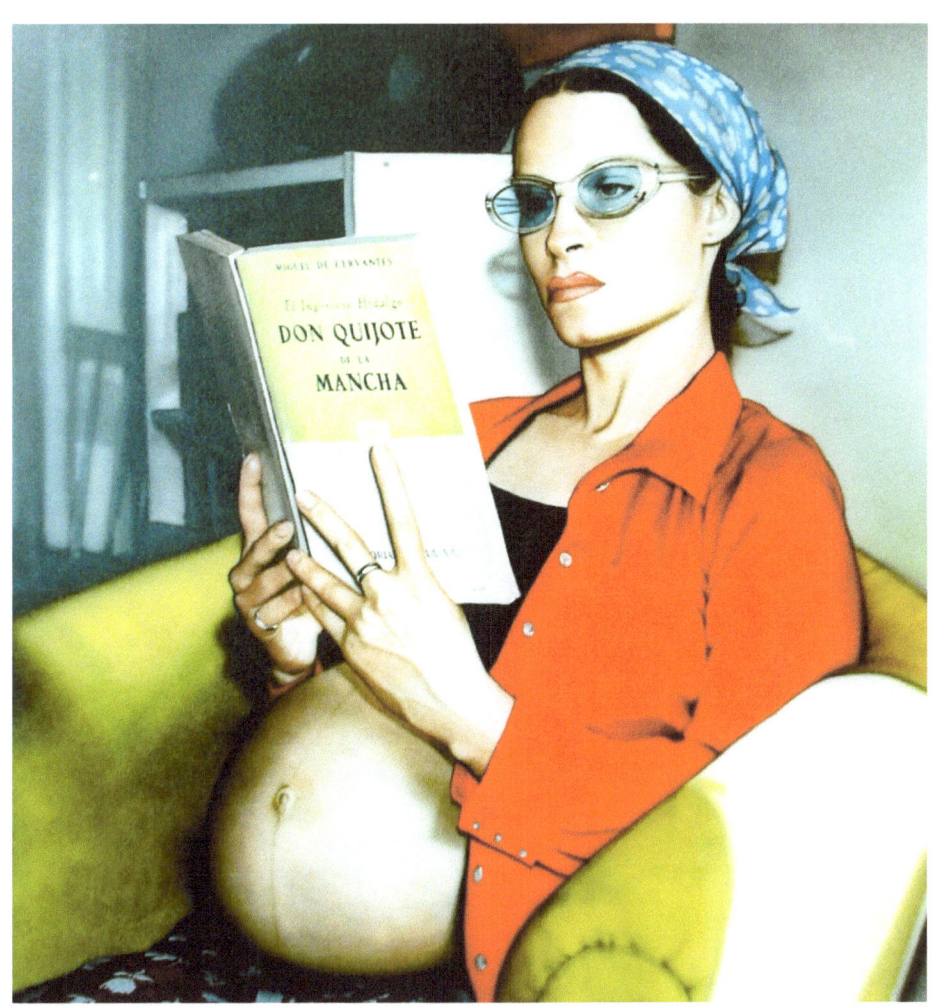

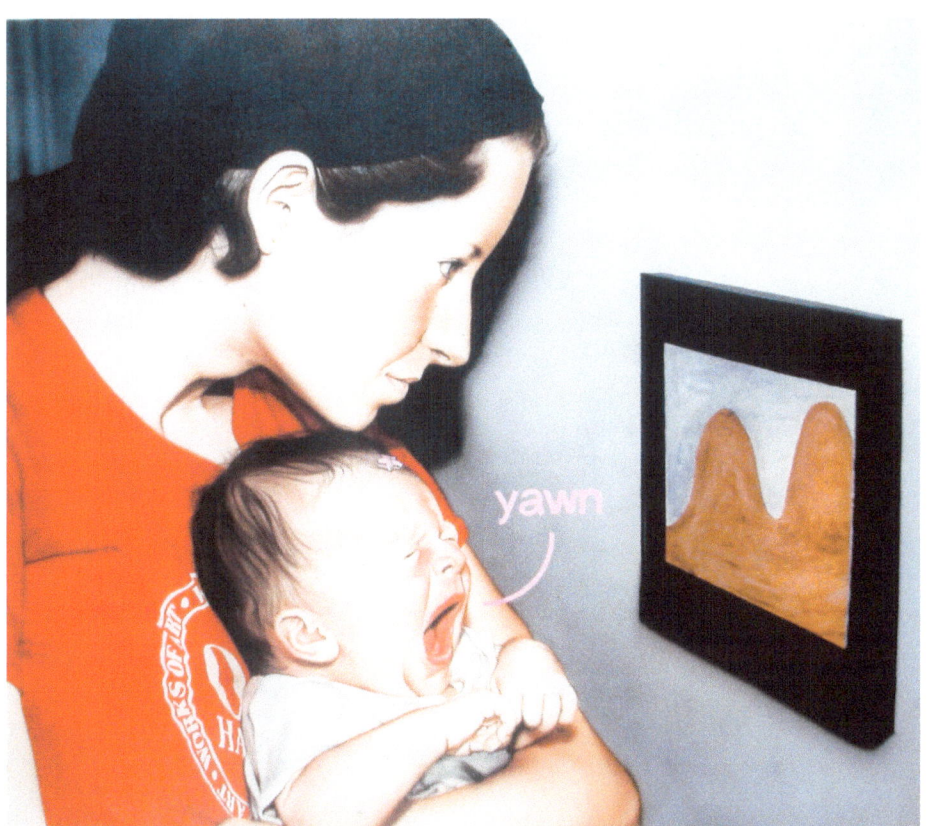

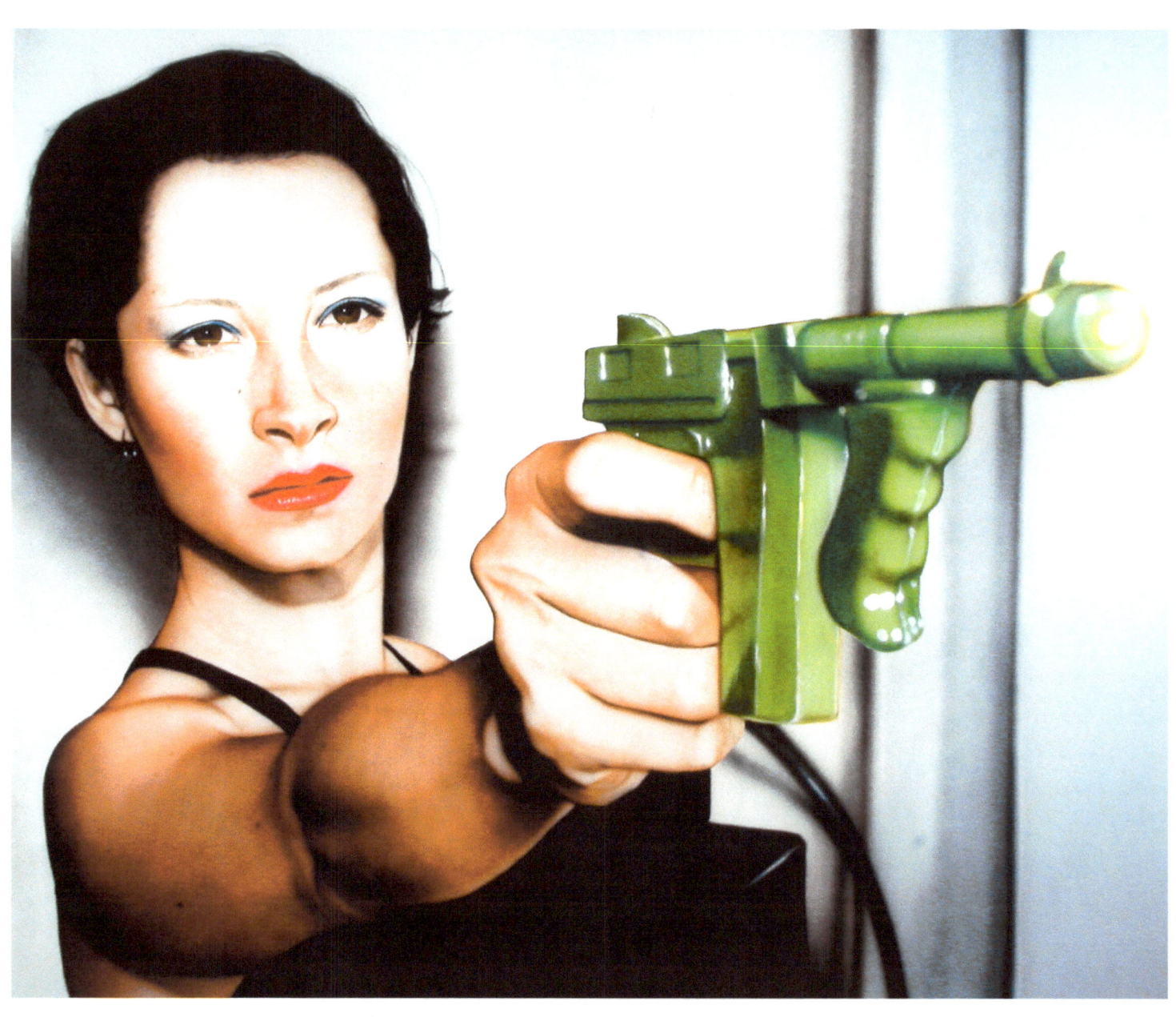

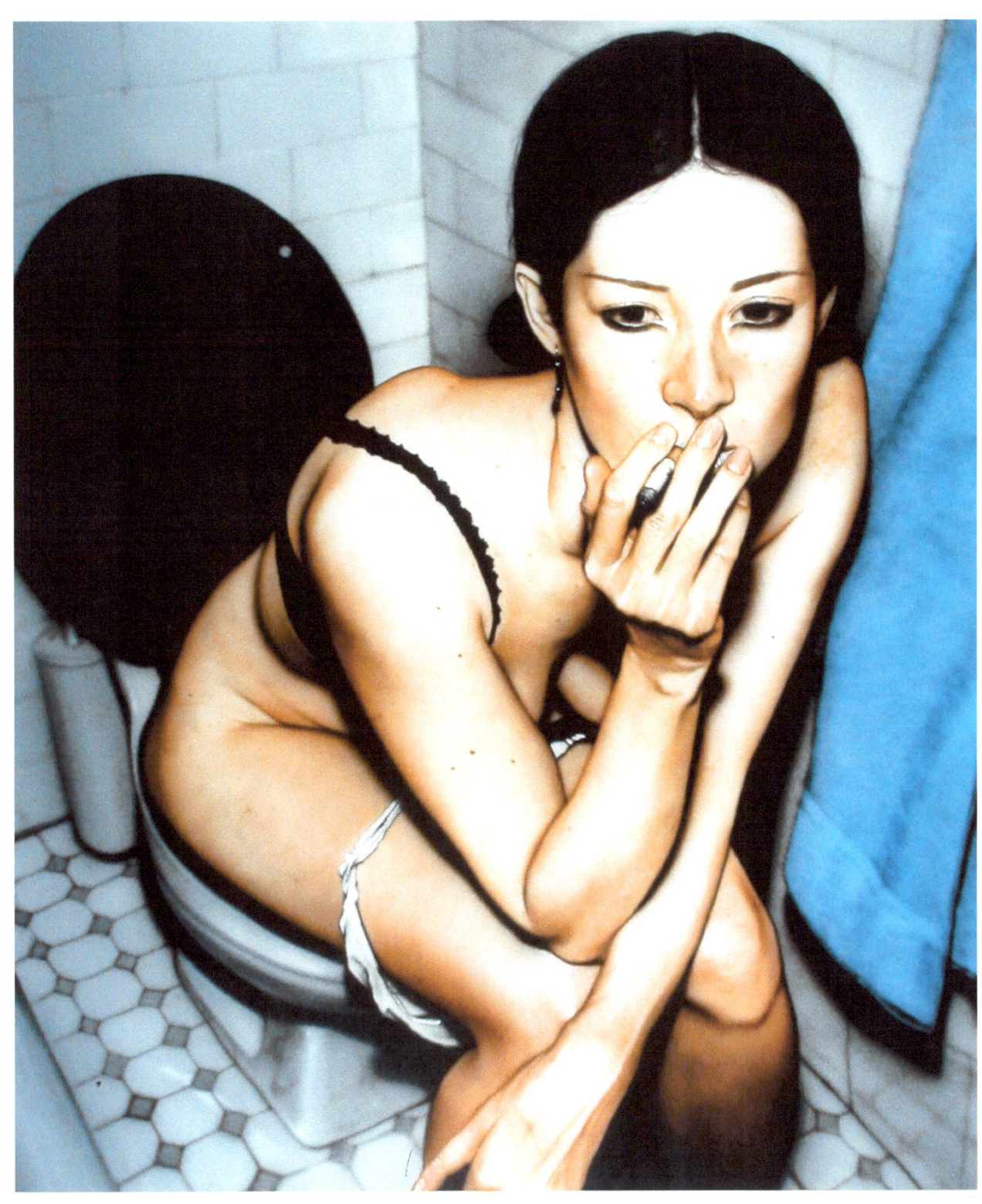

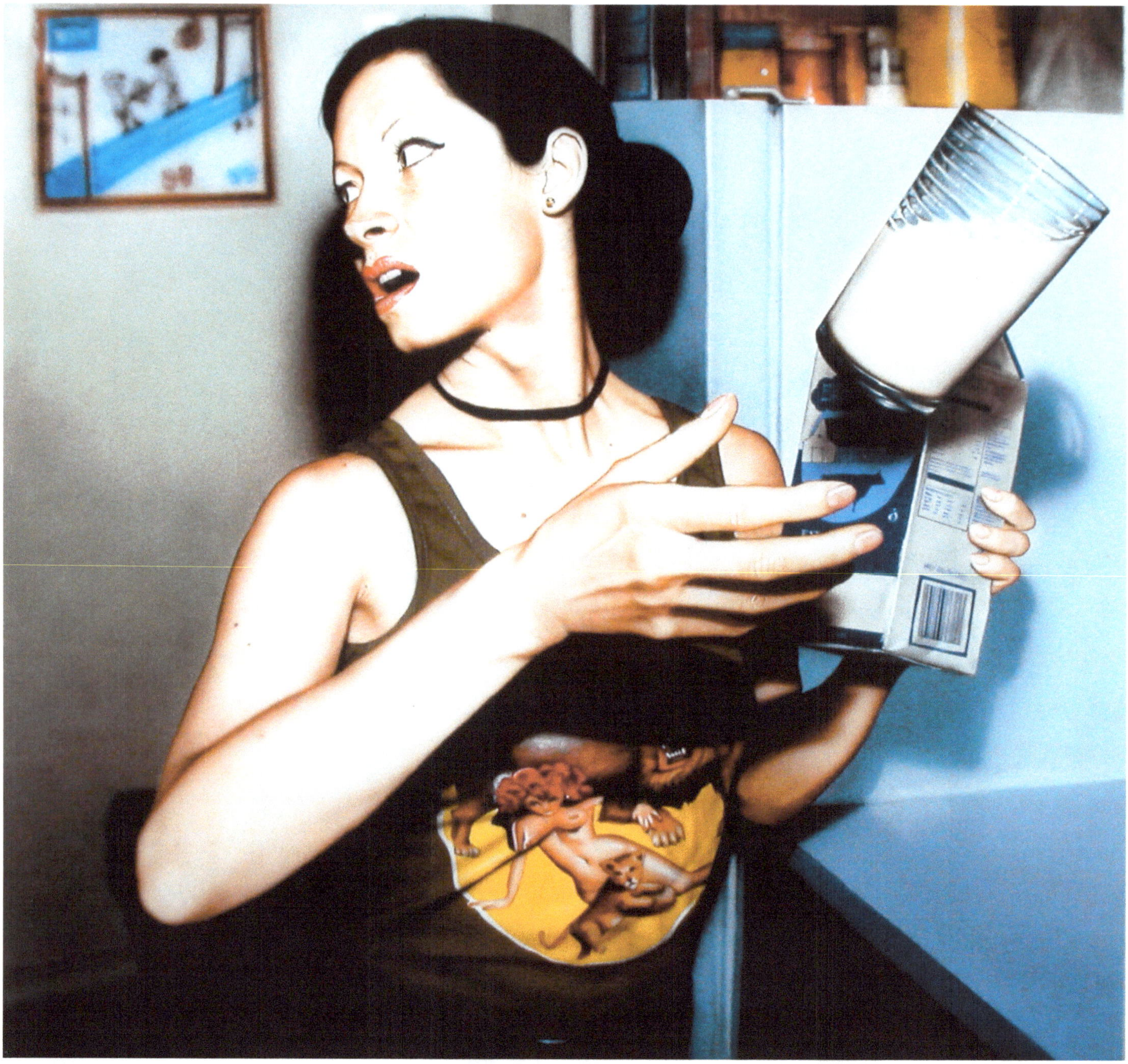

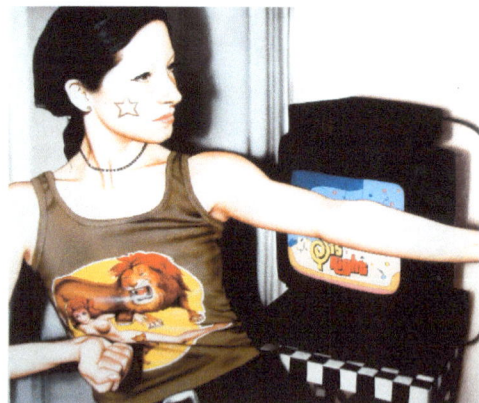

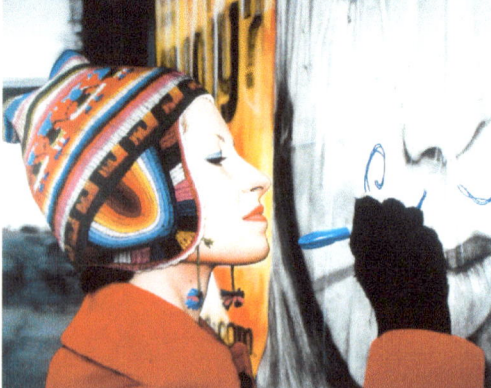

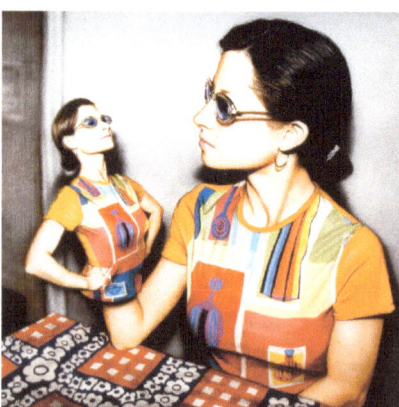

^ ACCIDENT 198 X 198 CMS 1999   > ABSTRACT PAINTING 198 X 148 CMS 1999

^ KUNG-FU 172 X 202 CMS 1999   ^ VANDAL 148 X 198 CMS 1999   ^ DIALOGUE 4 198 X 198 CMS 1999

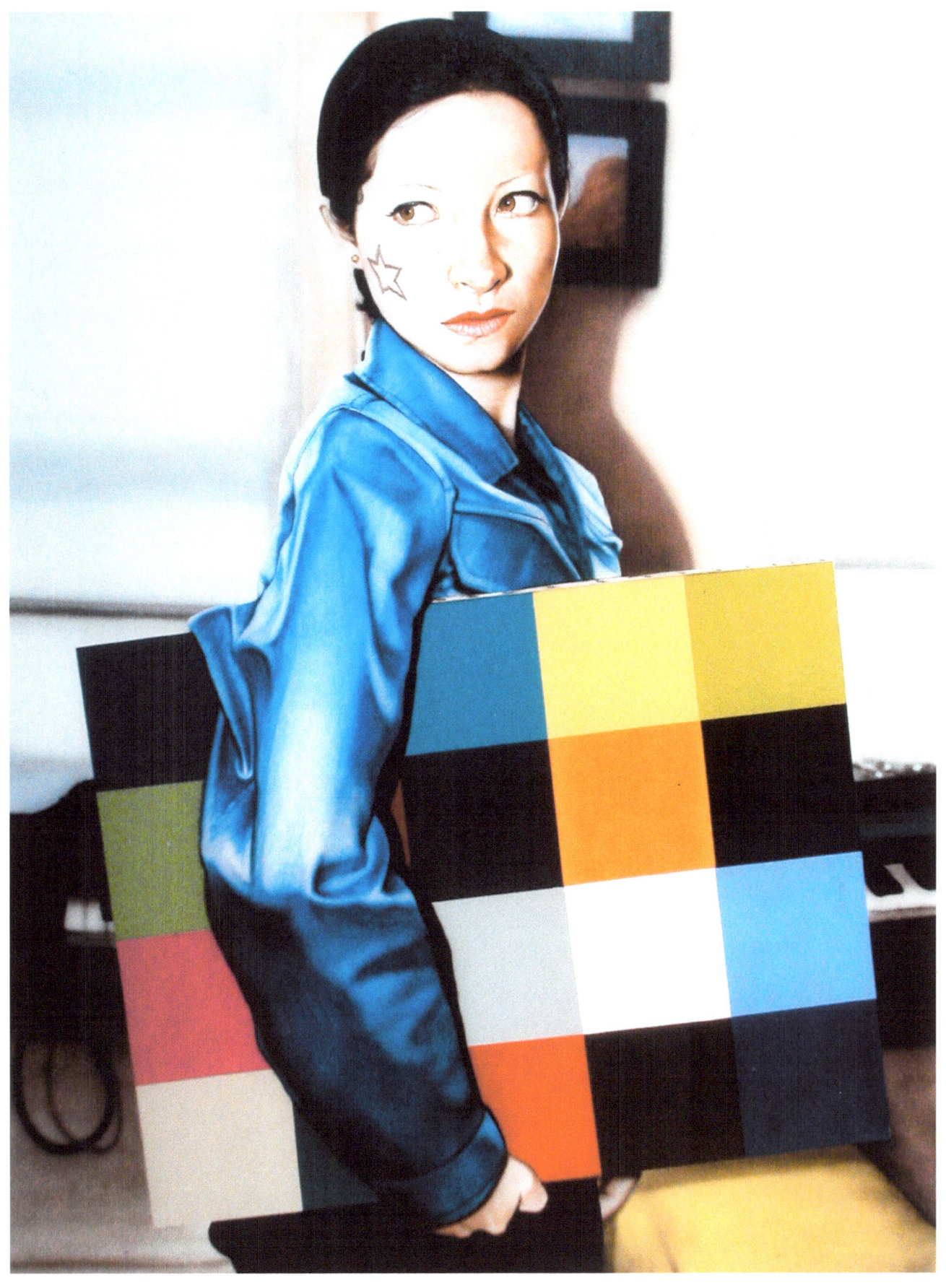

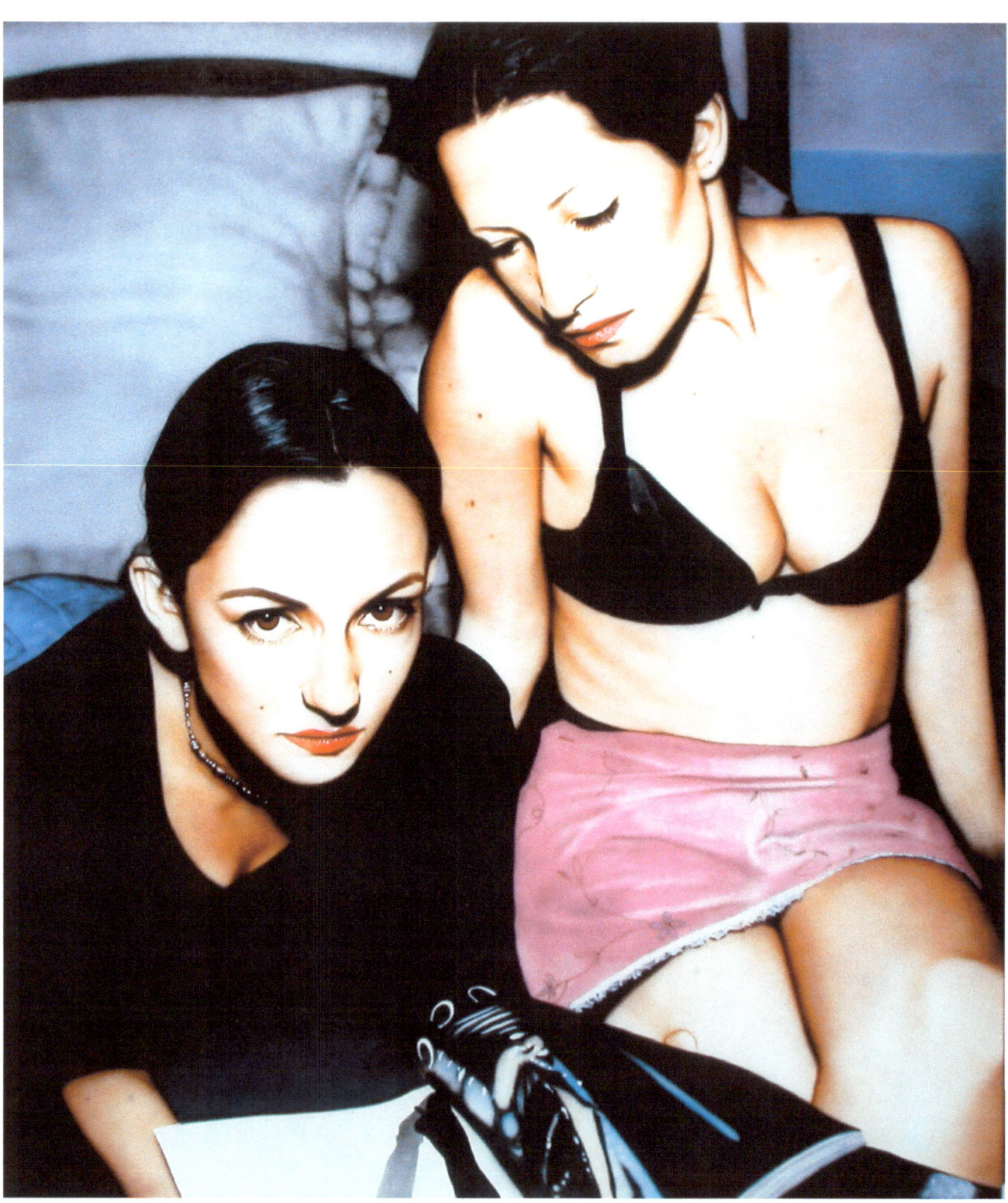

^ TWO GIRLS 202 X 172 CMS 1999
> DEVIL-BOY 202 X 172 CMS 1999

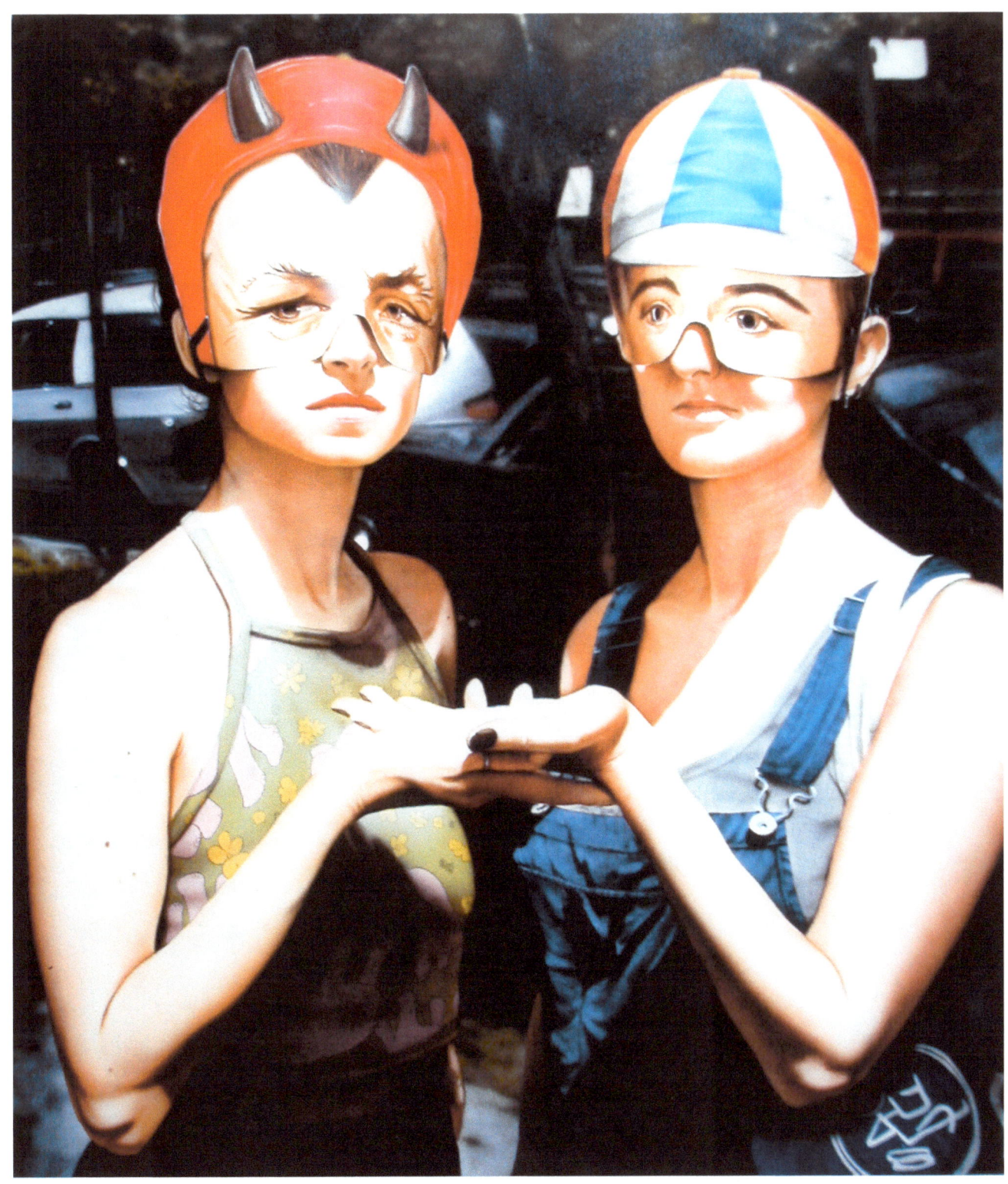

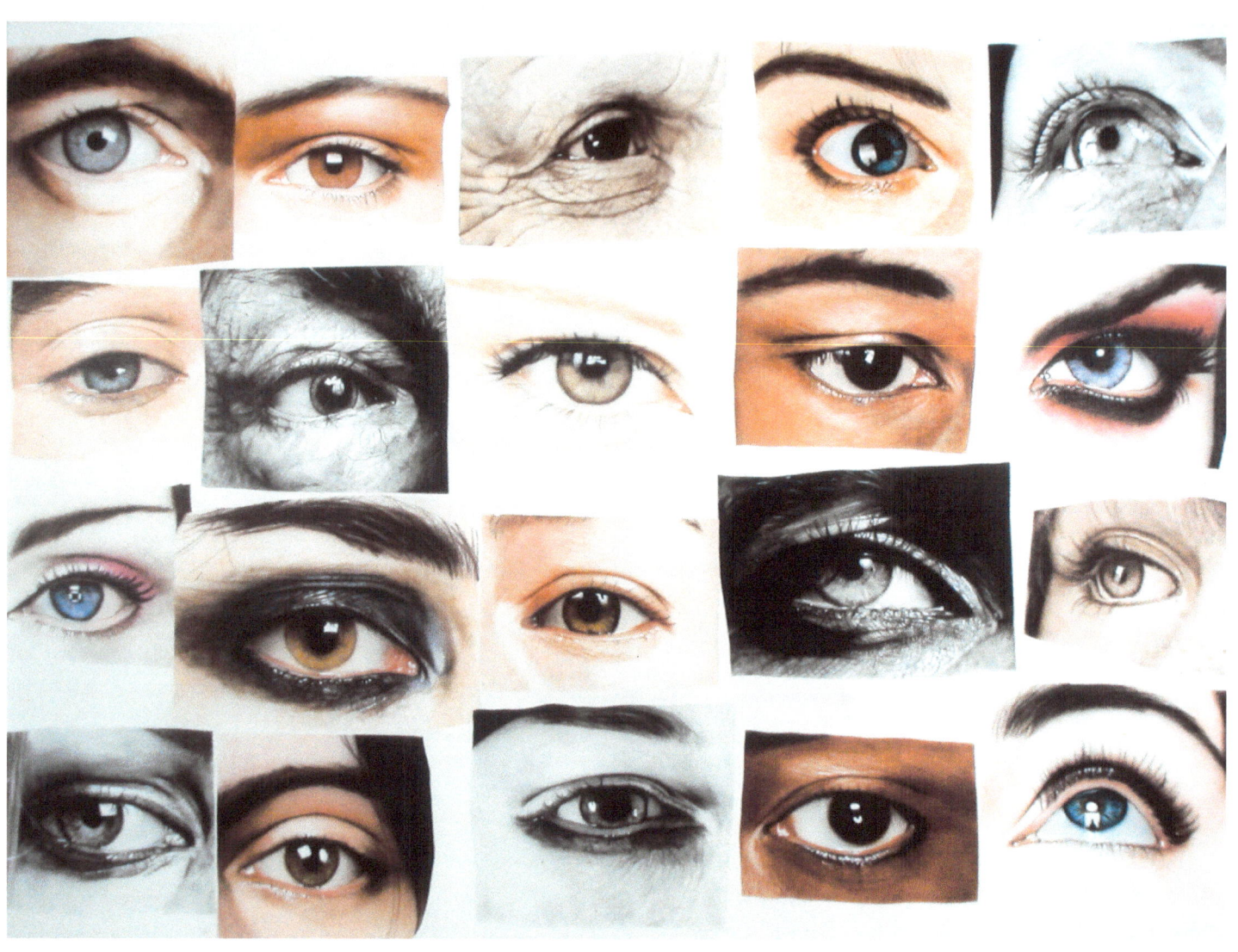

^ TWENTY EYES 148 X 198 CMS 1999

> CRAZY BUDDHA 172 X 202 CMS 1999   > TWO HEADS 148 X 198 CMS 1999

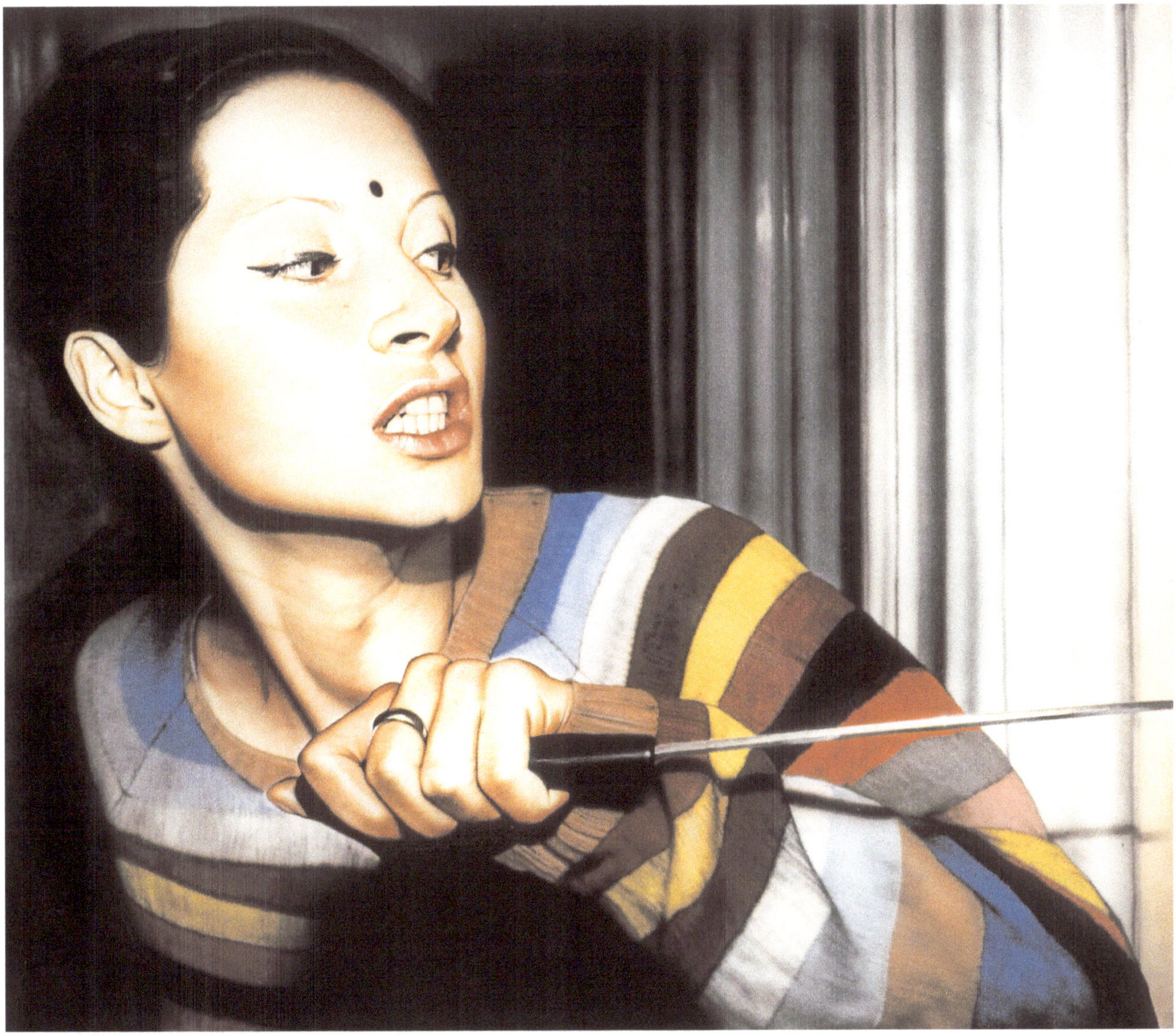

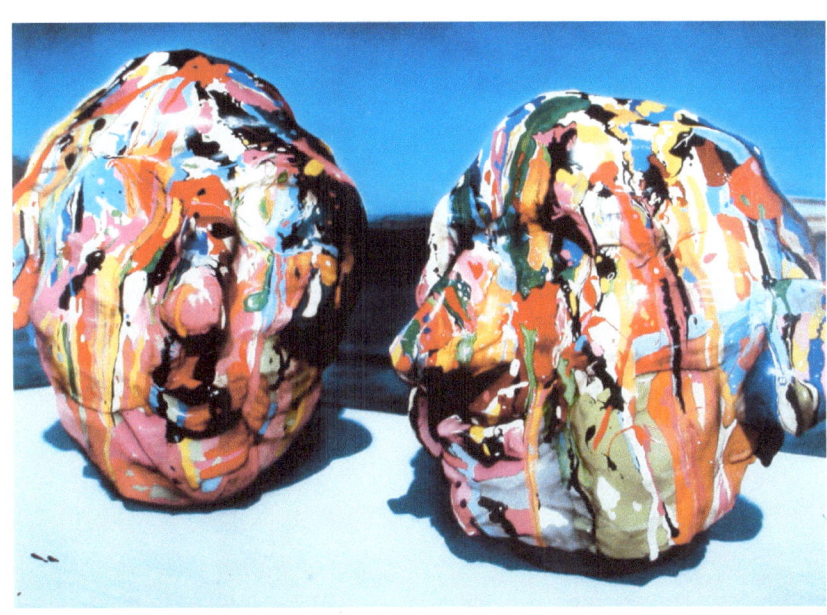

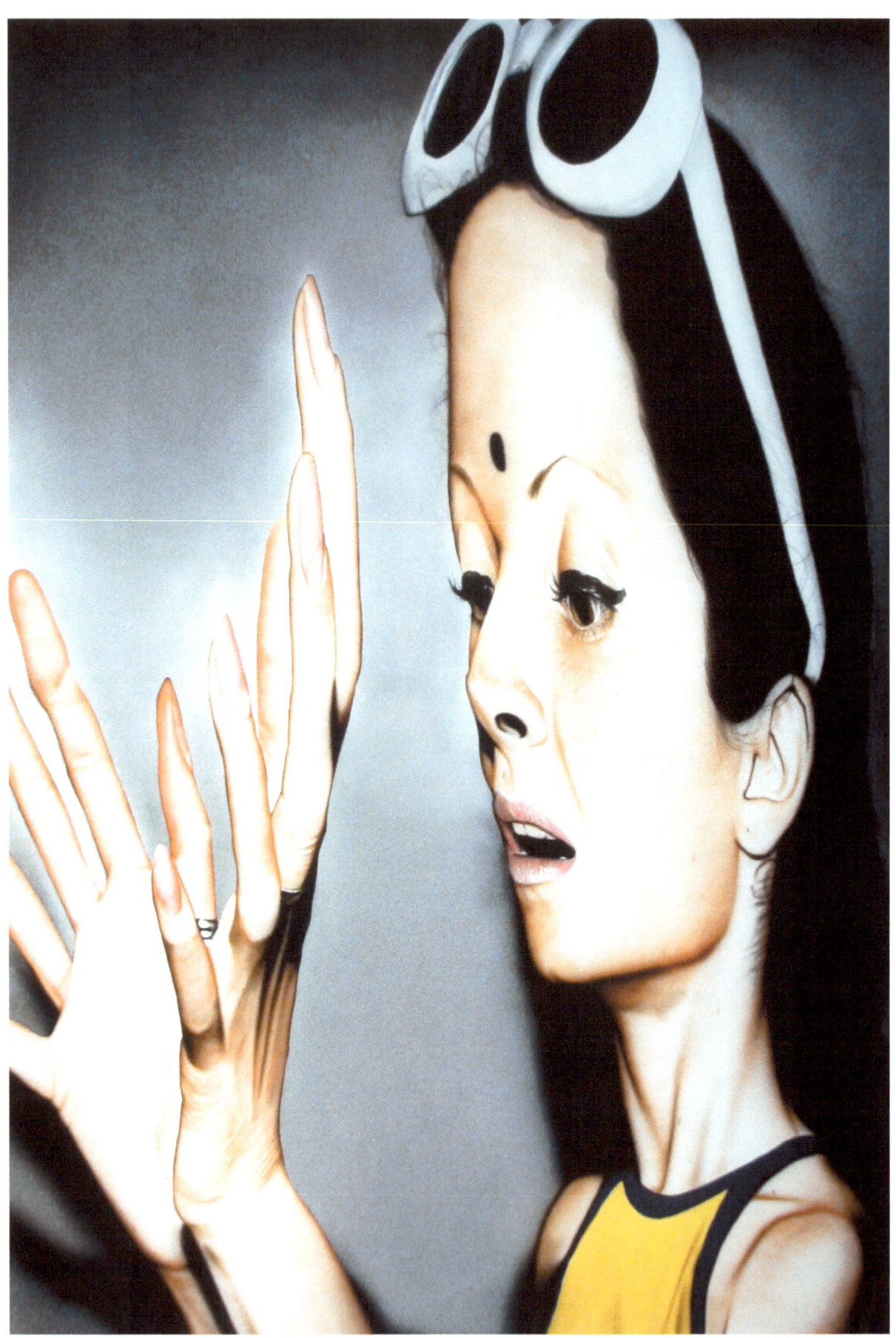

CATHEDRAL 228 X 152 CMS 1999

POWDER BOX 198 X 198 CMS 2000   POWDER BOX 2 148 X 198 CMS 2000

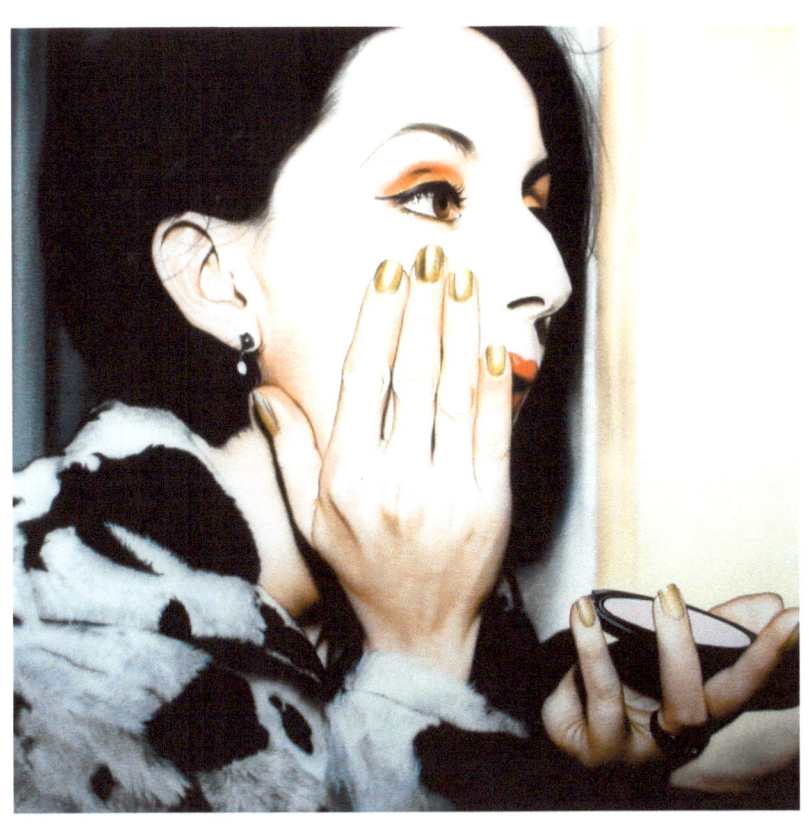

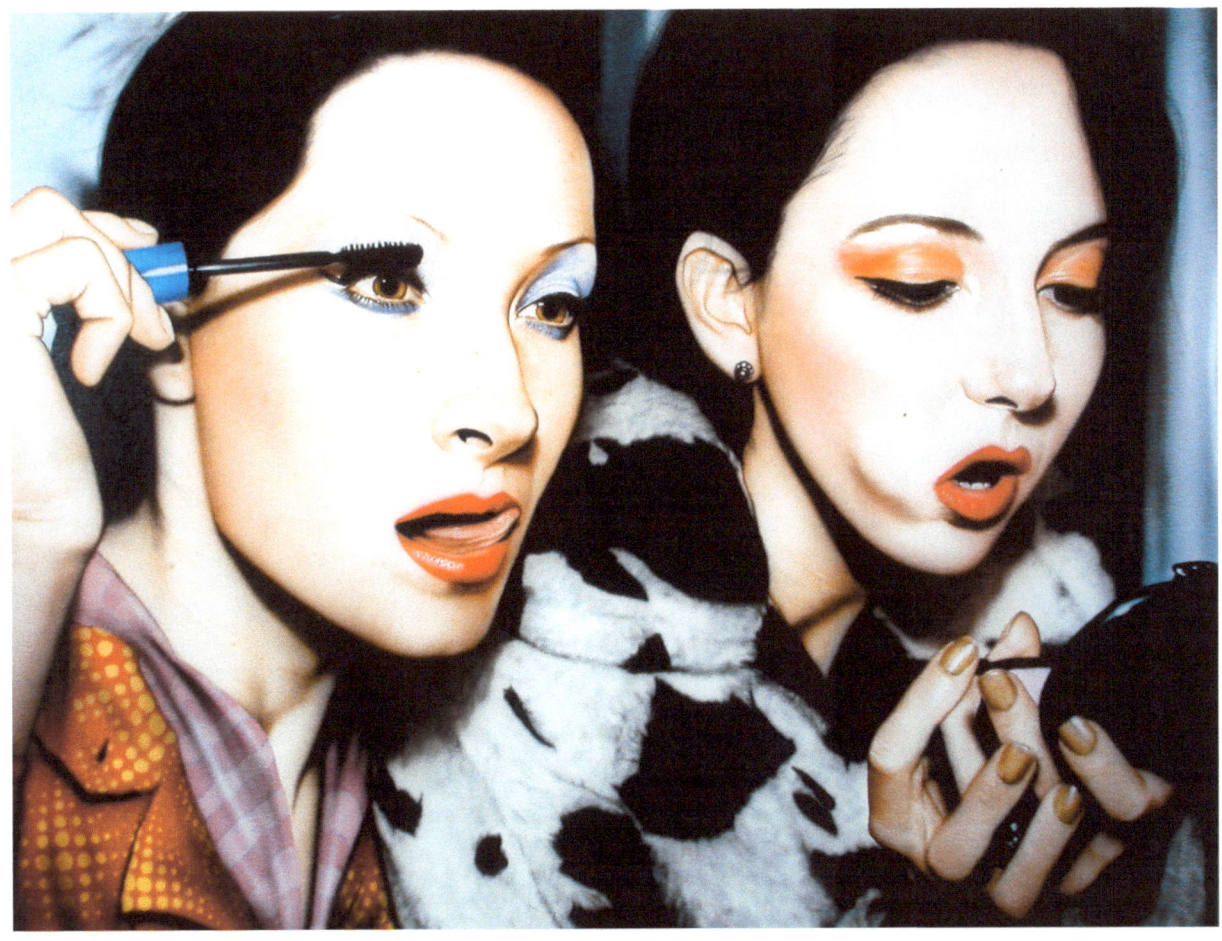

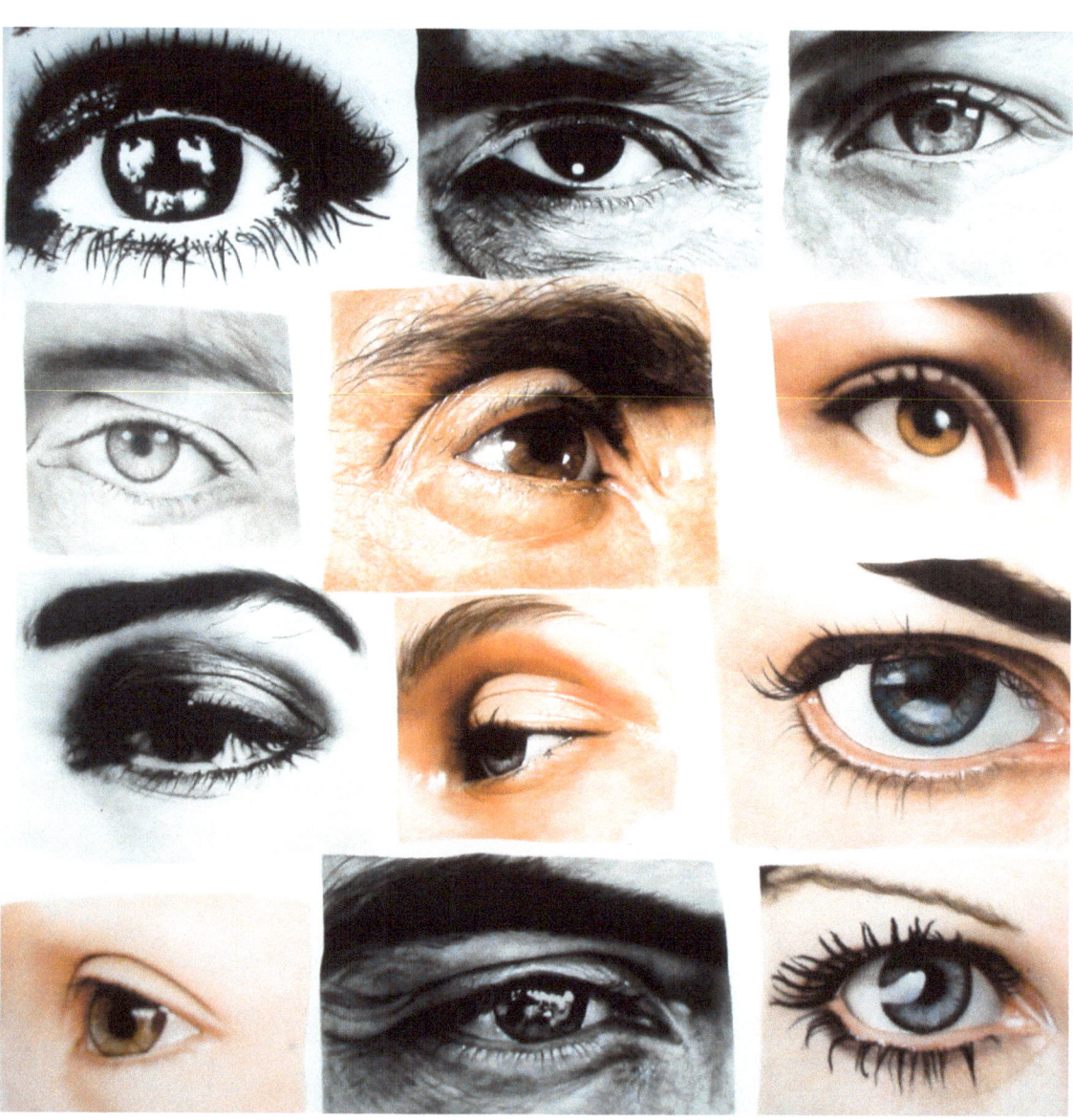

^ TWELVE EYES 172 X 172 CMS 2000
> TWO METHODS 172 X 172 CMS 2000

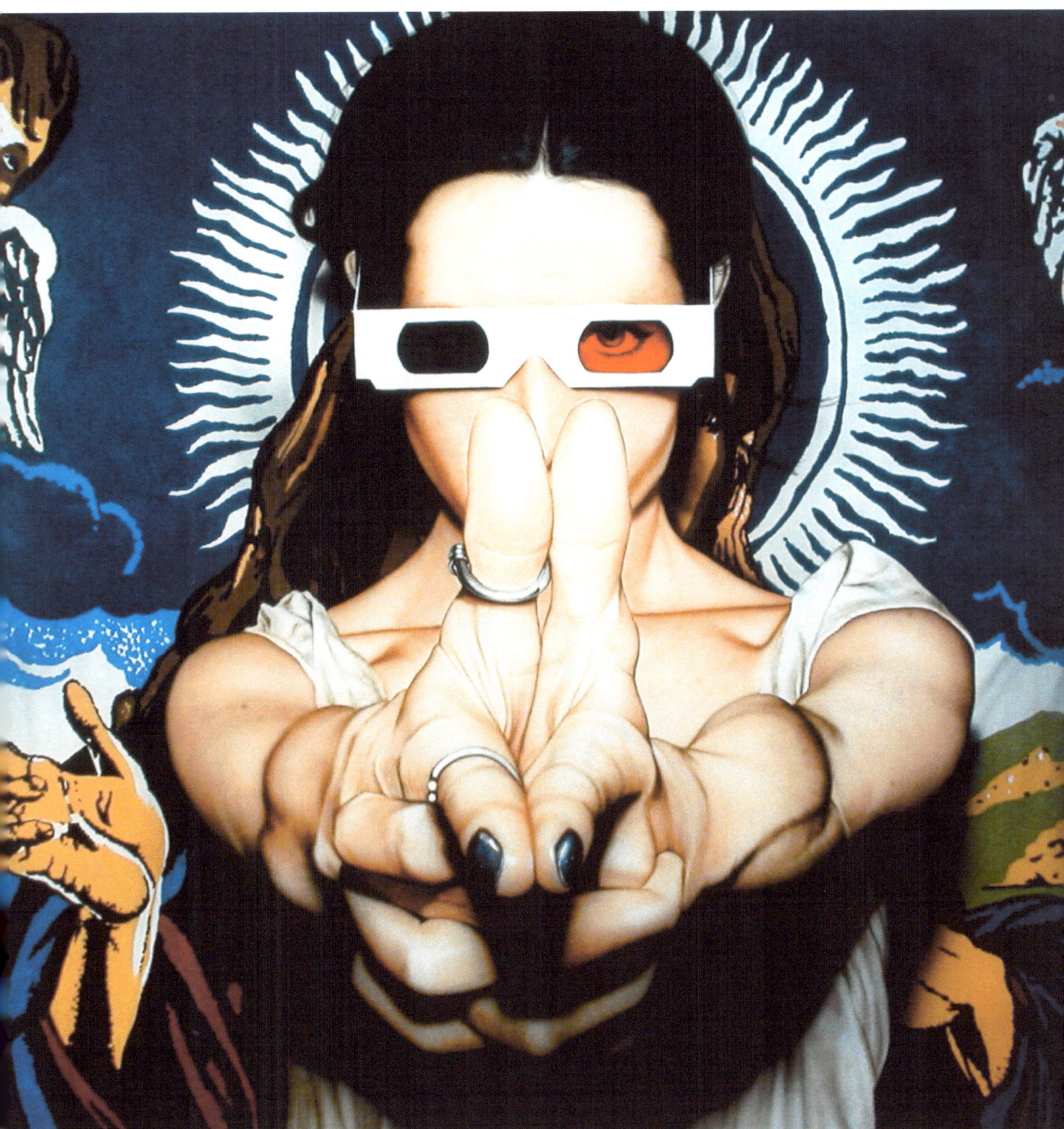

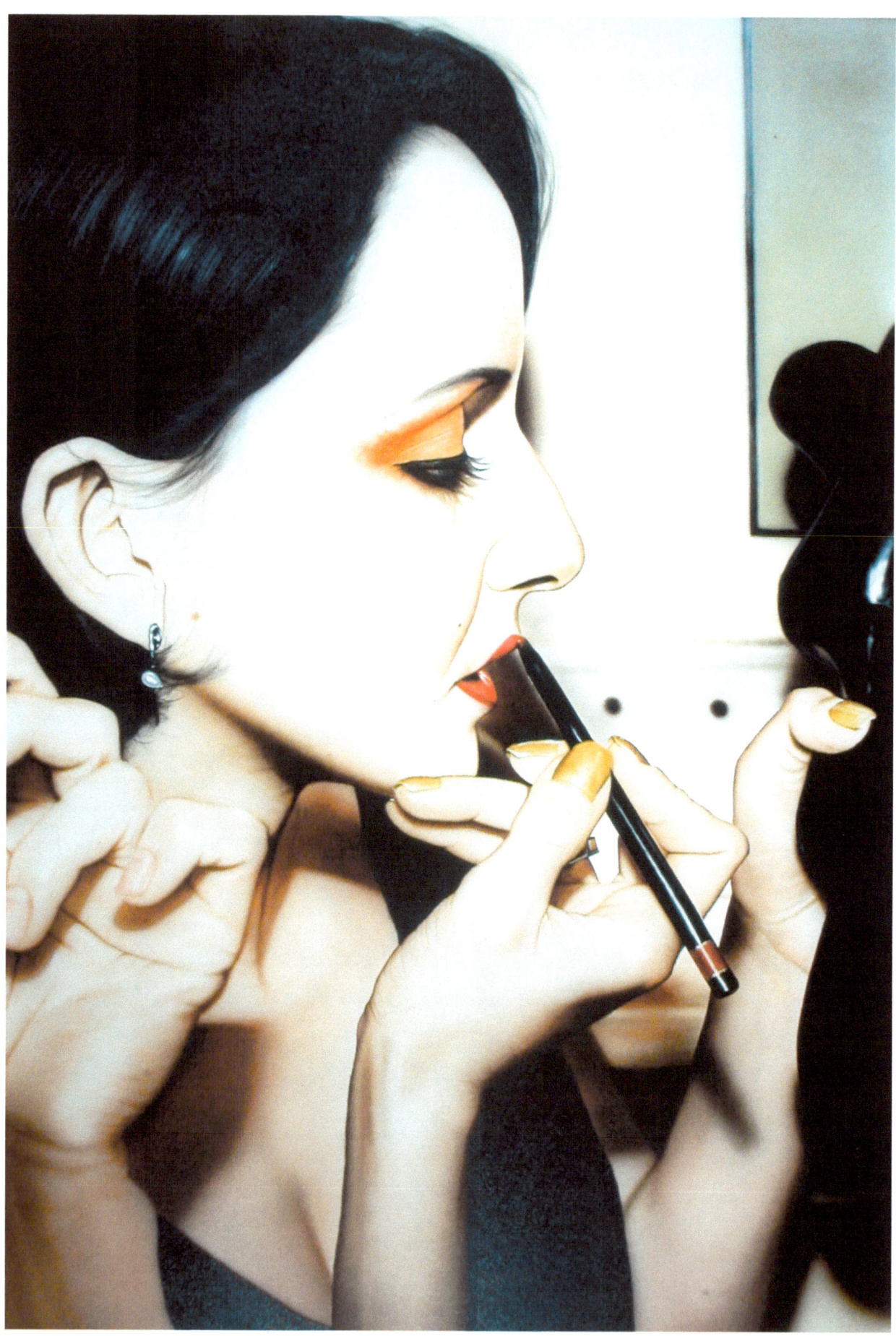

^ POWDER BOX 3 228 X 152 CMS 2000

> MERMAID 172 X 202 CMS 2000   > POWDER BOX 4 198 X 148 CMS 2000

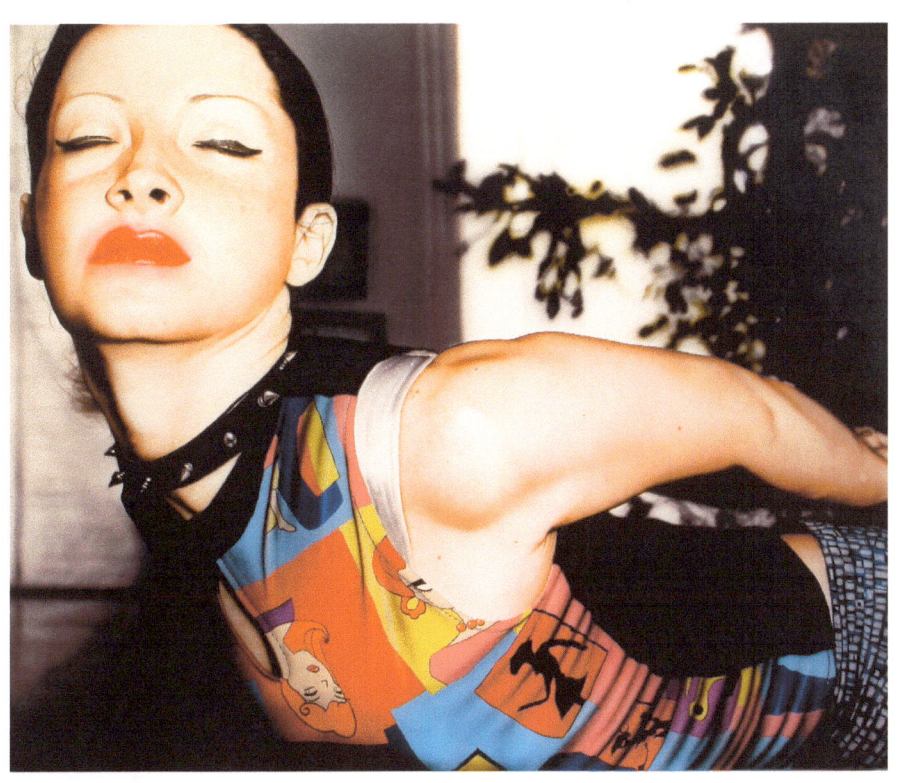

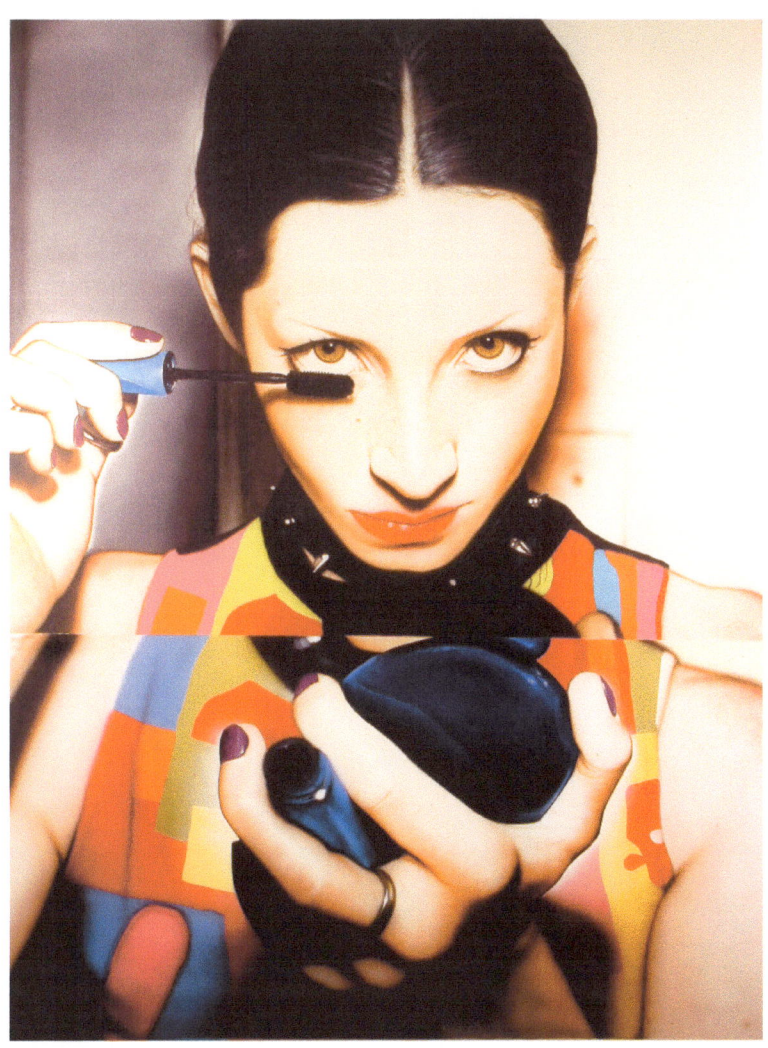

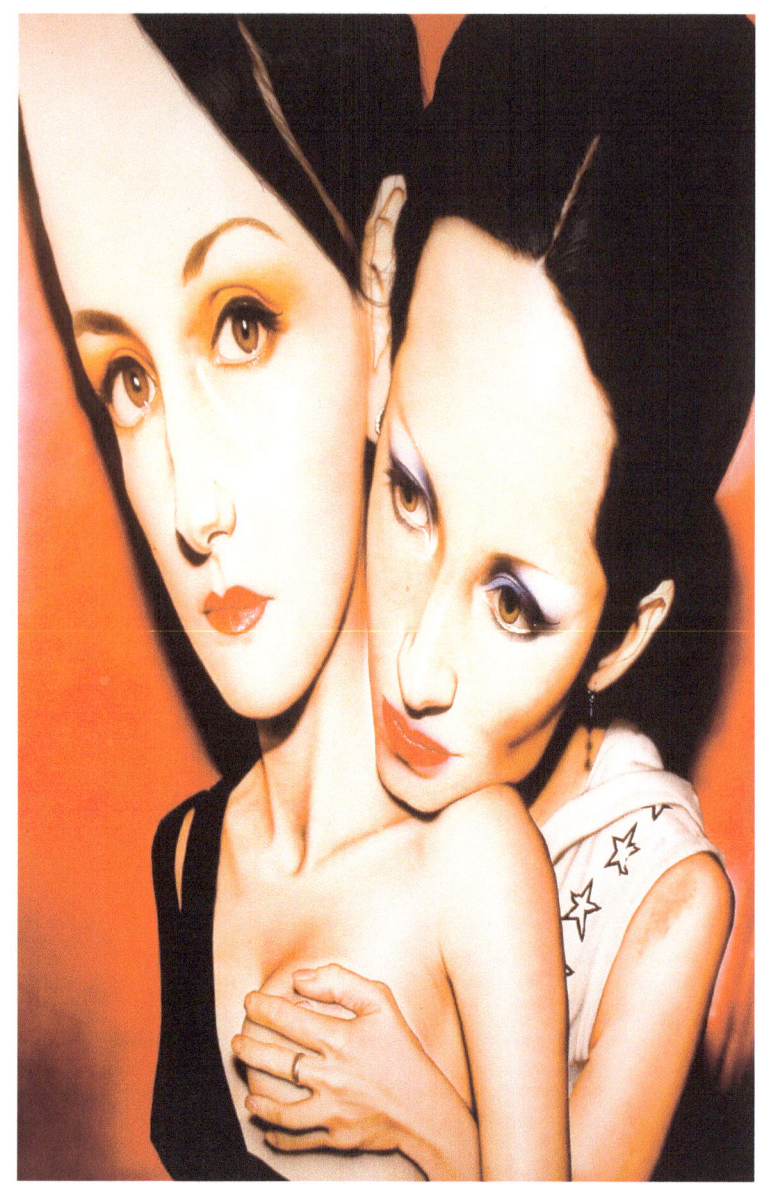

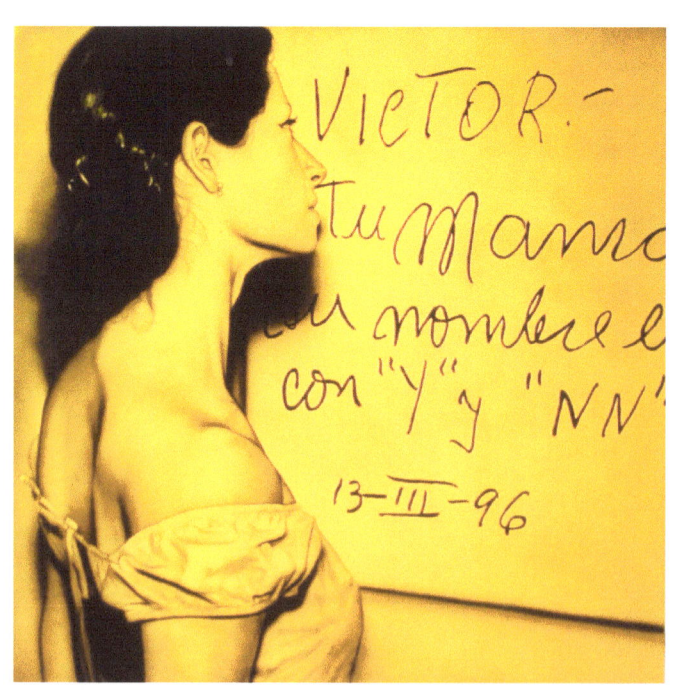

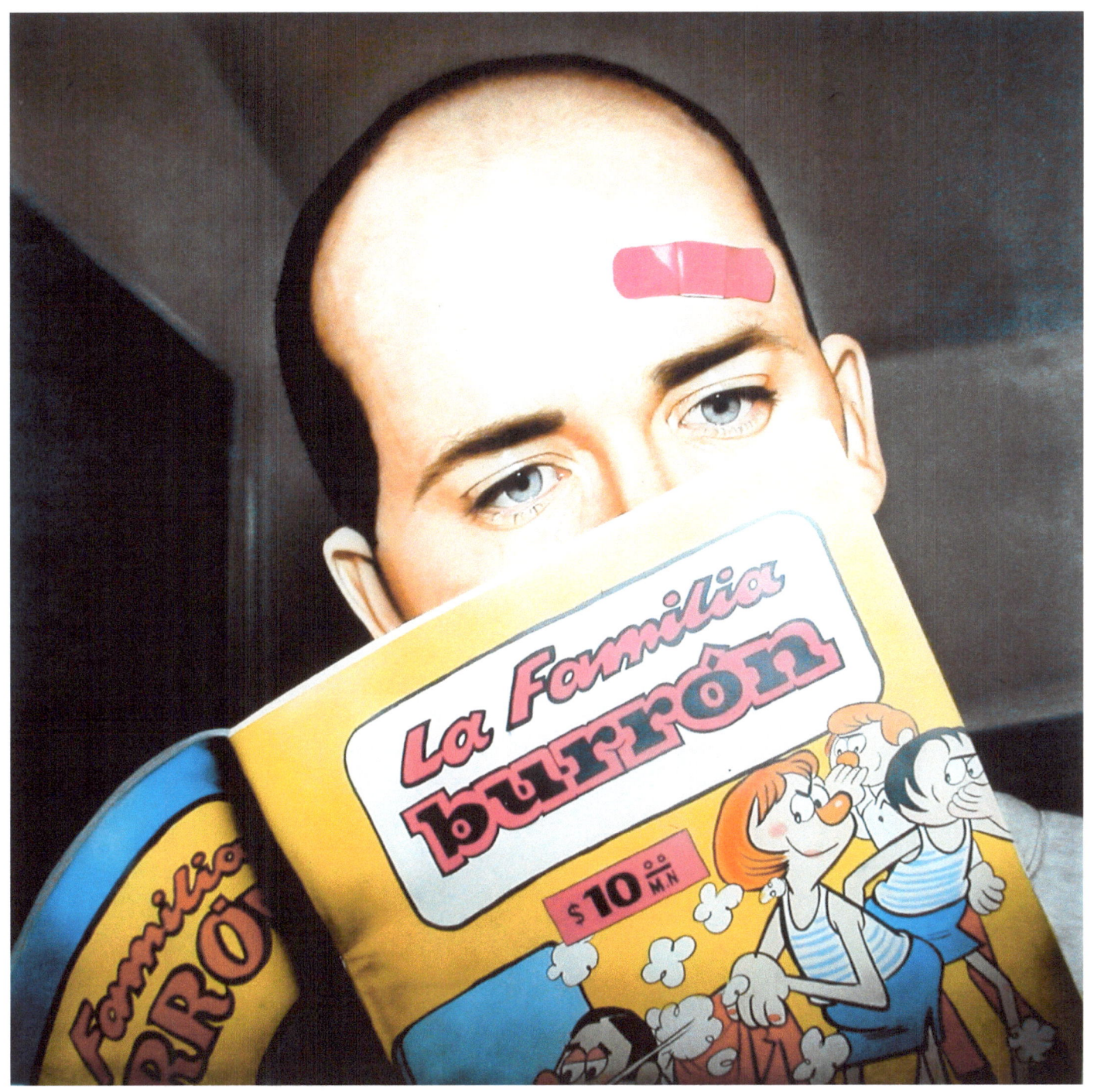

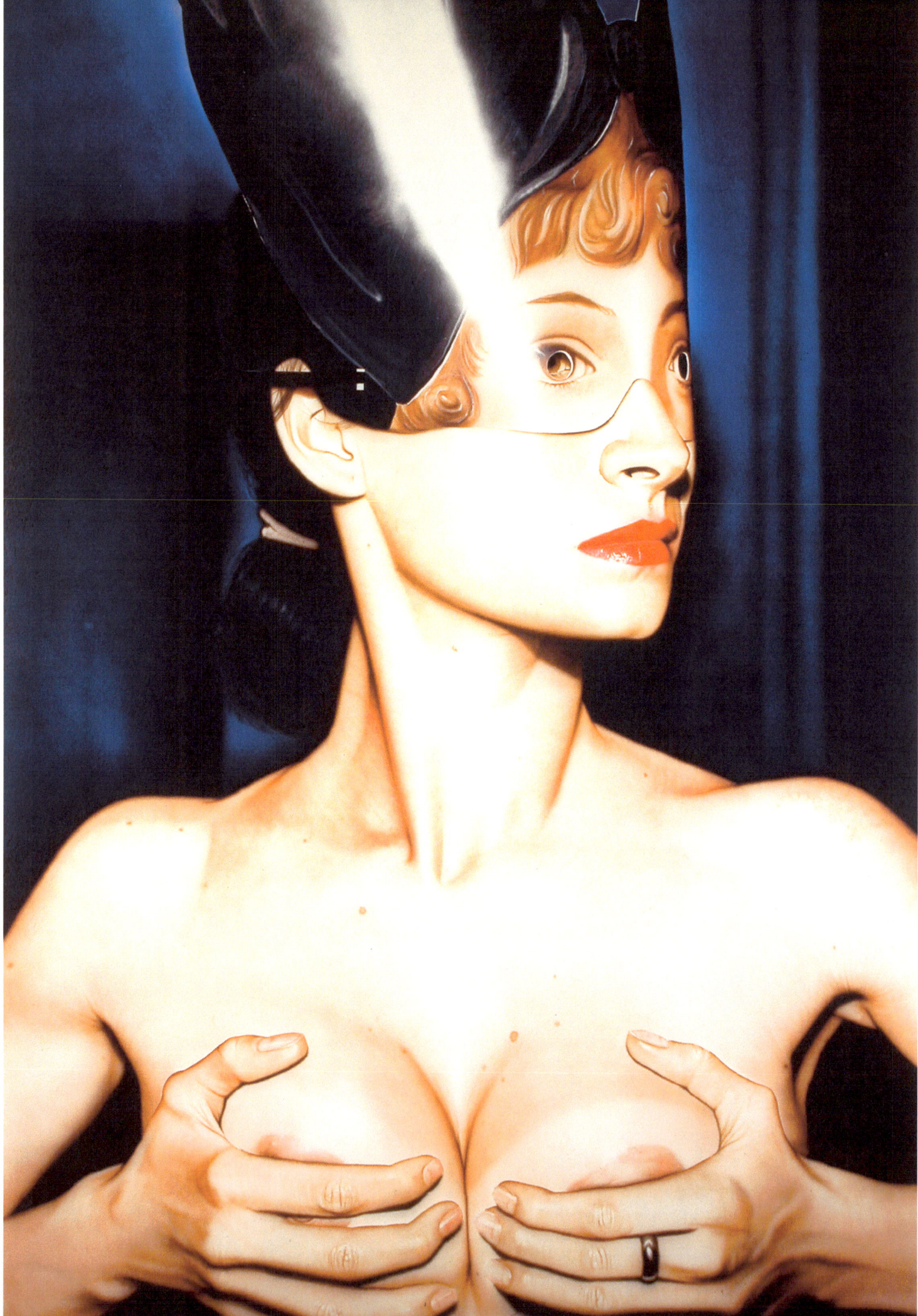

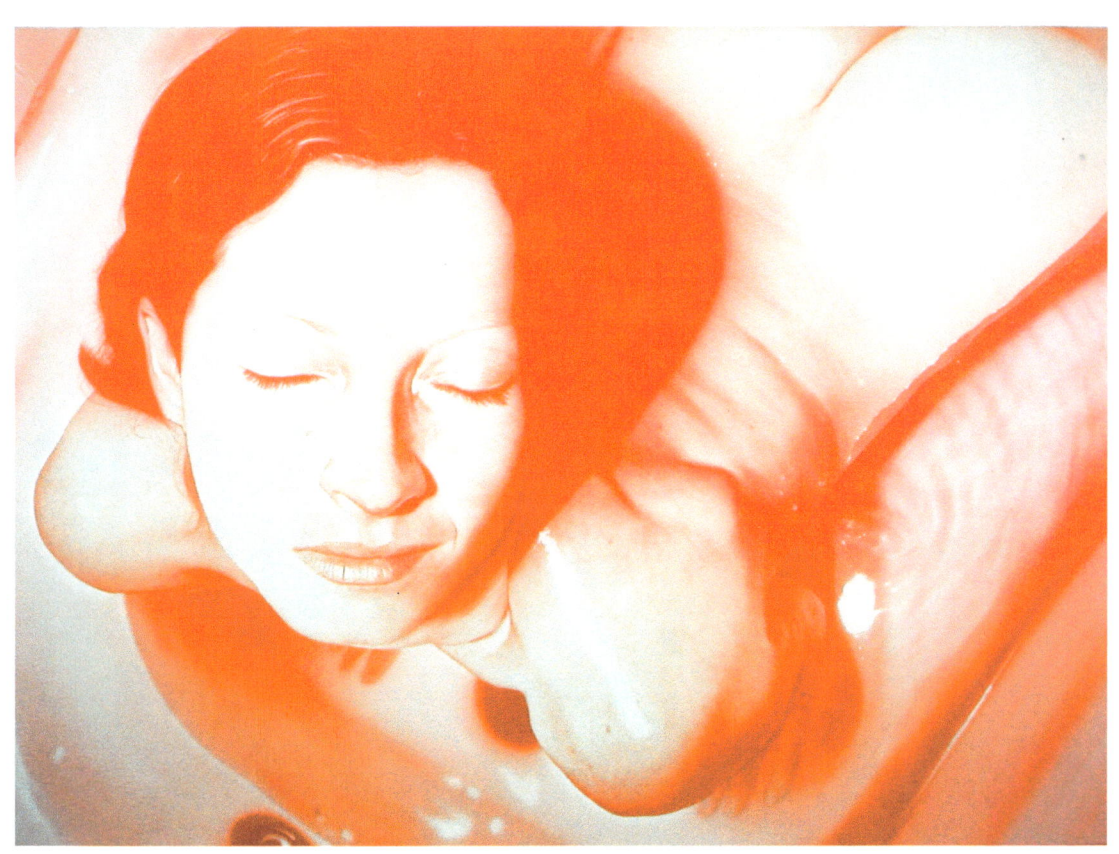

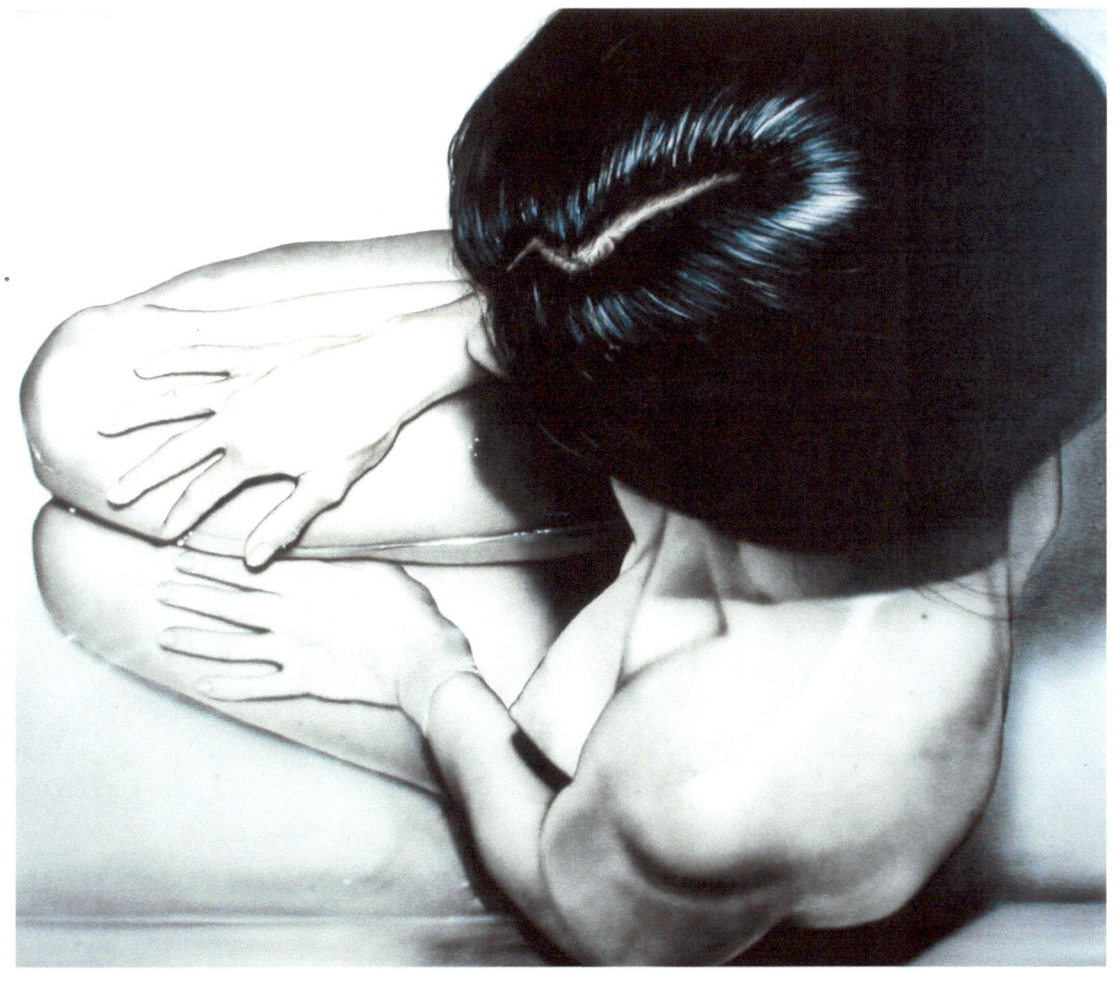

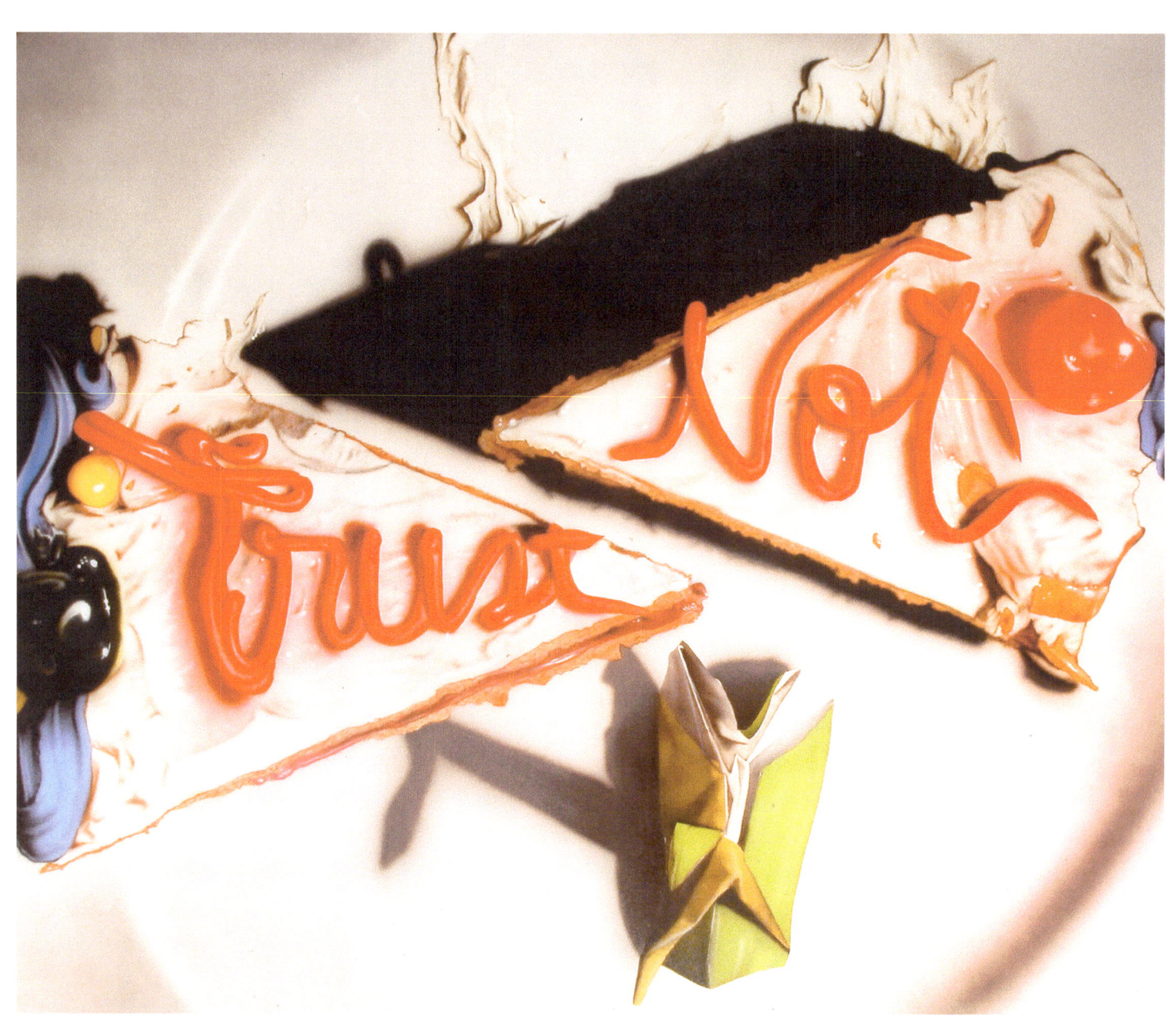

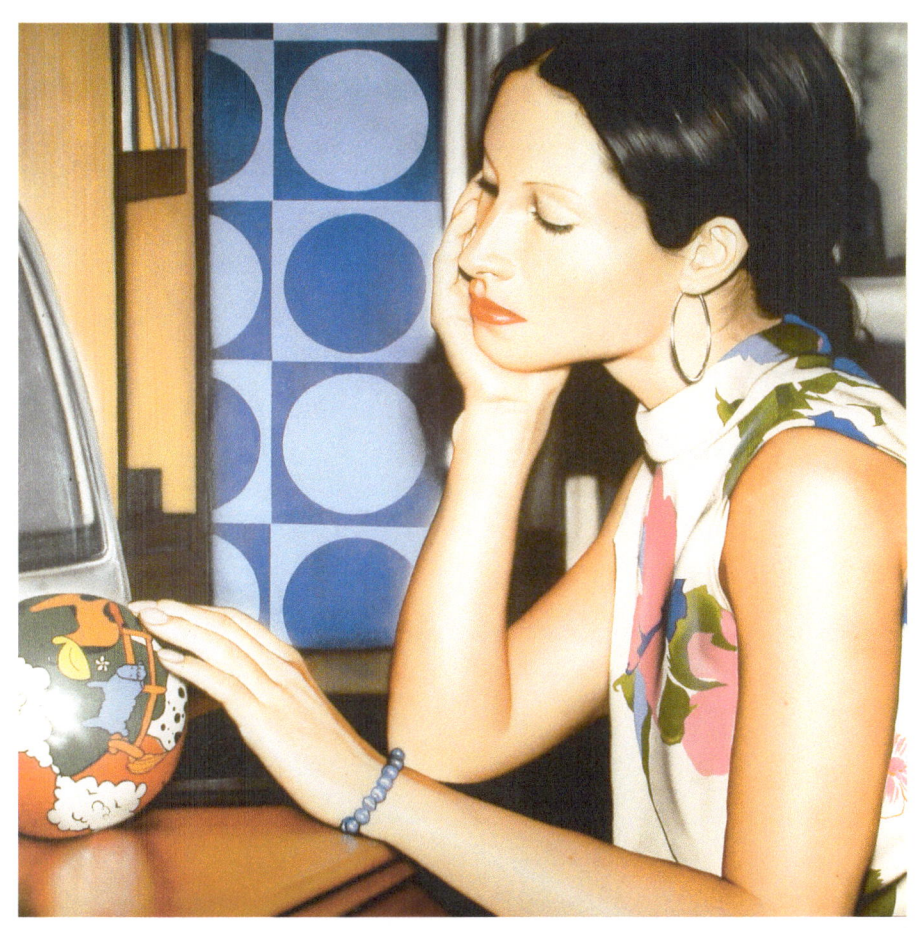

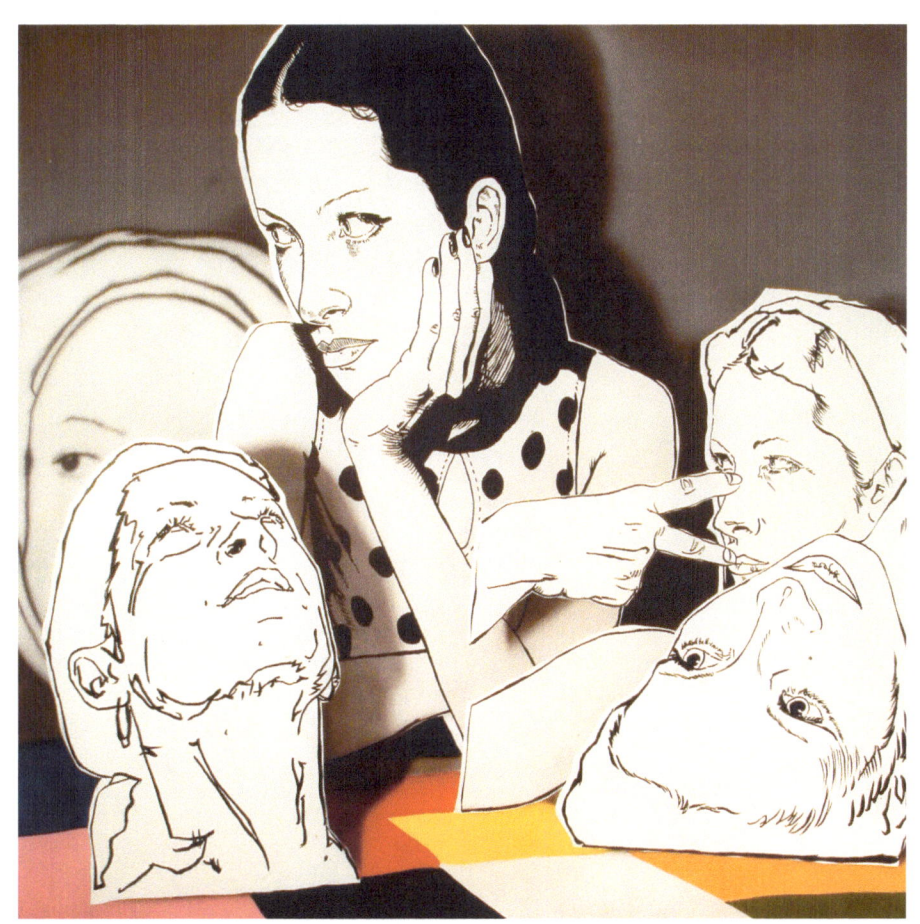

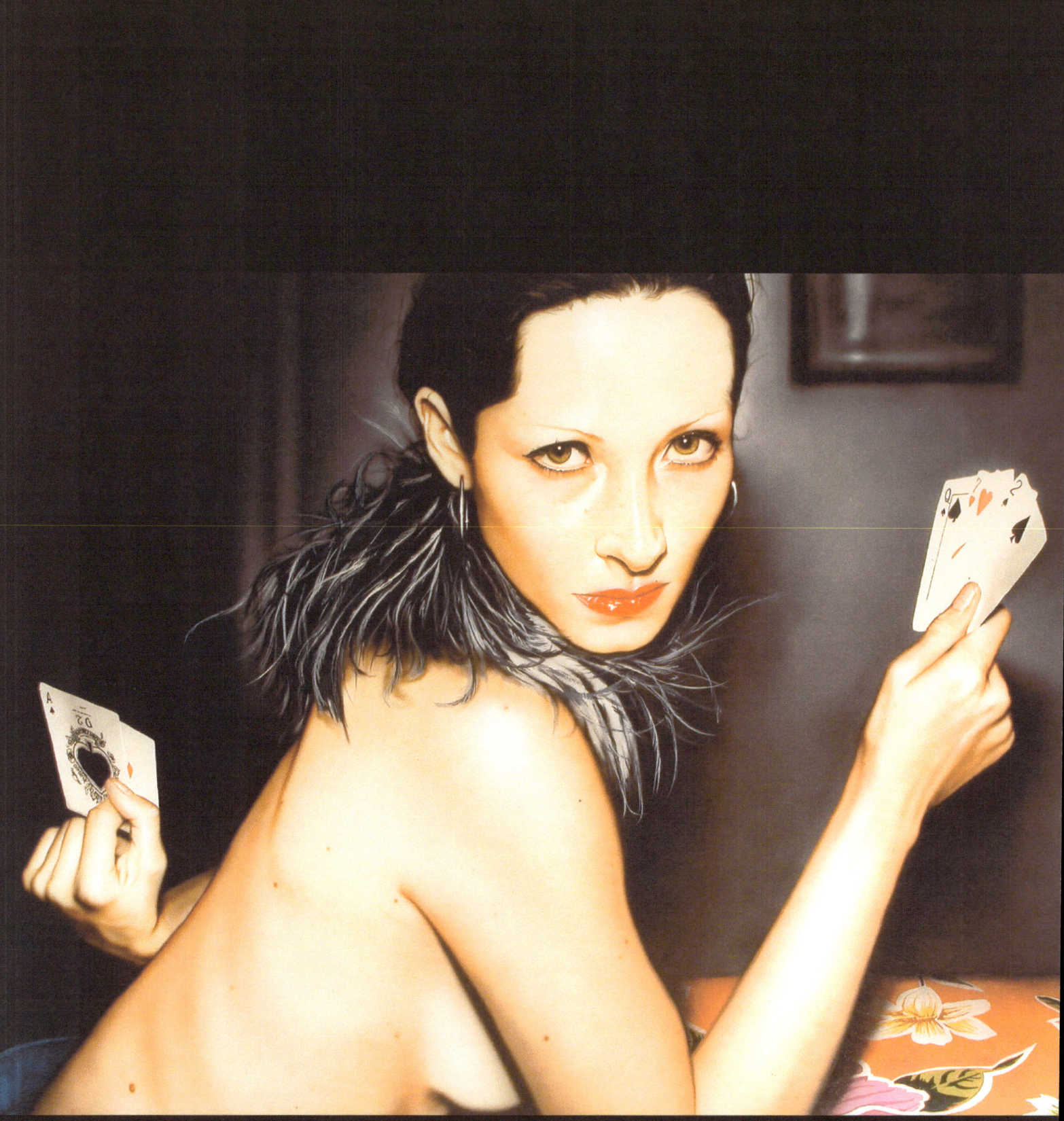

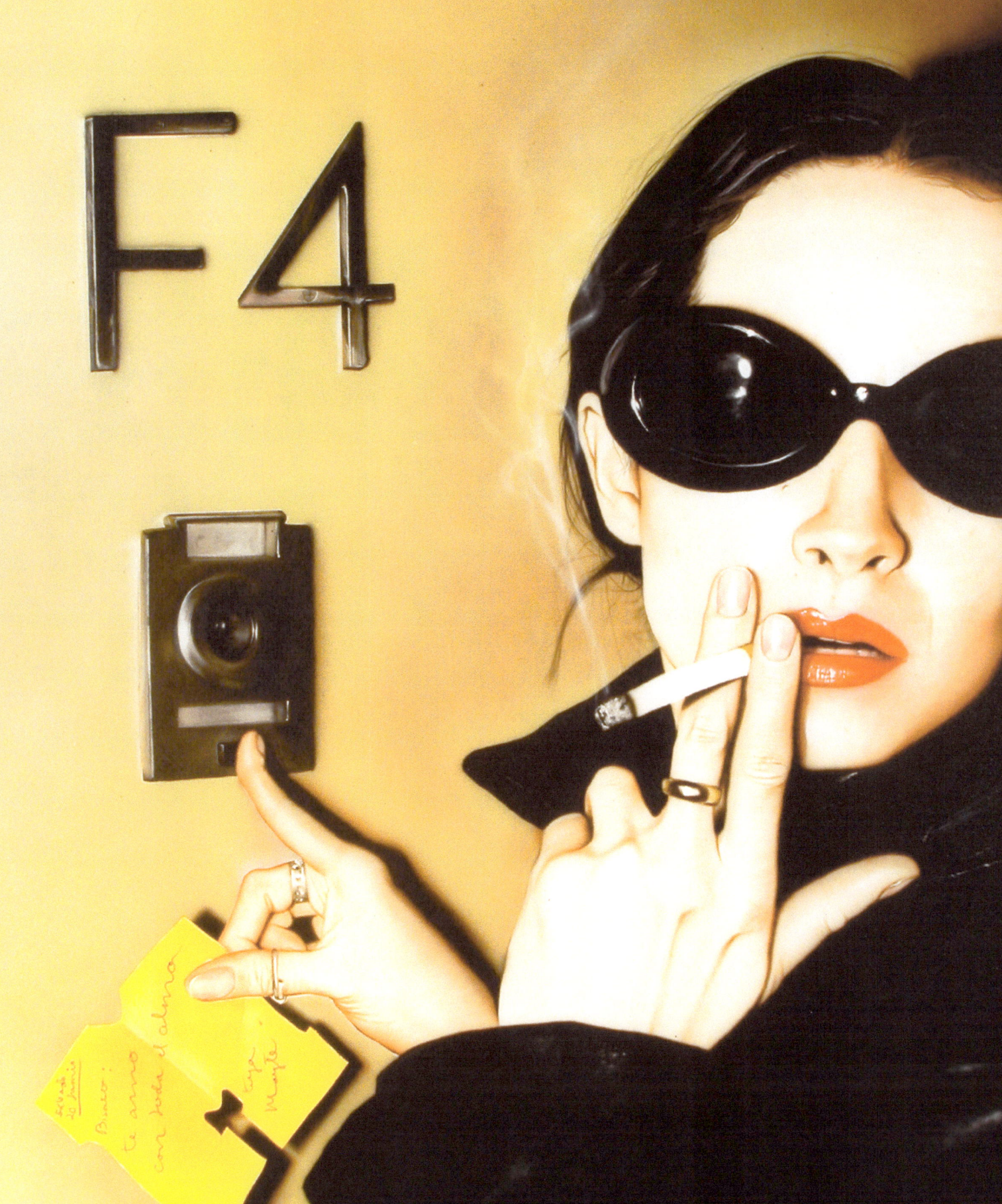

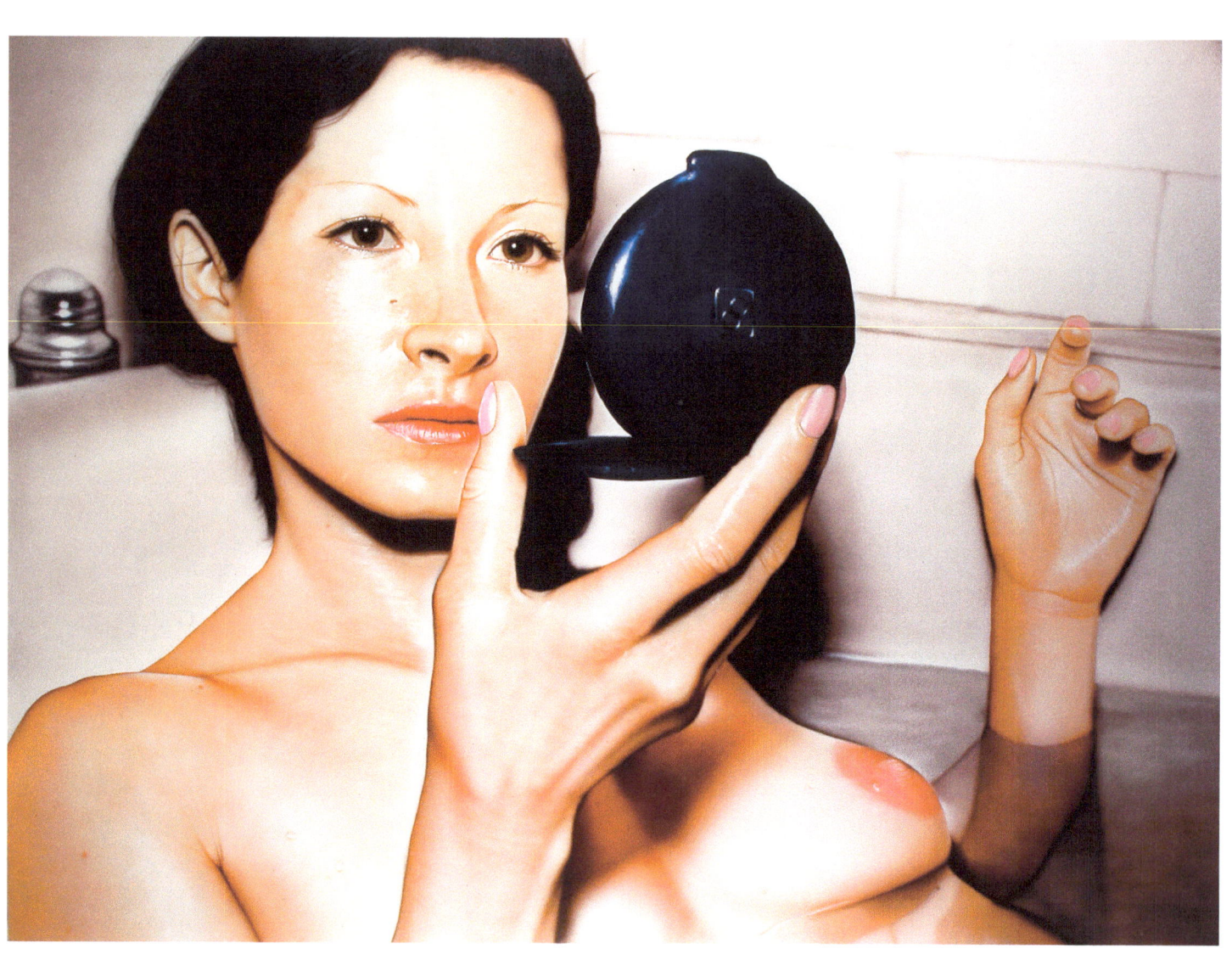

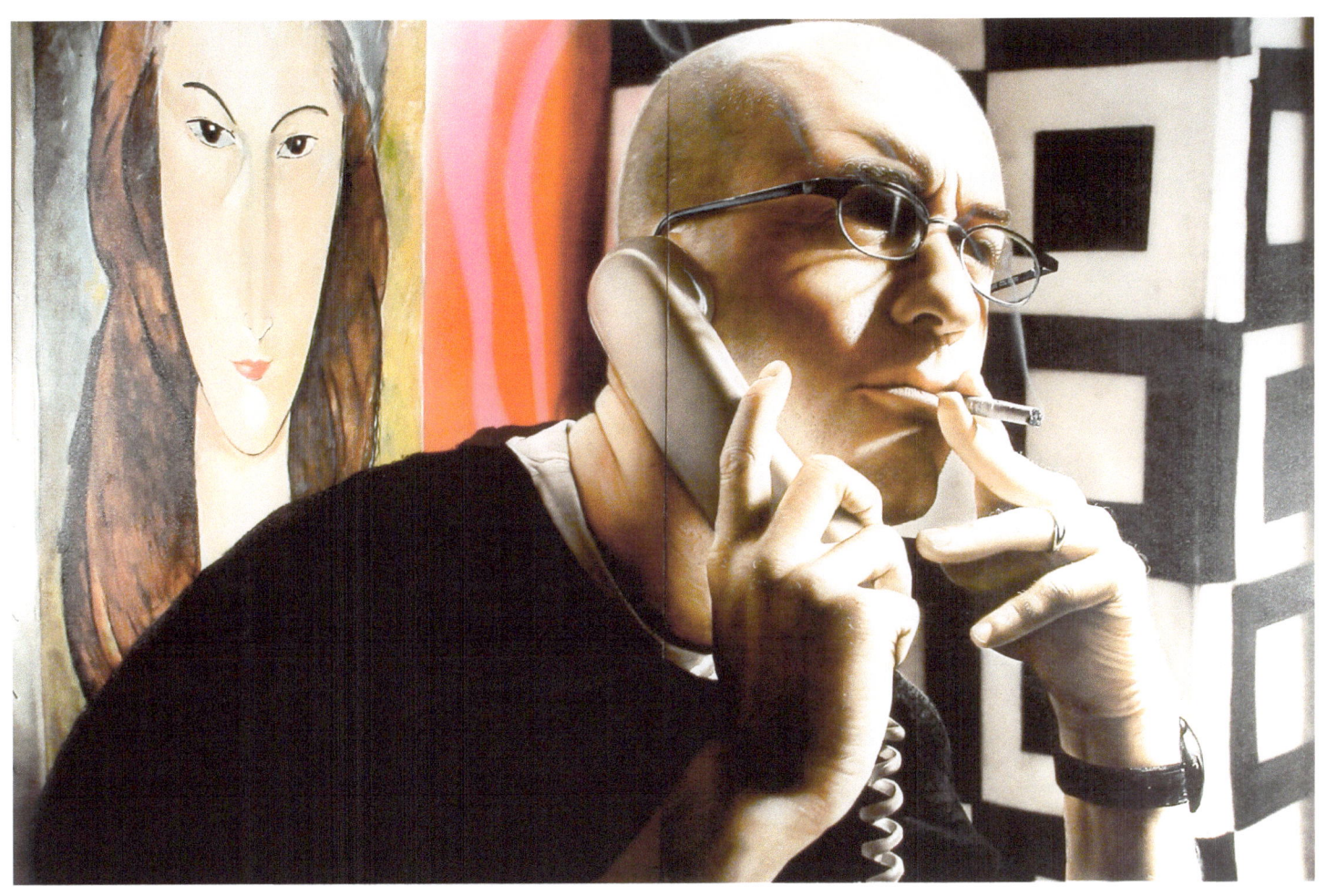

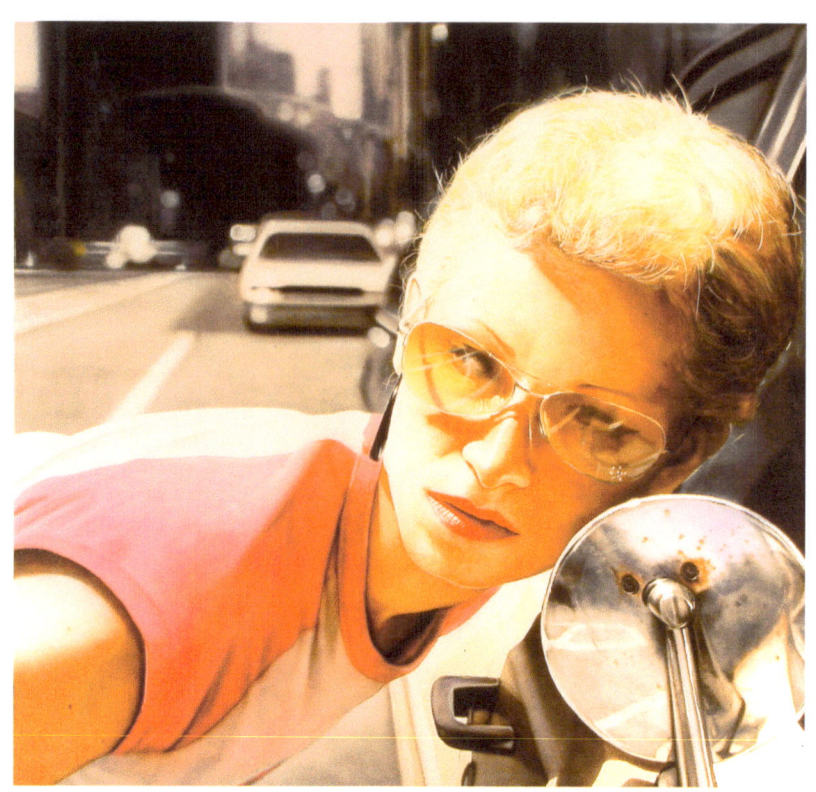

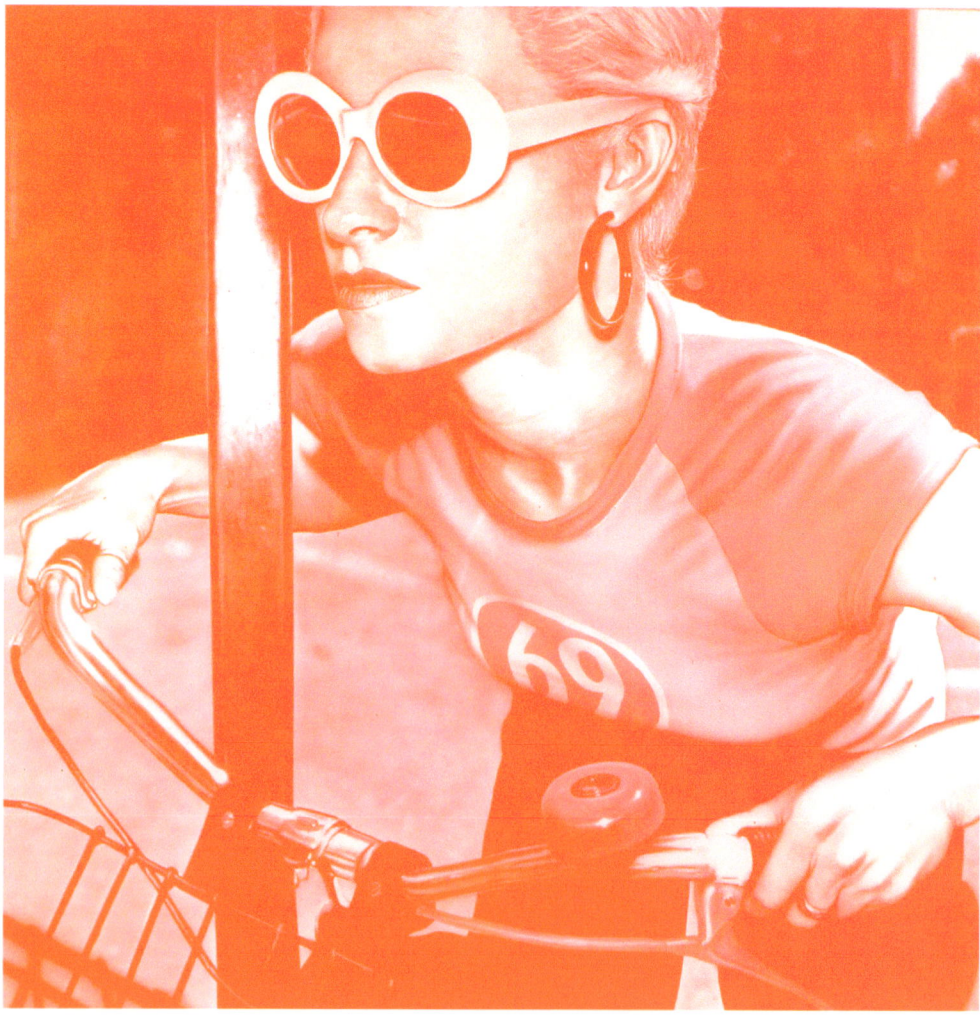

^ BUBBLE-GUM CAR   198 X 198 CMS 2001   ^ BICYCLE THIEF   198 X 198 CMS 2001

> BLUE MAGDALENE   202 X 202 CMS 2001

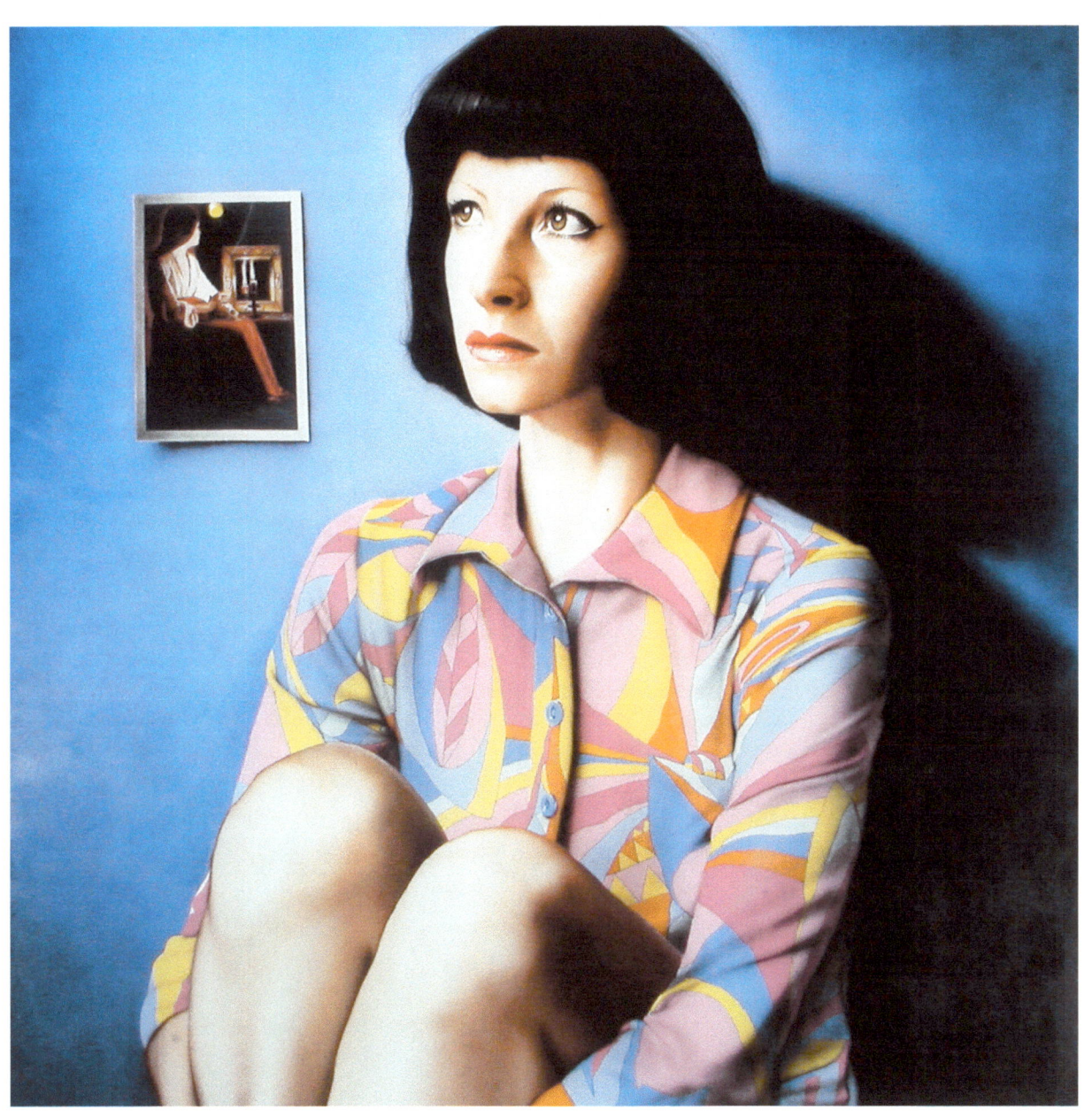

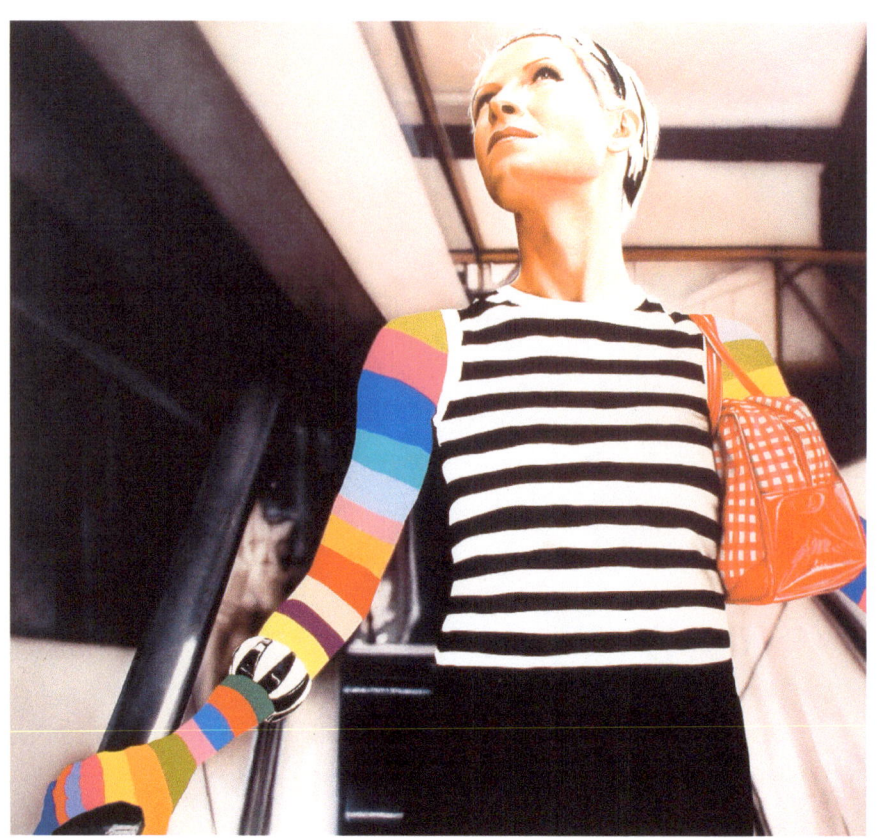

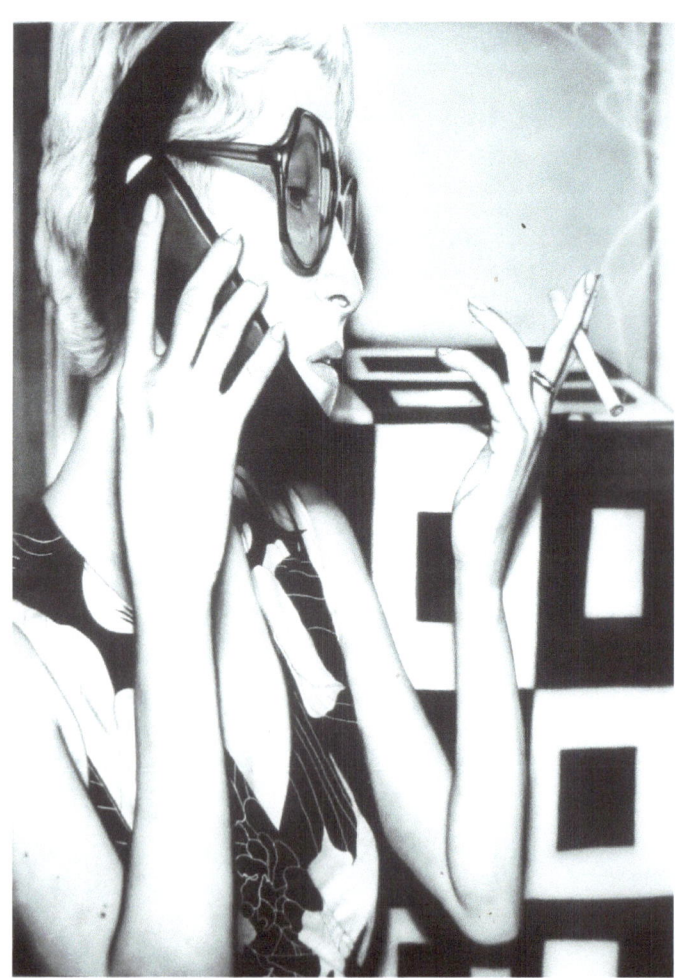

^ DANTE'S STAIRS 202 X 212 CMS 2001   ^ PHONE CALL 2 212 X 148 CMS 2001

> BUNNY 202 X 202 CMS 2001

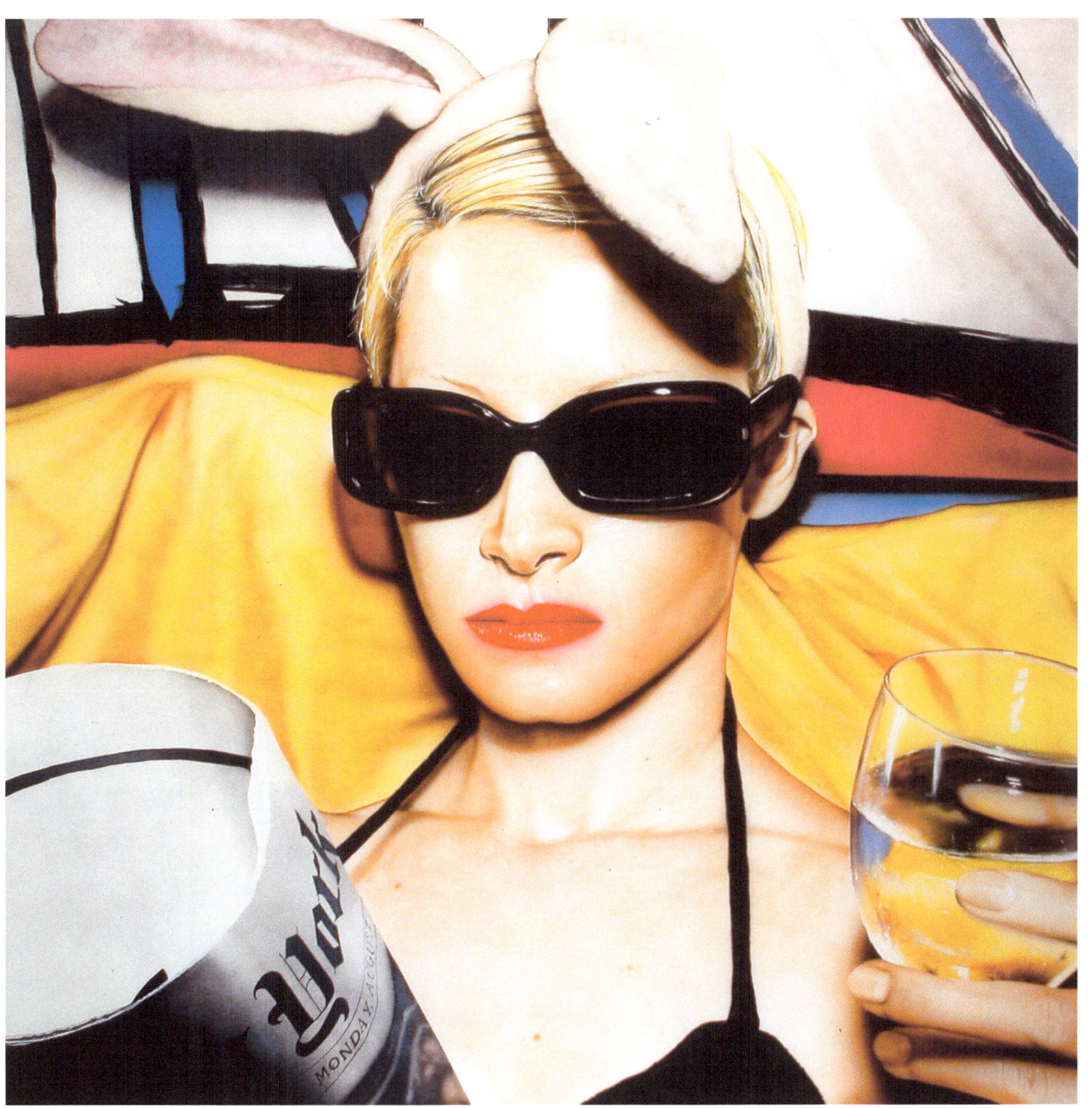

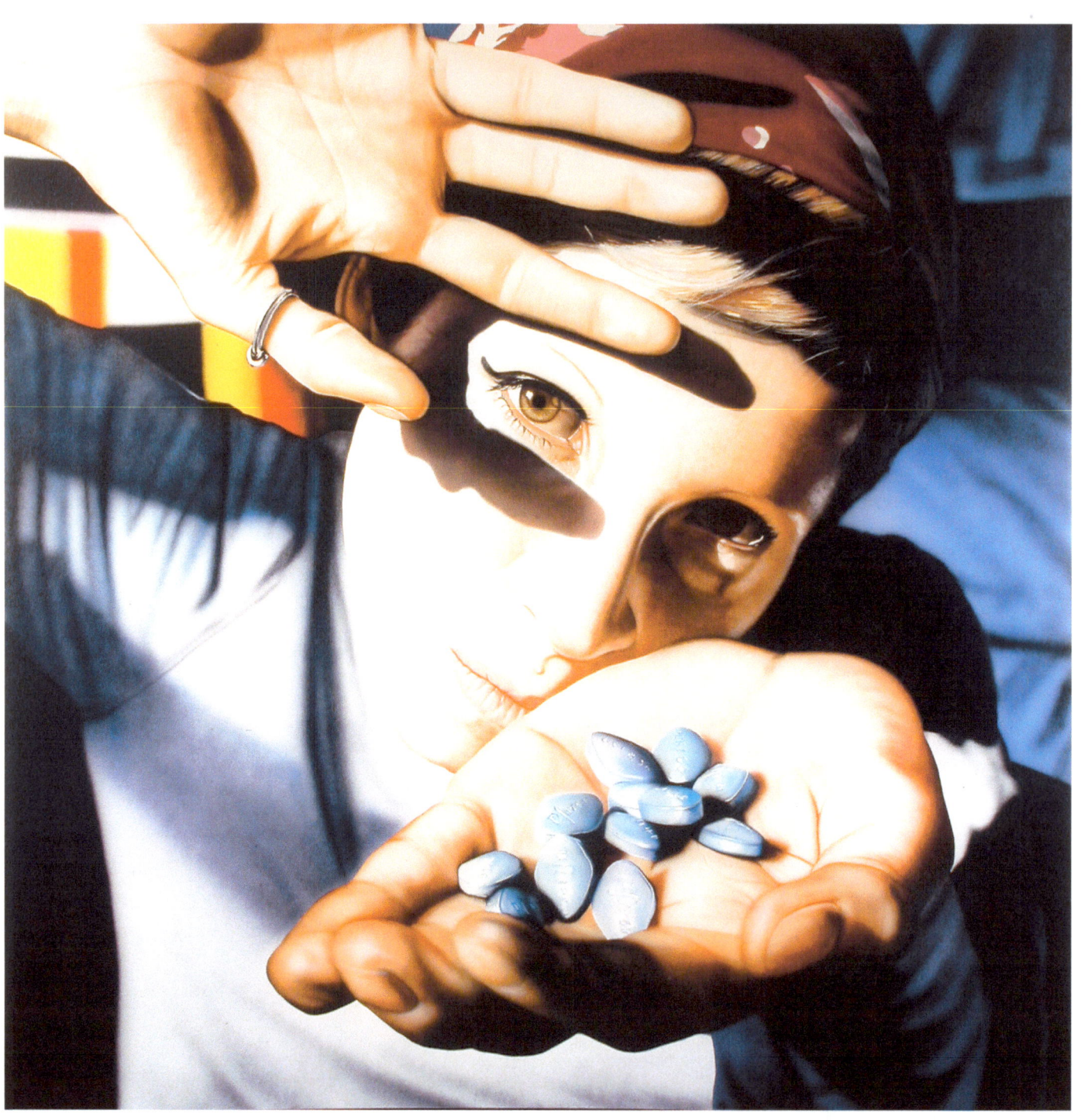

^ BLUE PILLS 198 X 198 CMS 2001

> CINEMA NOTEBOOKS I 243 X 152 CMS 2001

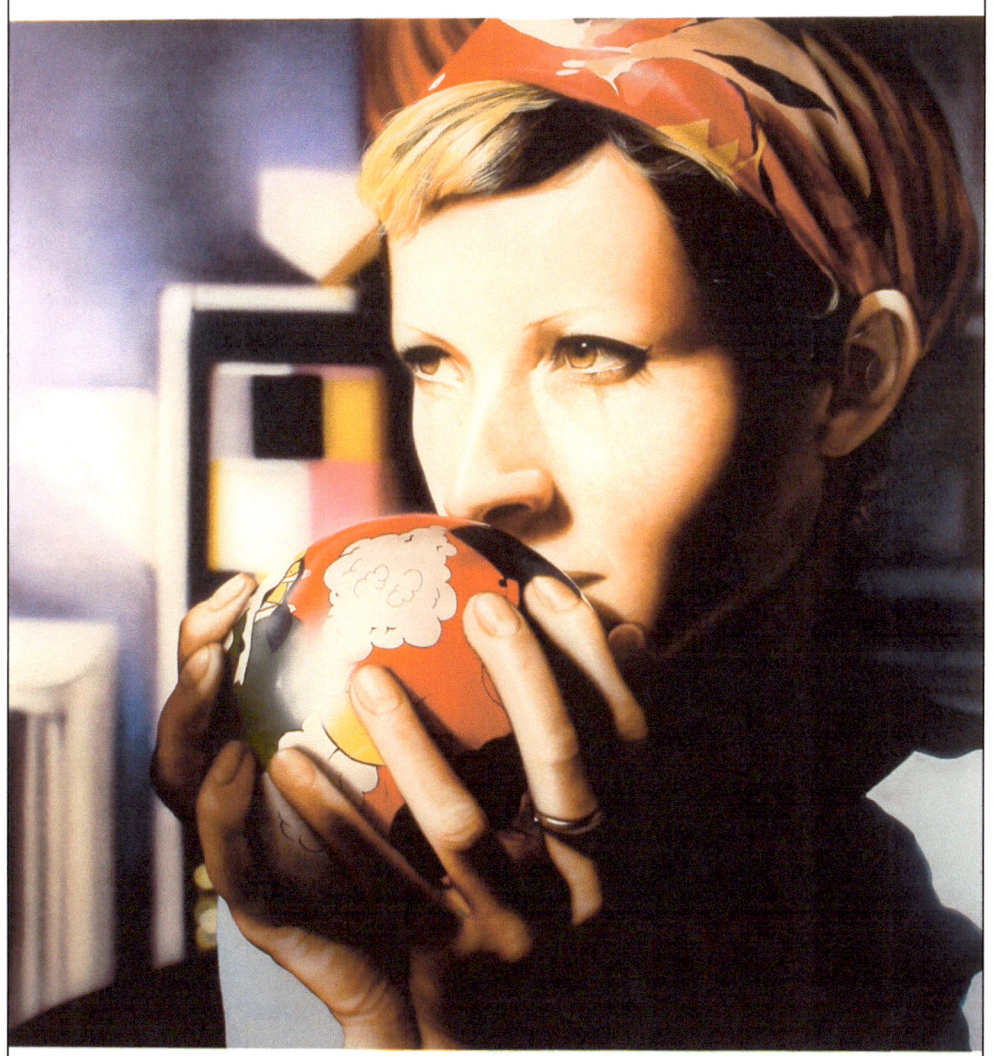

CAHIERS
DU CINÉMA

143 ★ REVUE MENSUELLE DE CINÉMA ● MAI 1963 ★ 143

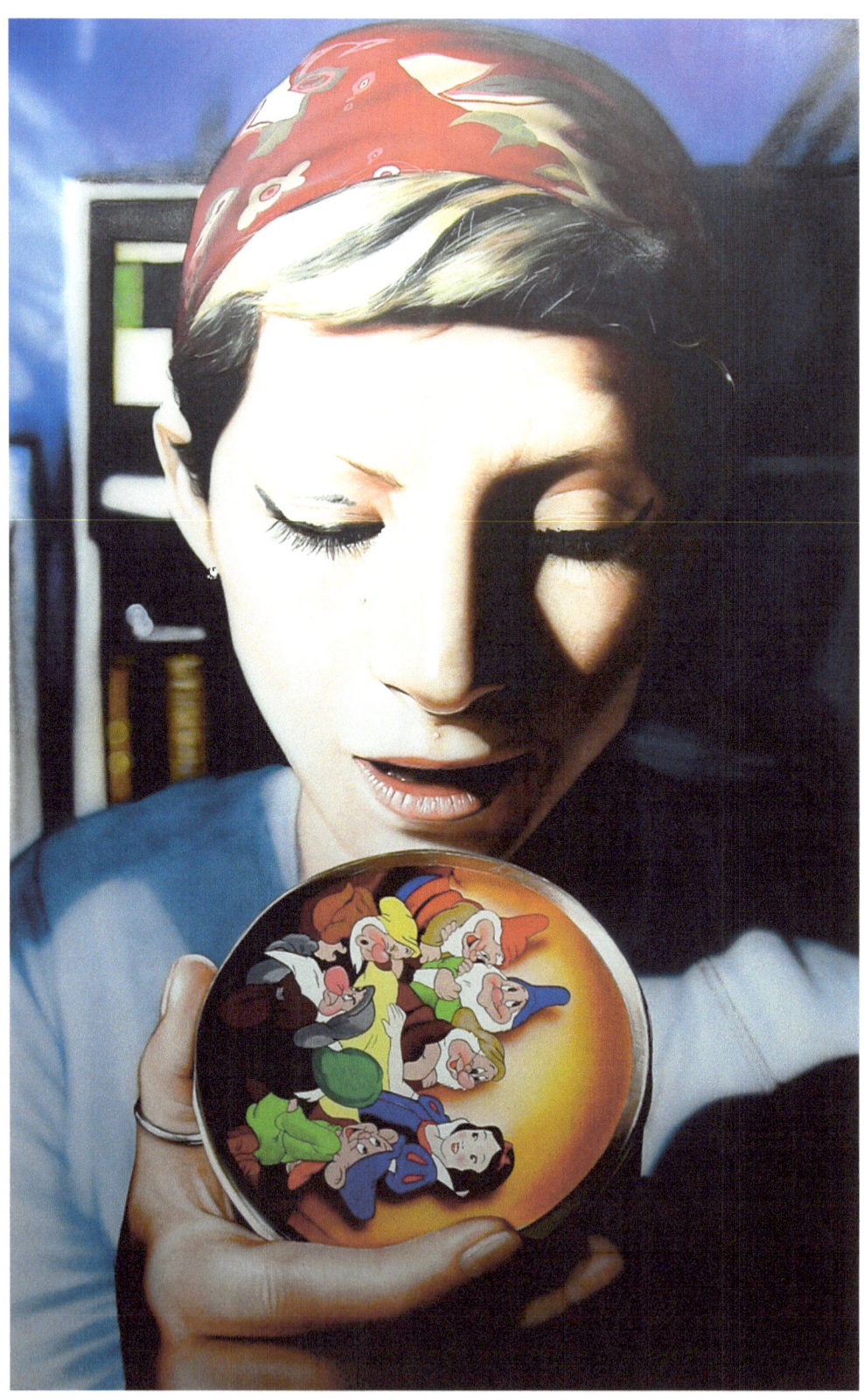

^ SNOW-BOX 243 X 152 CMS 2001
> SEPTEMBER 2 198 X 148 CMS 2001

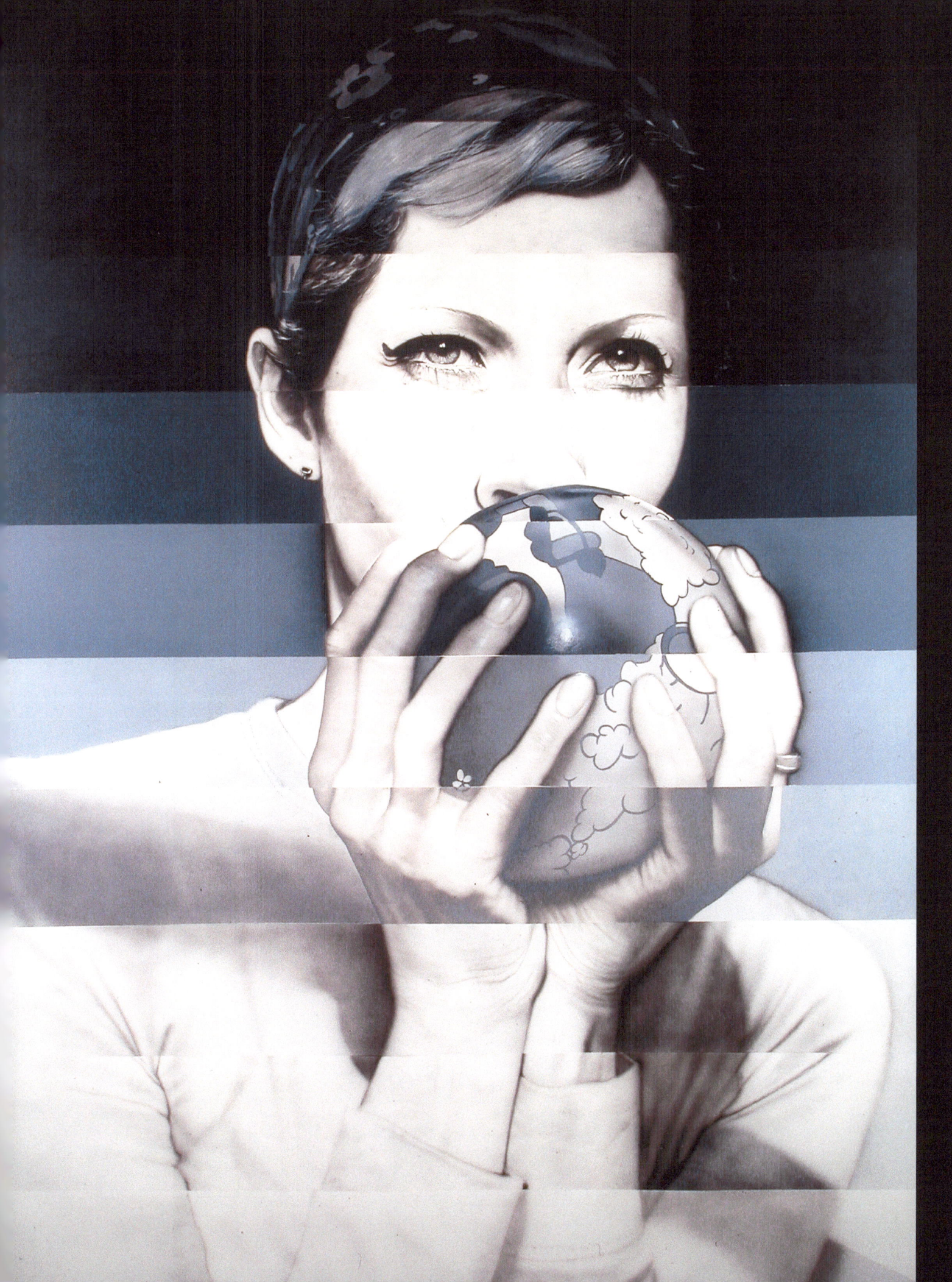

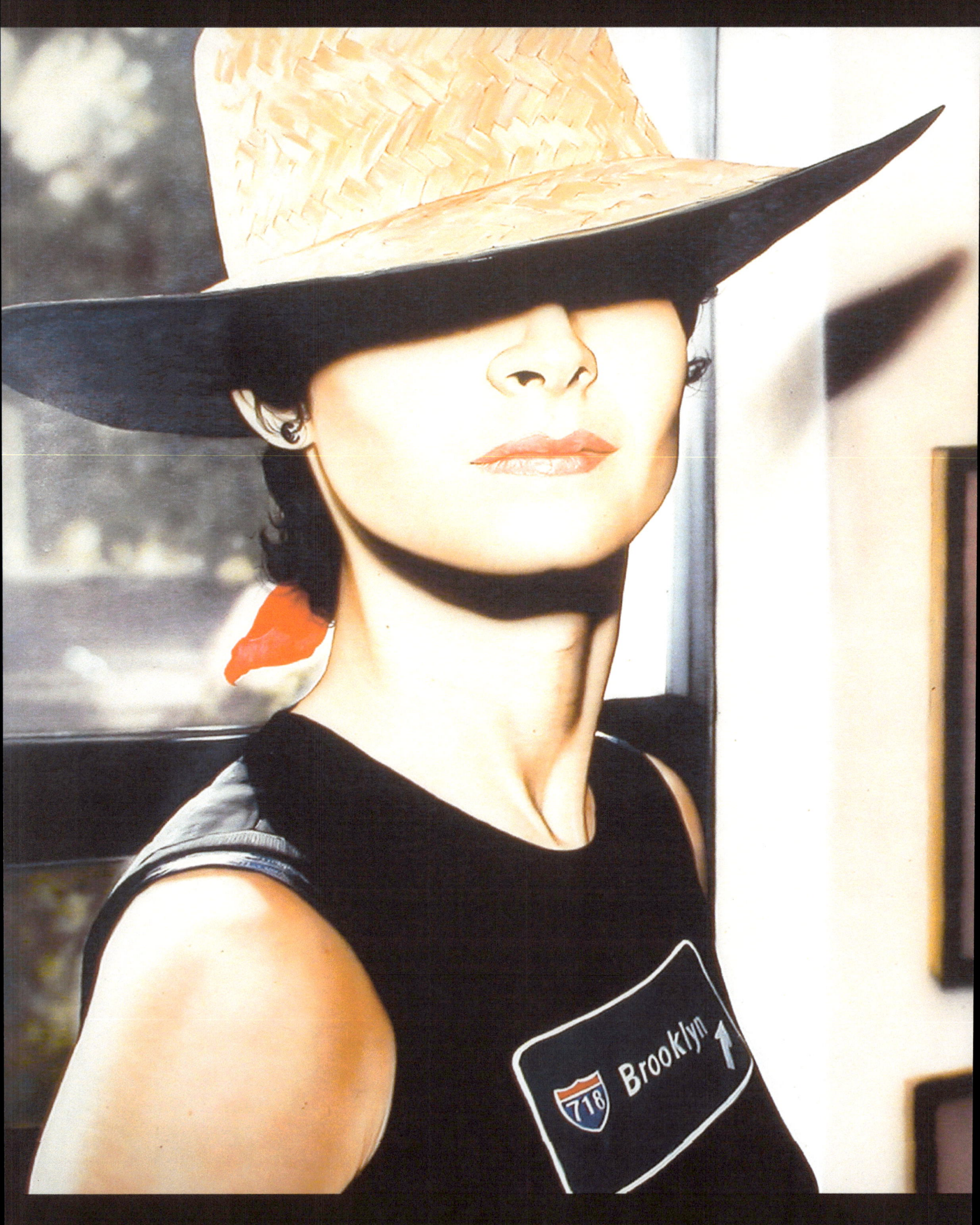

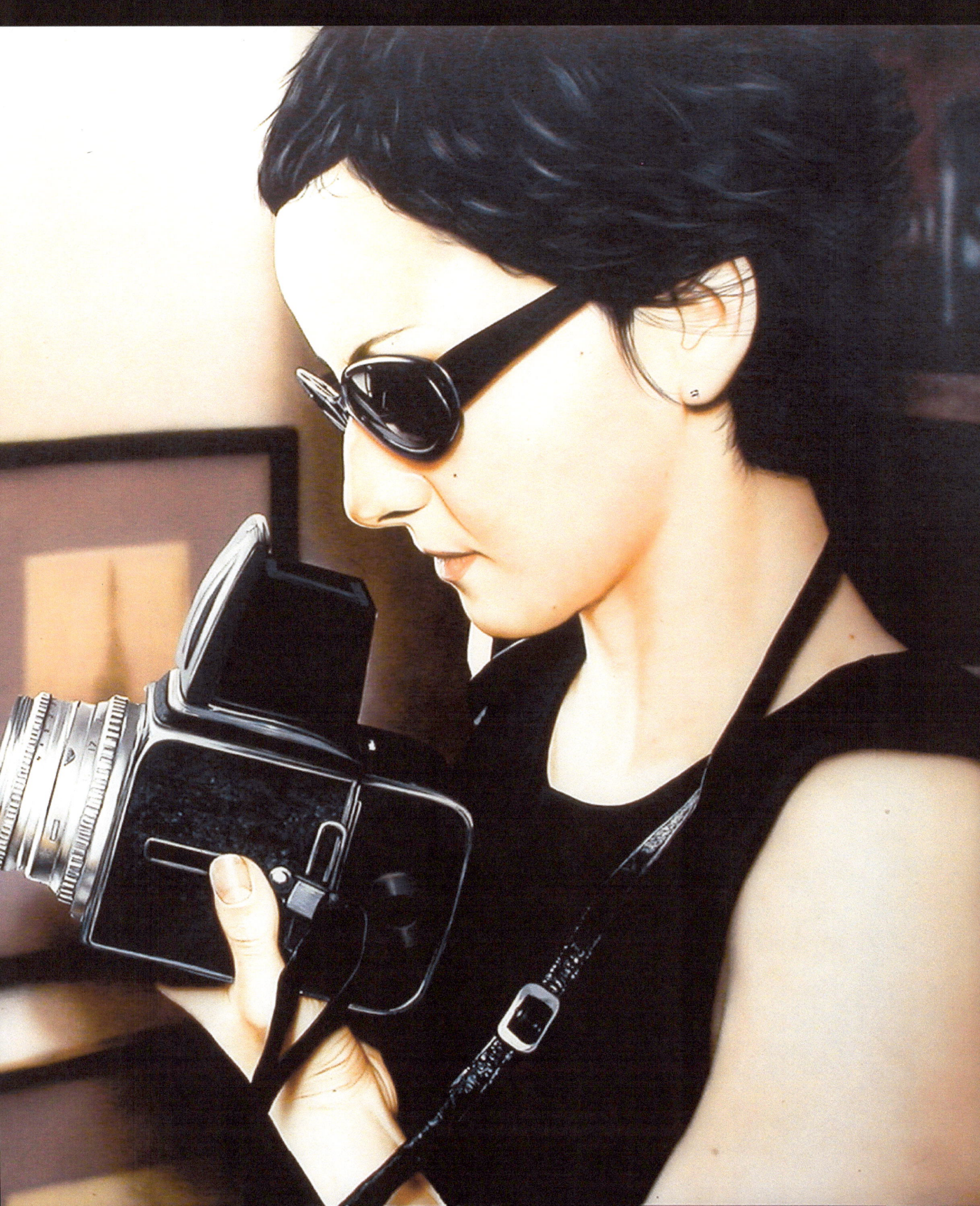

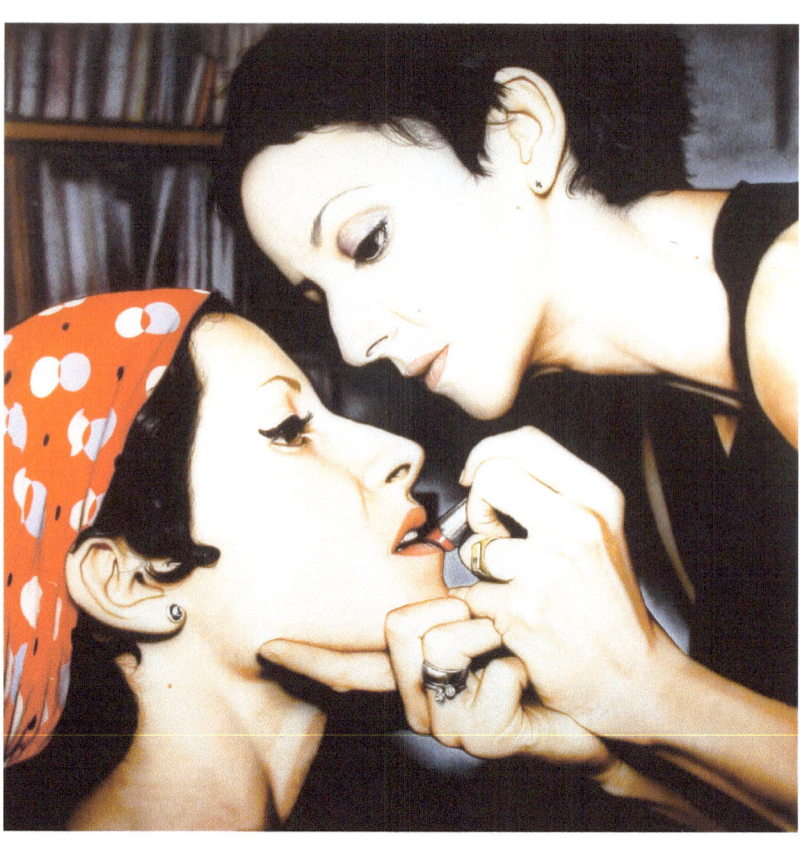

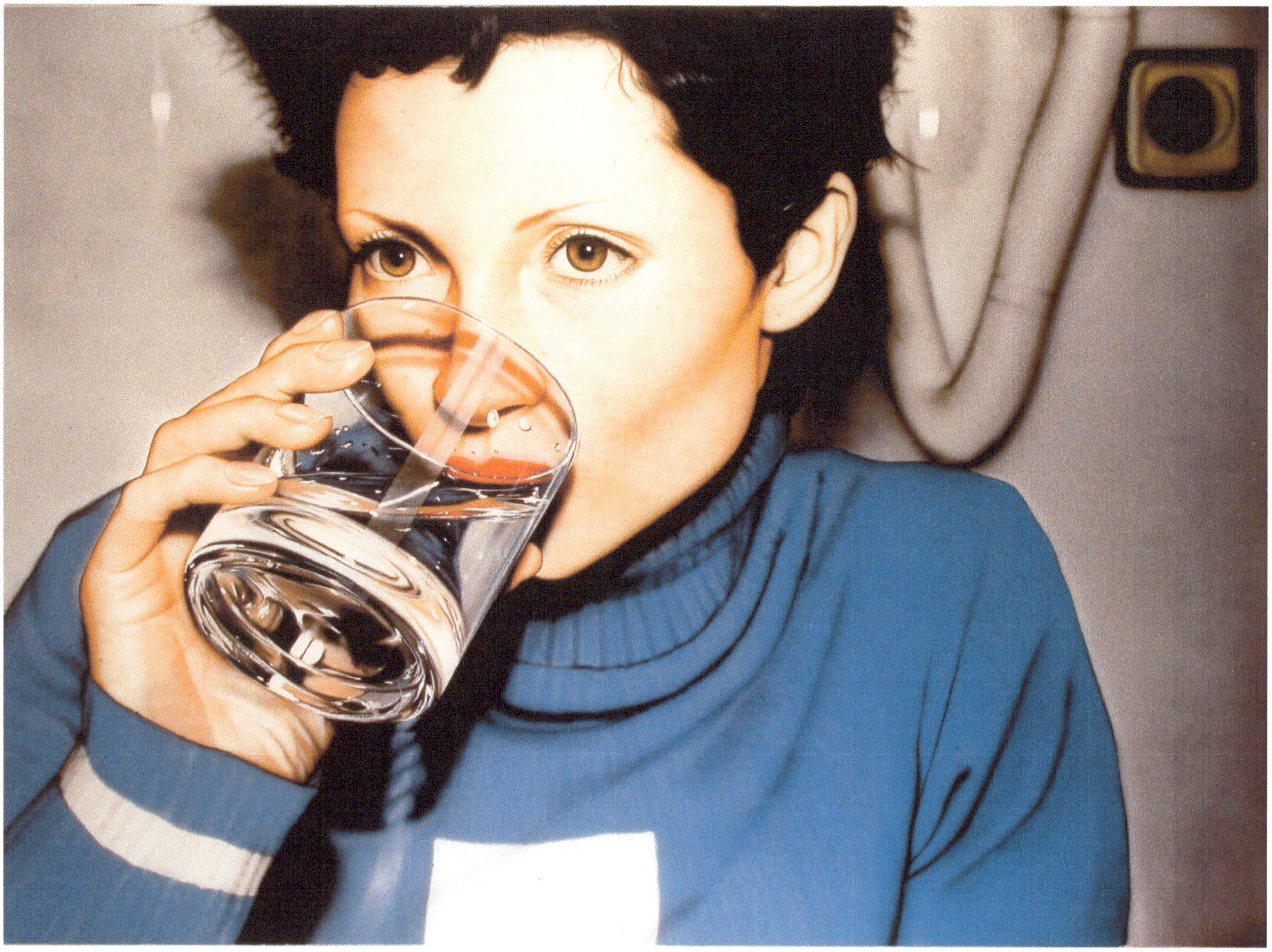

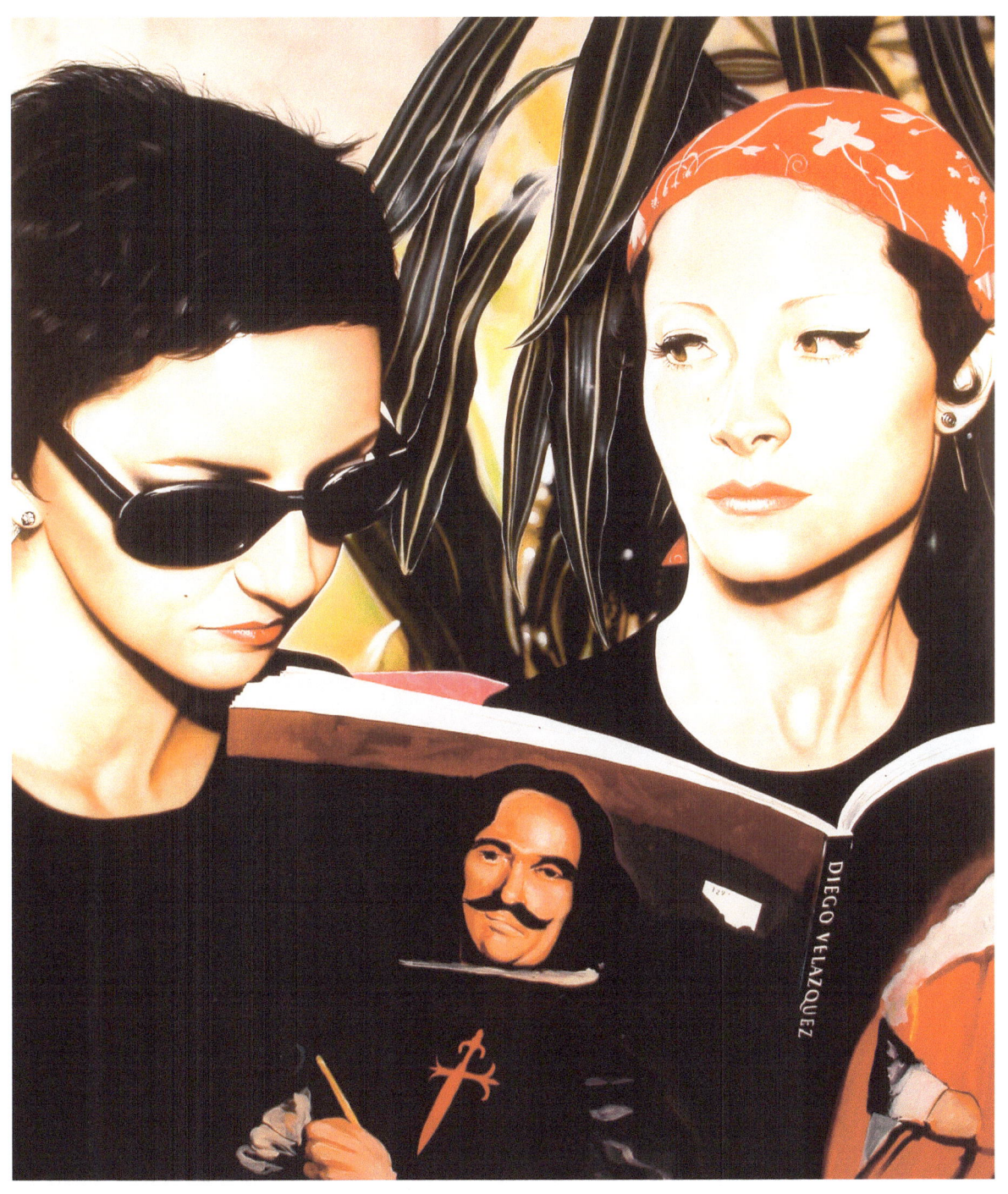

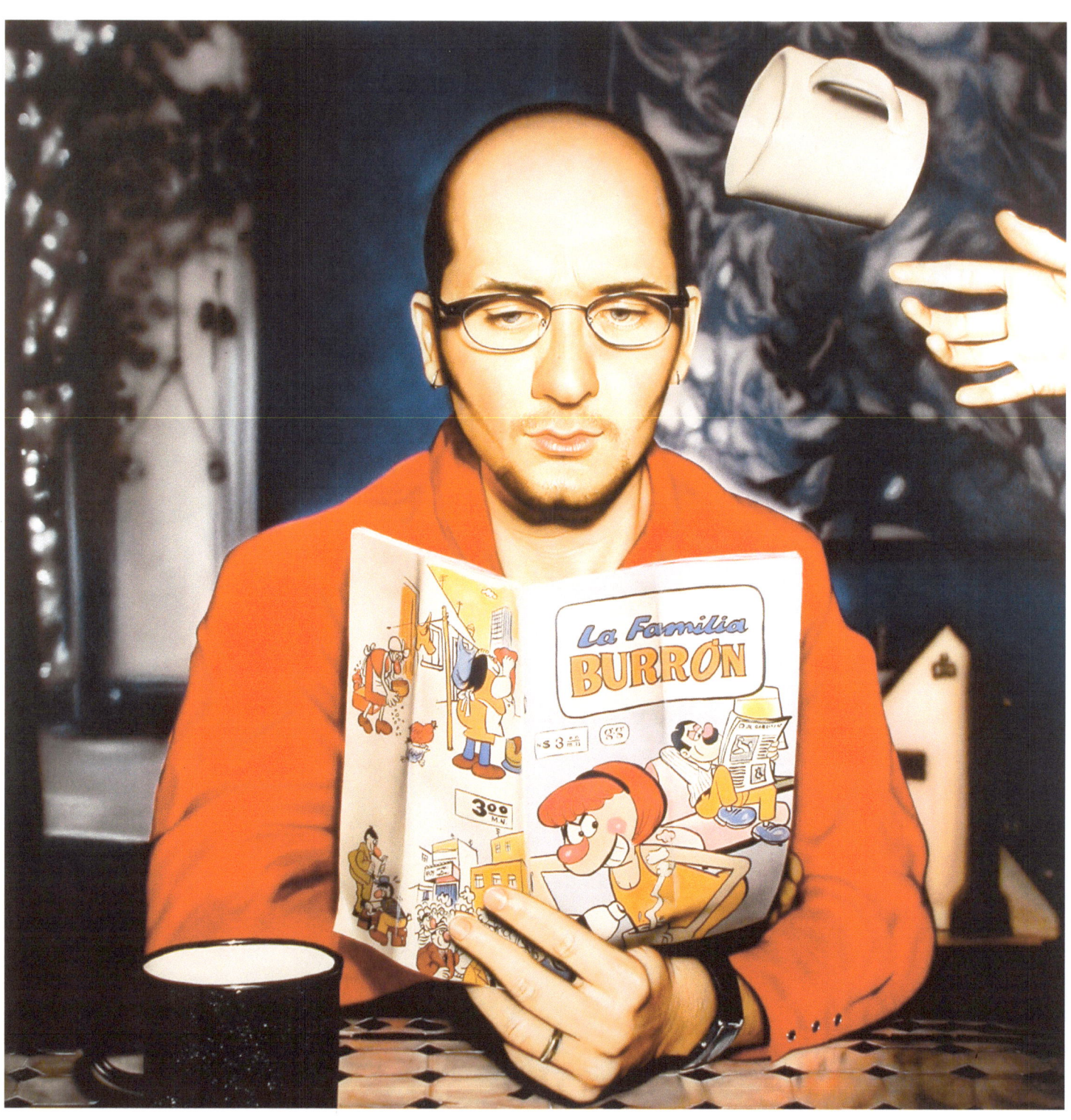

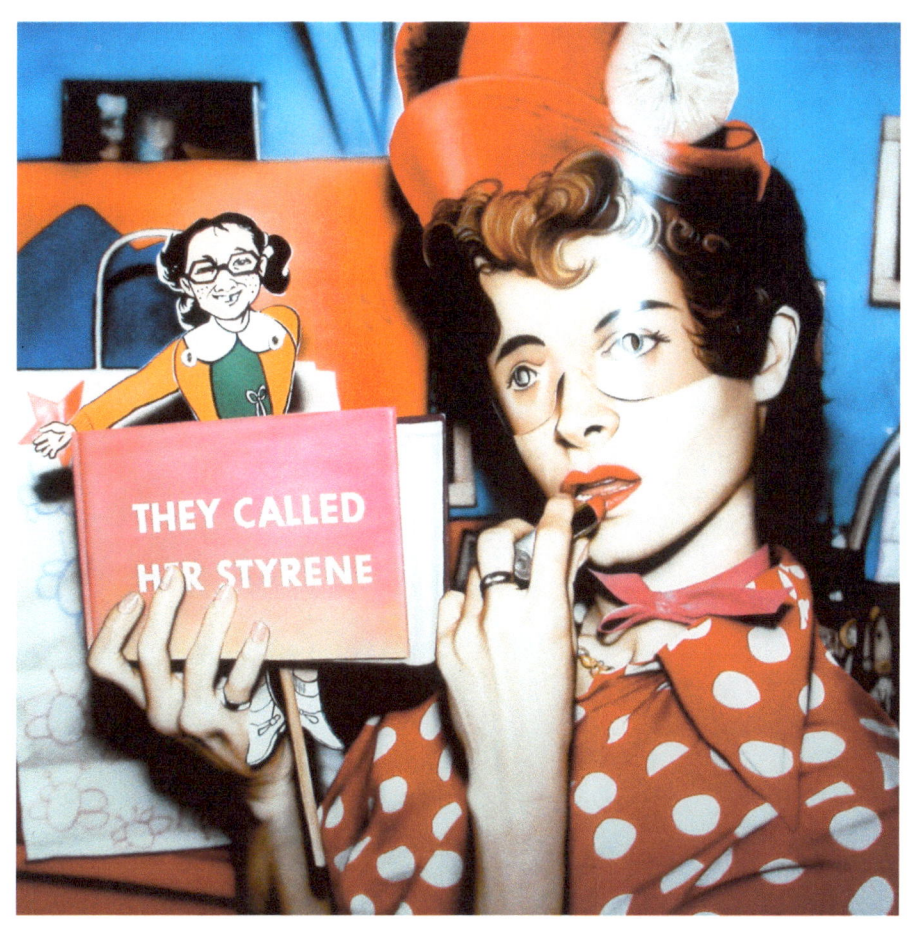

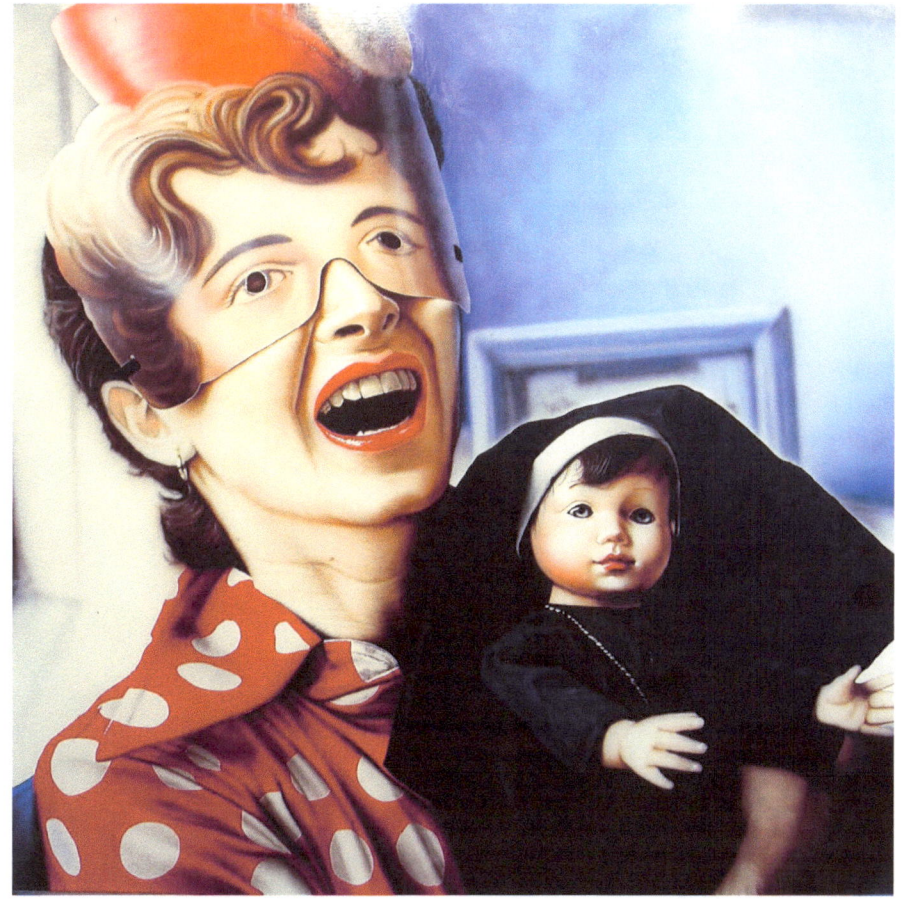

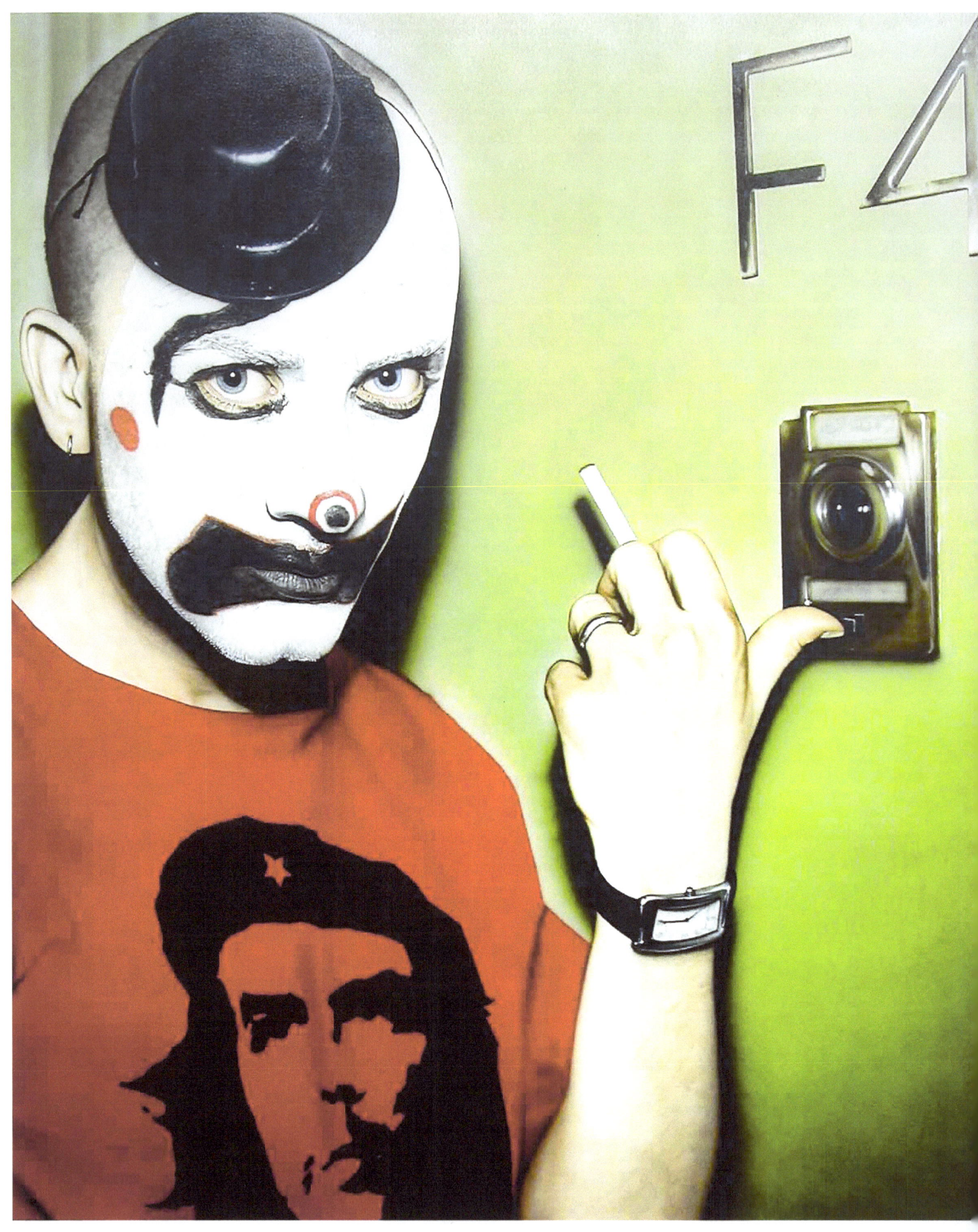

^ F4 2 198 X 152 CMS 2002

> ROUND CLOWN WITH SKULL 91 CMS DIAMETER 2003   > TWO YEARS 198 X 198 CMS 2002   > GREAT ESCAPE 162 X 198 CMS 2002

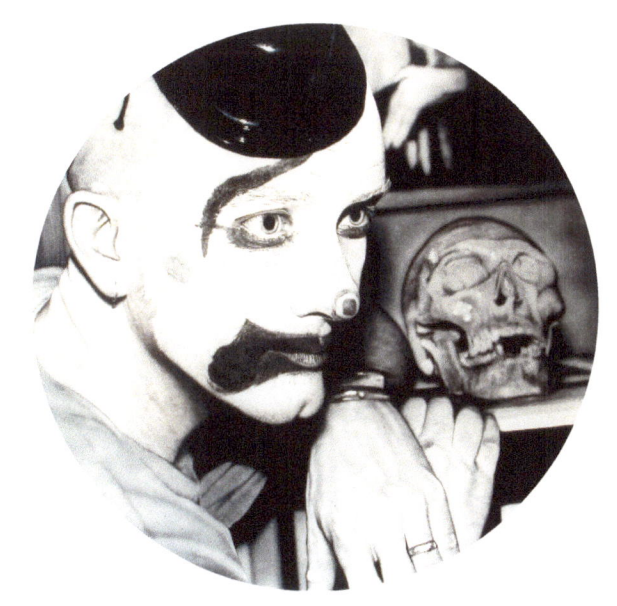

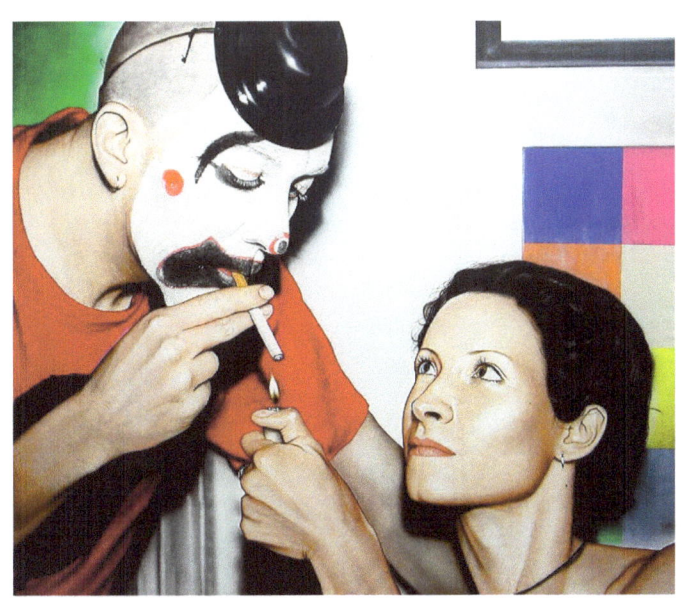

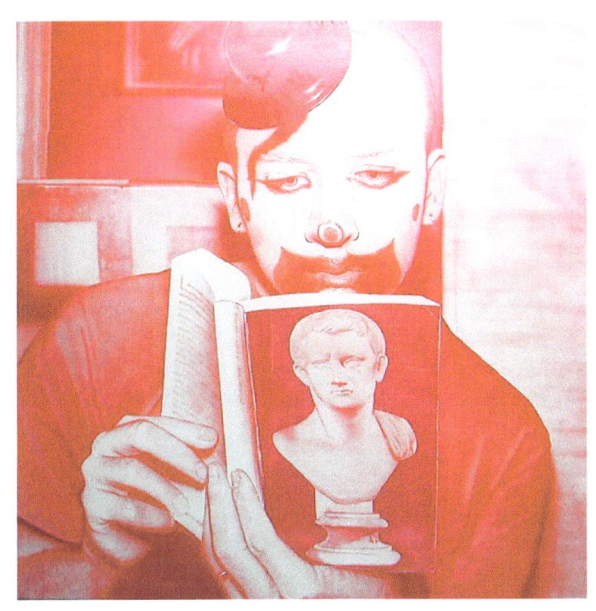

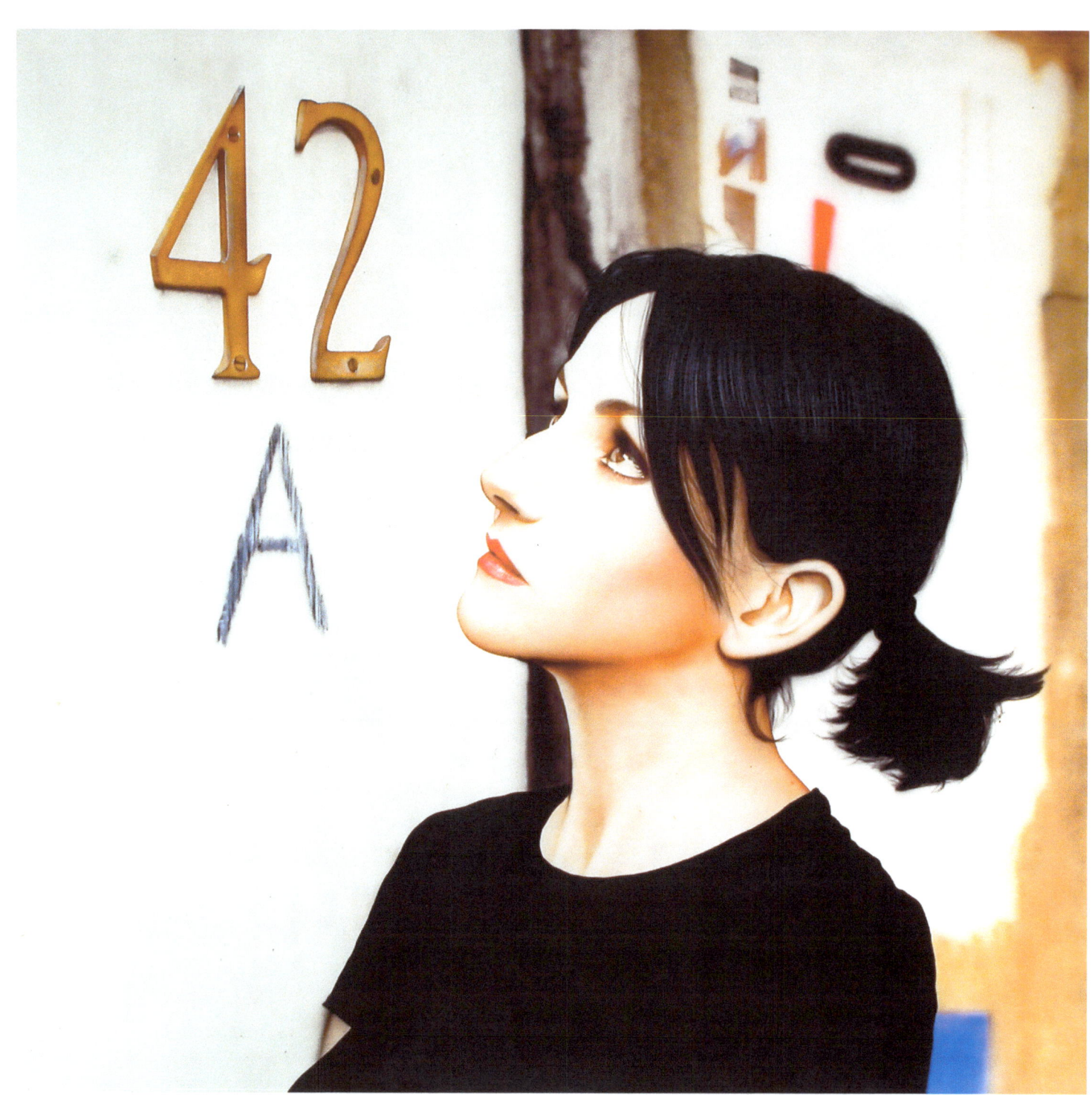

^ MAGDALENE 42A 198 X 198 CMS 2003
> JACOB'S DREAM 172 X 202 CMS 2003

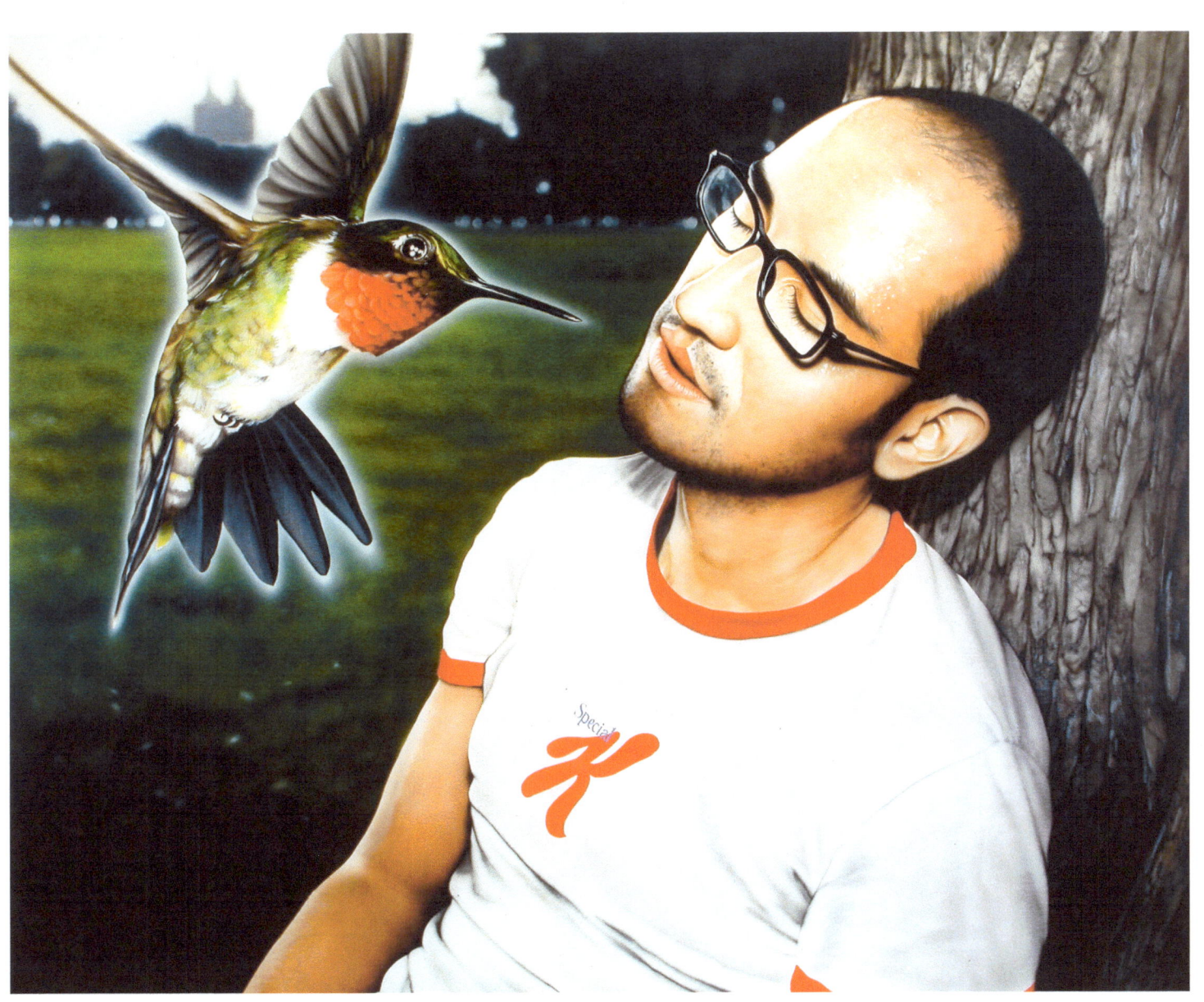

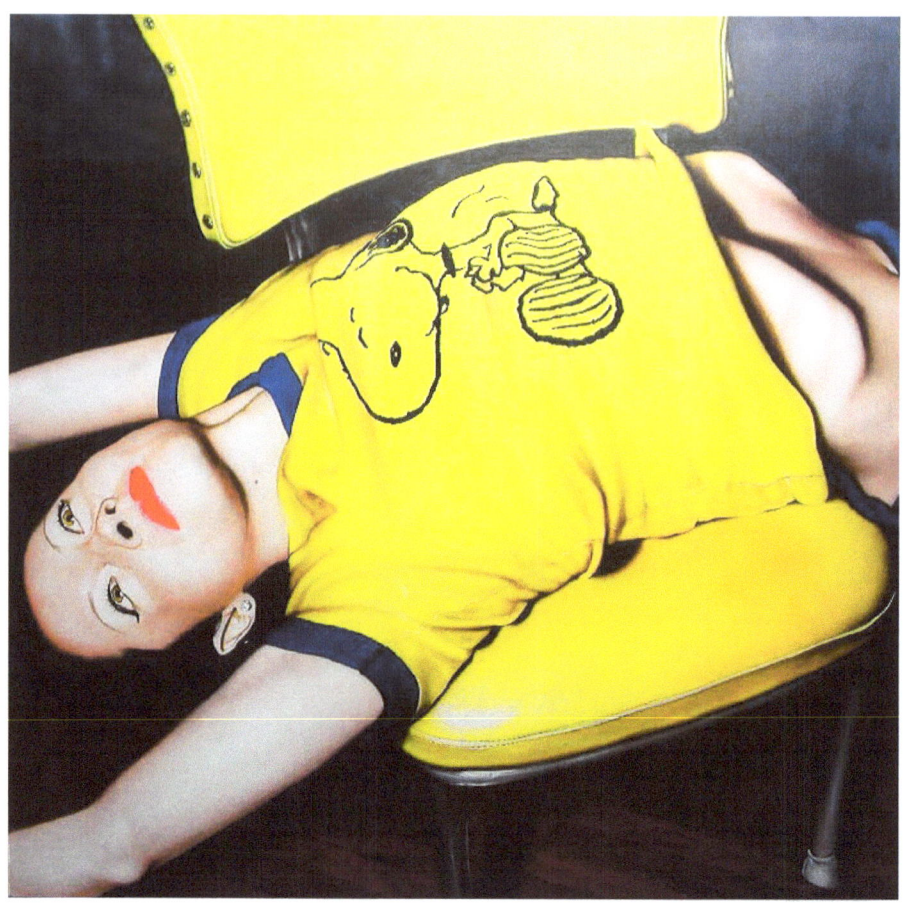

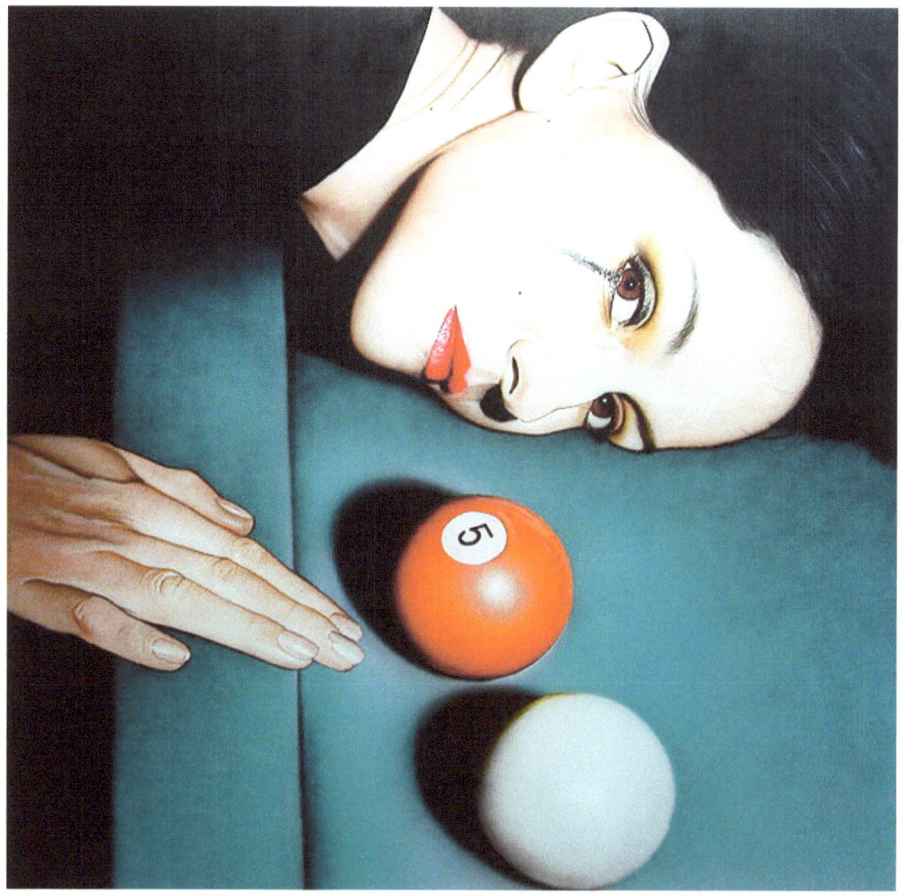

^ ST. BARTHOLOMEW 198 X 198 CMS 2003   ^ MAGDALENE 2 198 X 198 CMS 2003

> DIAMOND GIRL 172 X 152 CMS 2003

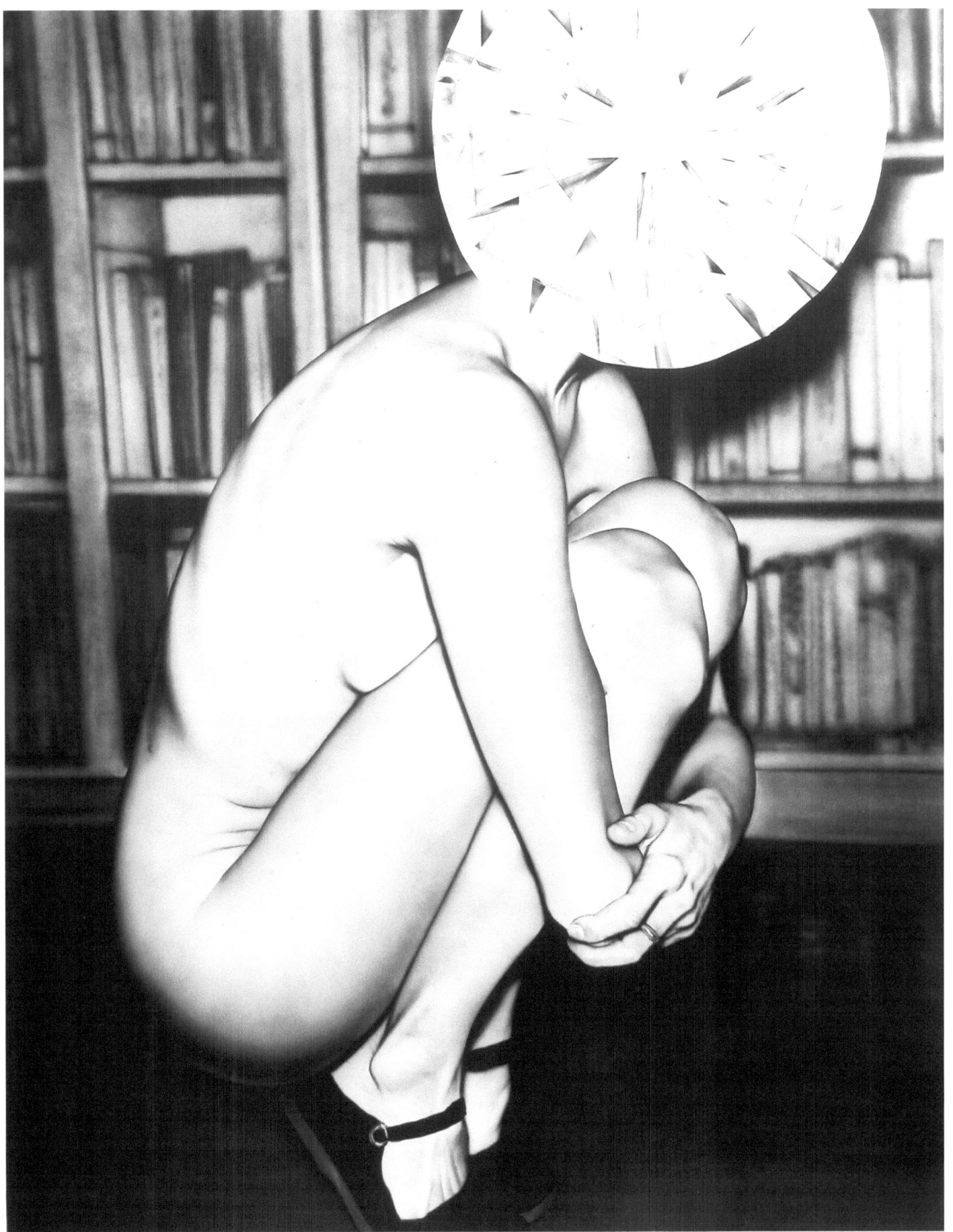

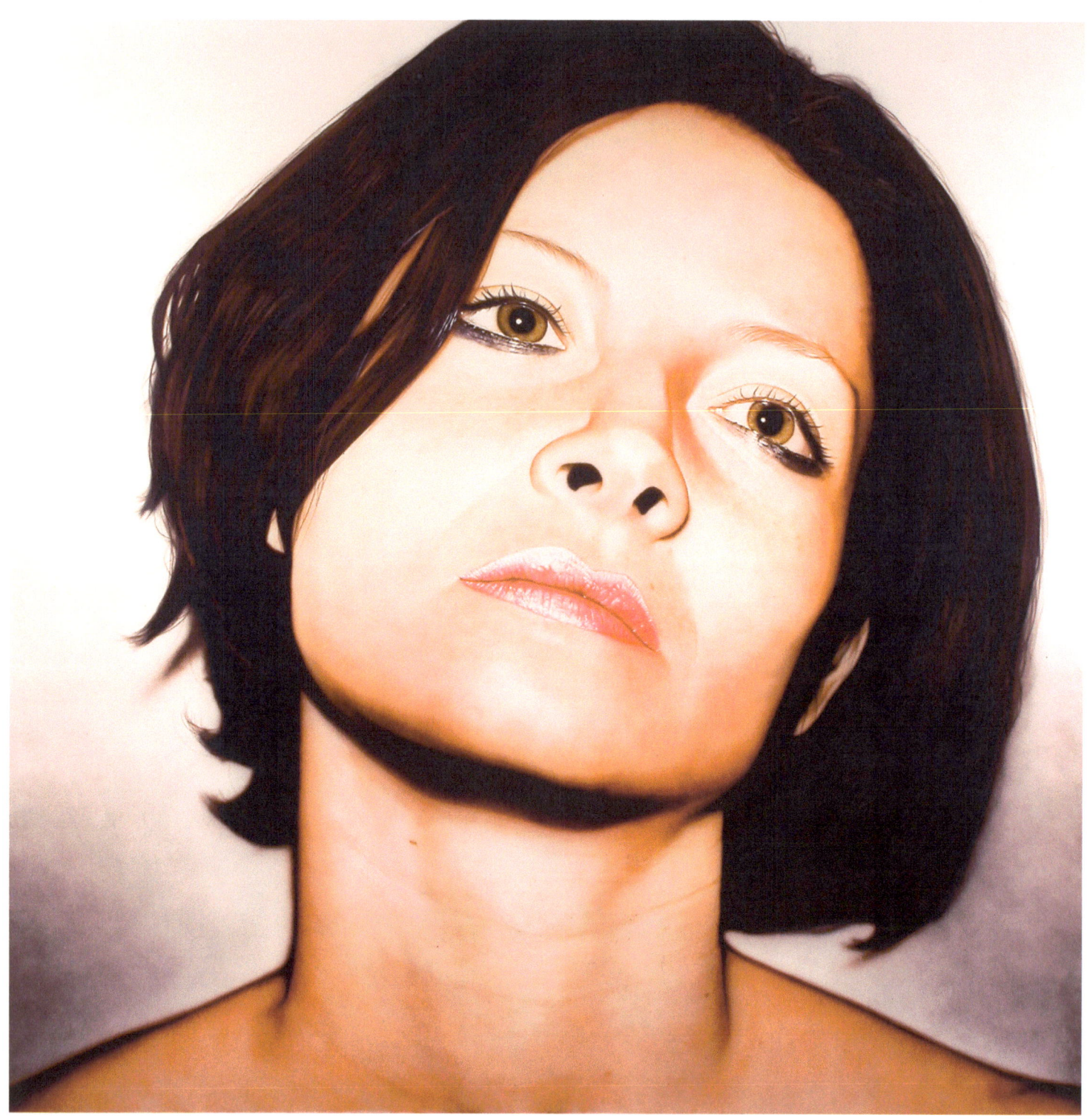

^ SILVER 198 X 198 CMS 2003
> BLACK 243 X 198 CMS 2003

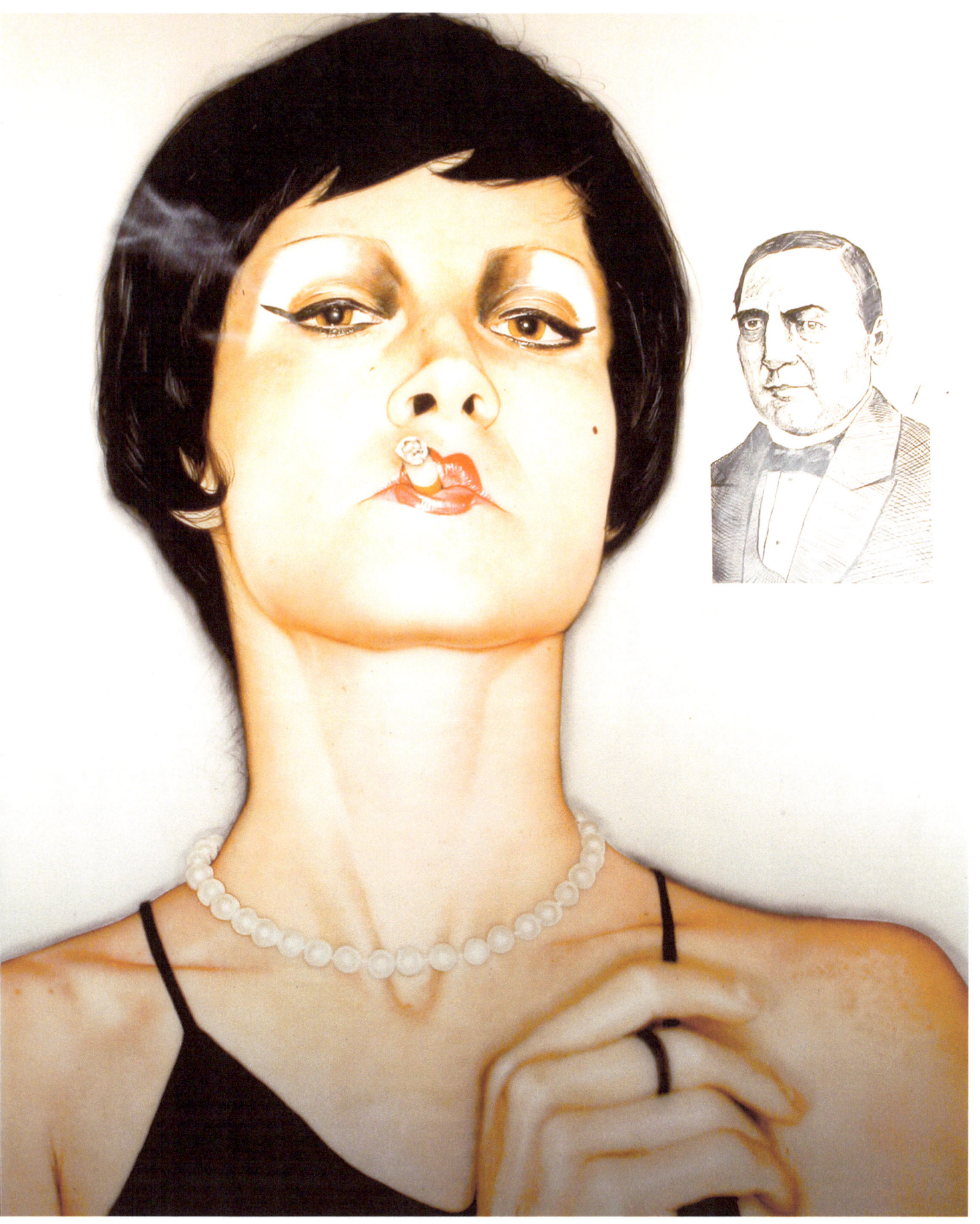

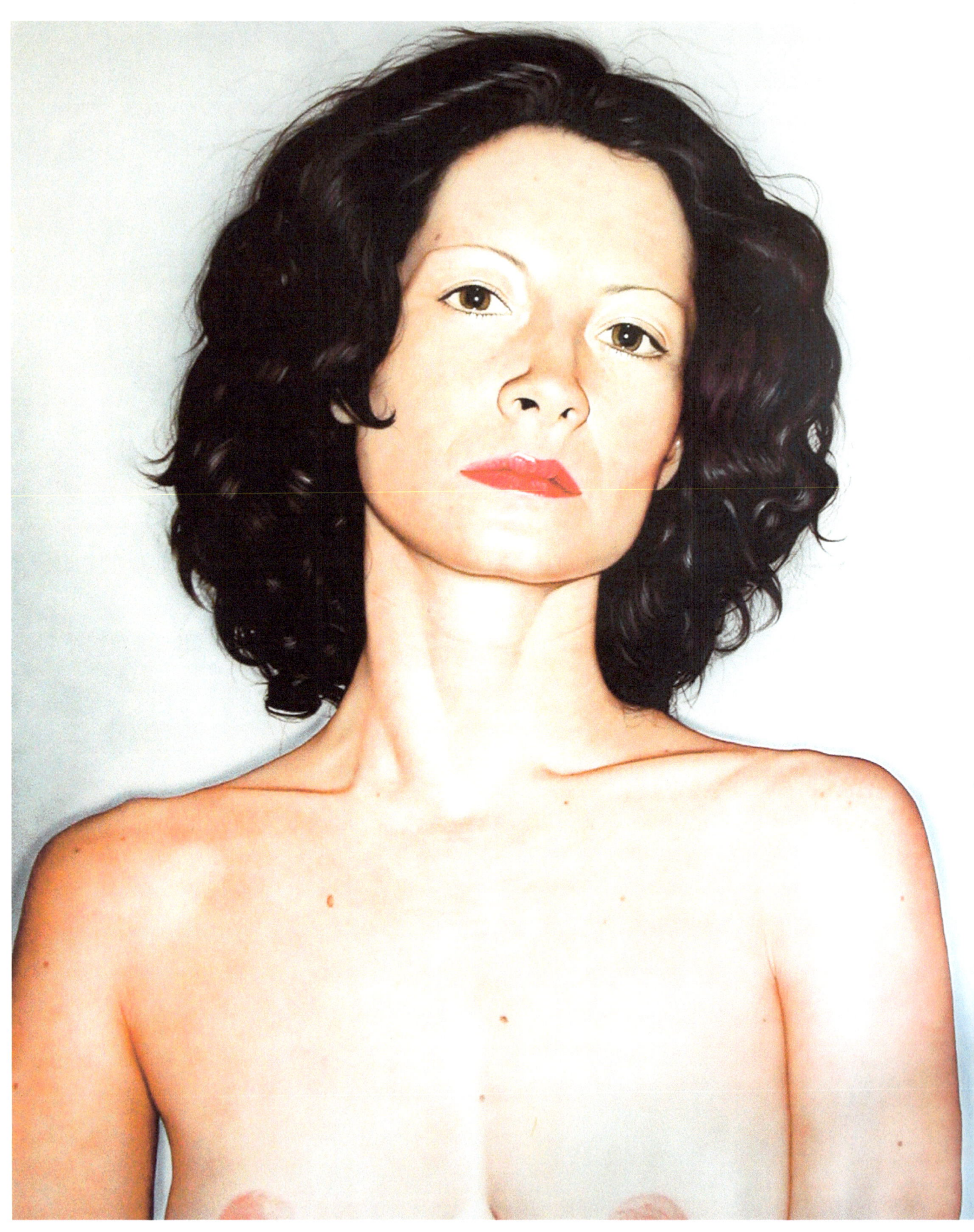

^ WHITE 198 X 198 CMS 2003
> GOLD 198 X 198 CMS 2003

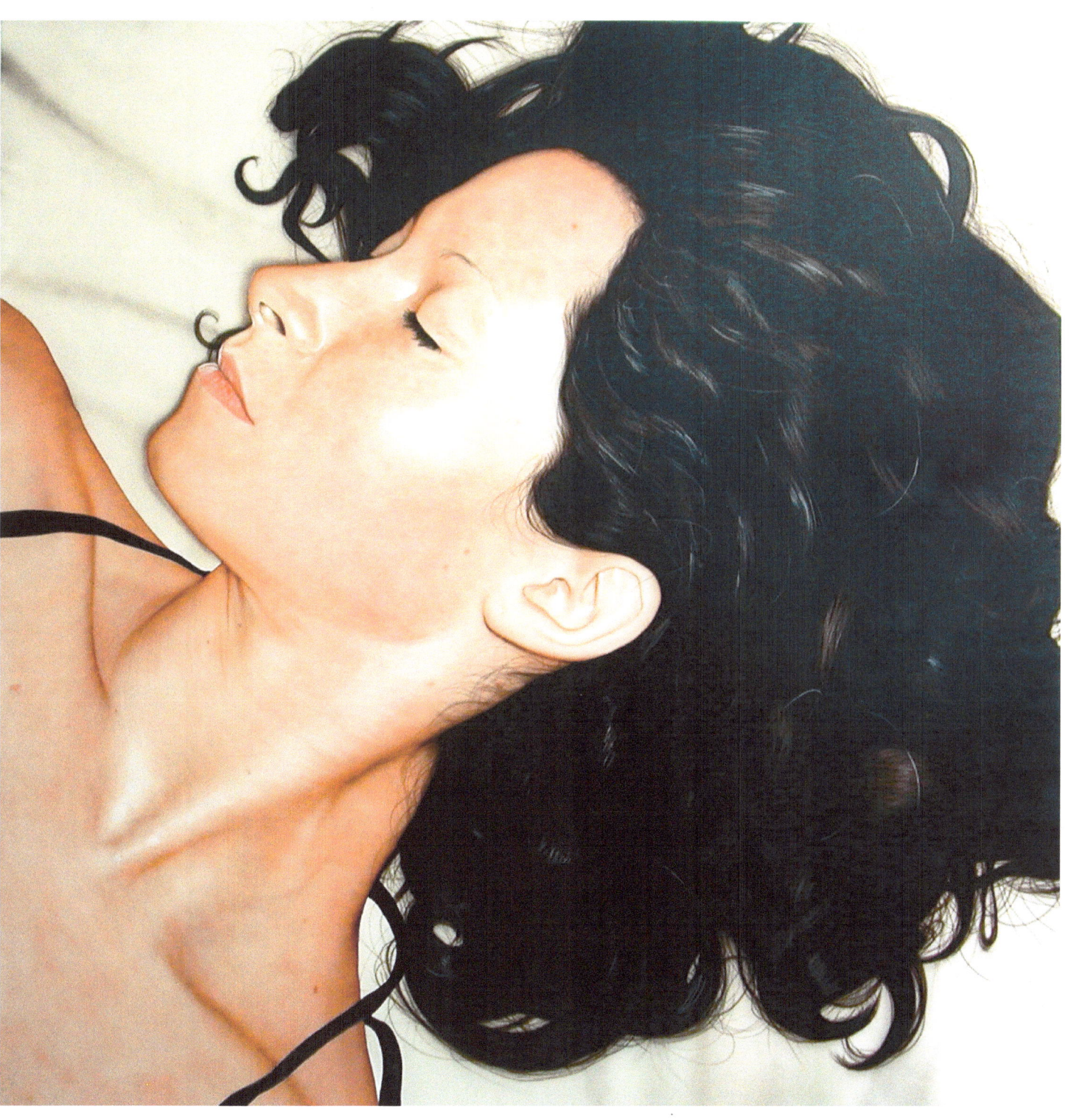

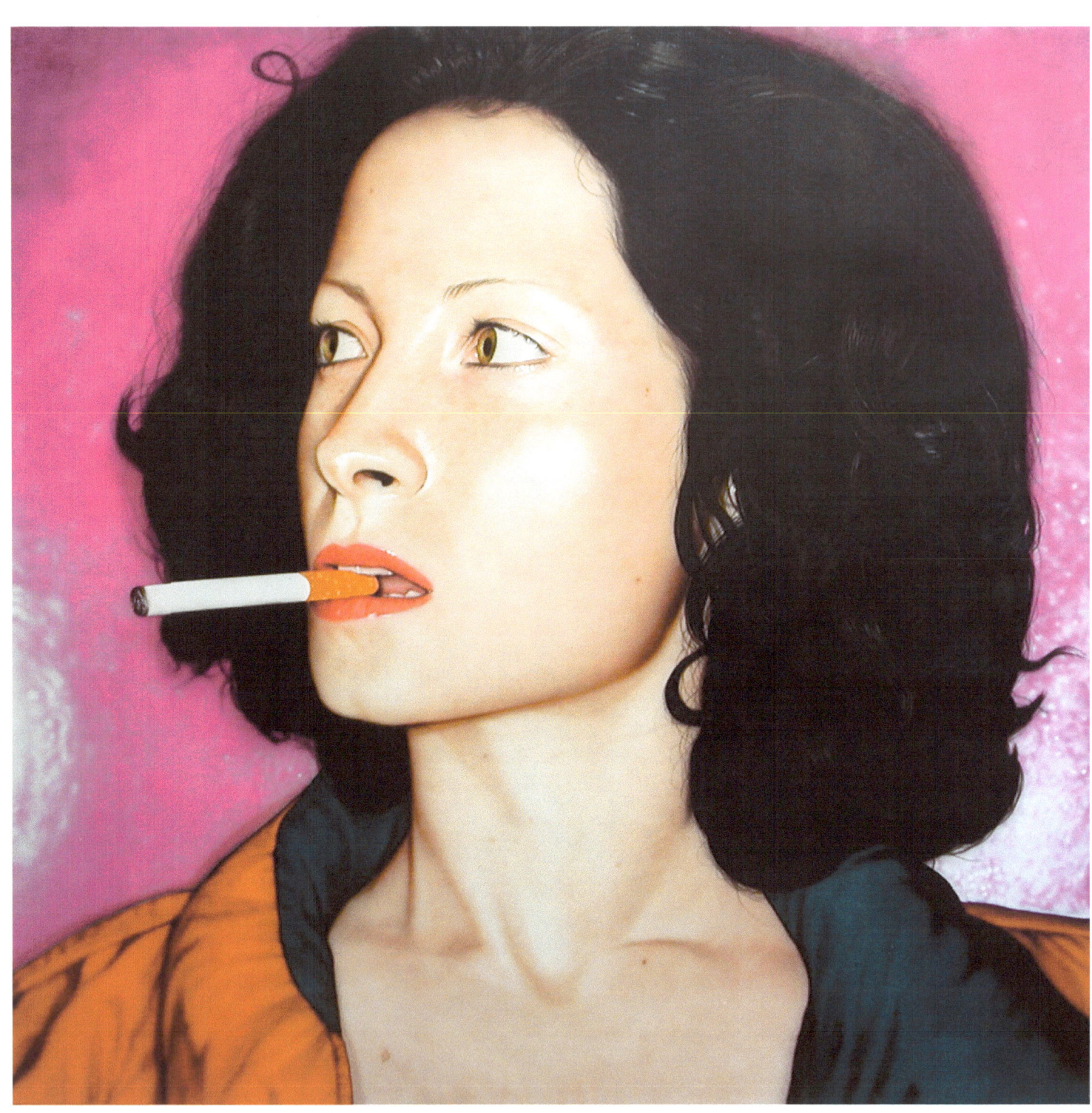

^ PINK 198 X 198 CMS 2003
> FEAR NOT 198 X 198 CMS 2003

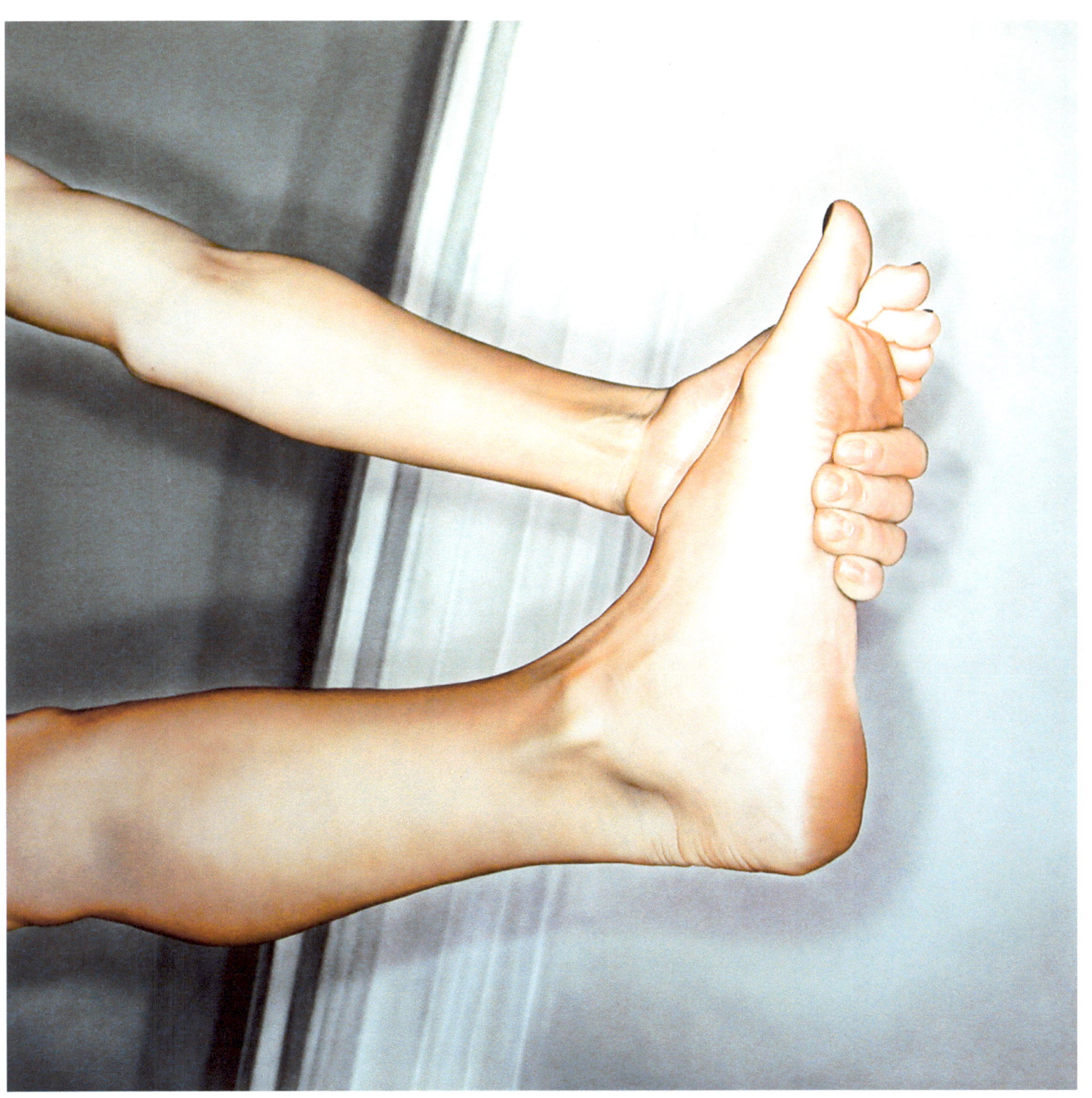

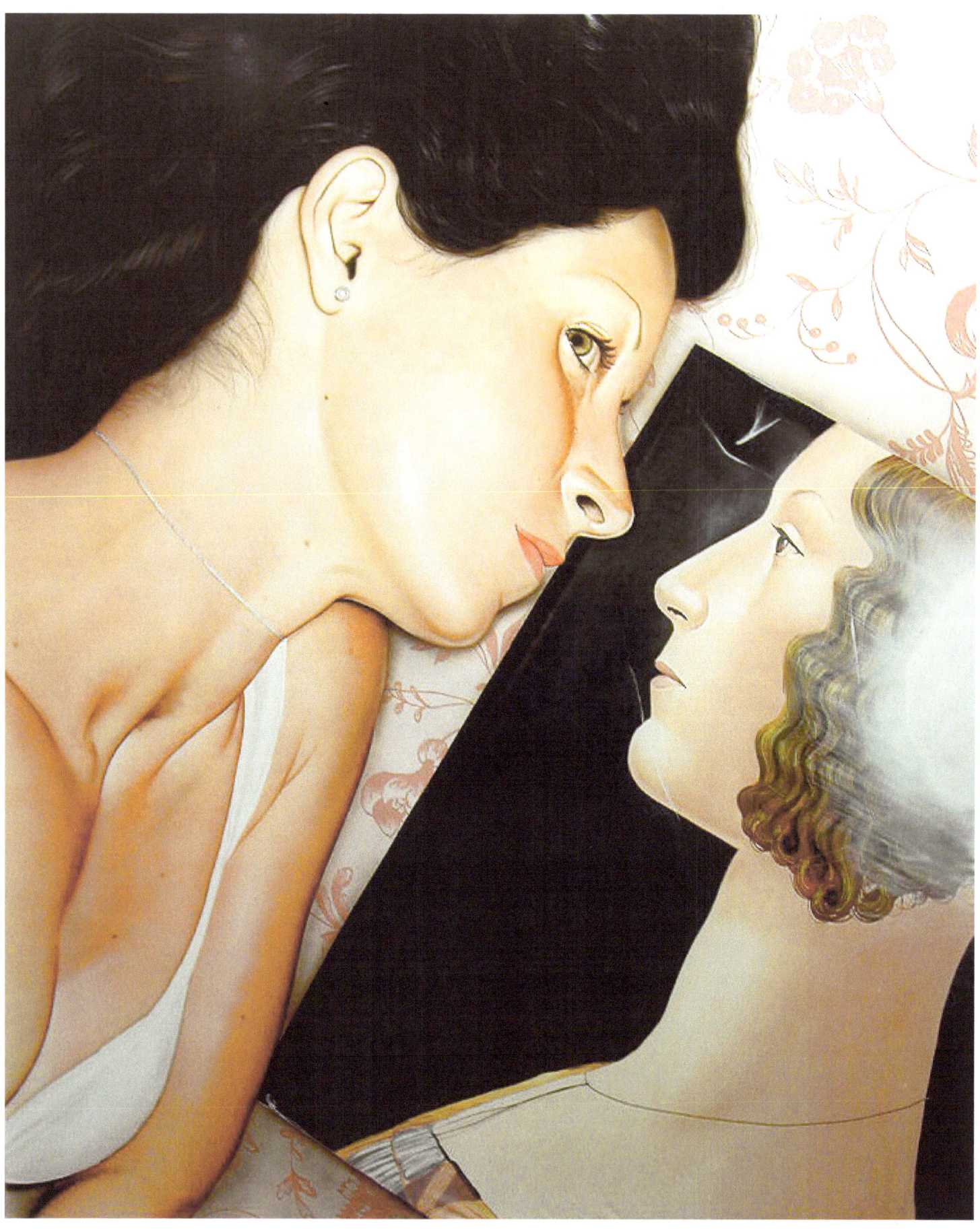

1993

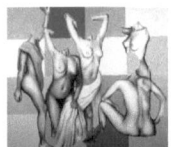
AVIGNON
160 X 150 CMS

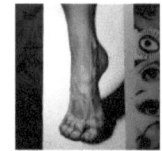
FLAG
150 X 160 CMS

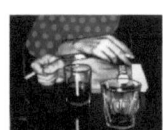
HANDS
80 X 100 CMS

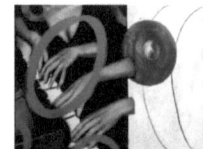
NIPPLE
100 X 200 CMS

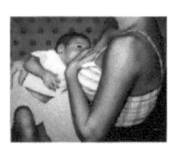
LIFE 3
100 X 120 CMS

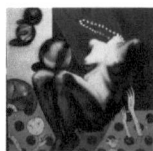
PEACOCK'S
FEATHER
214 X 218 CMS

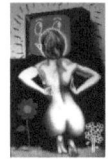
TV
150 X 90 CMS

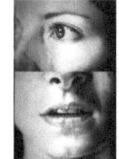
SKIN
210 X 120 CMS

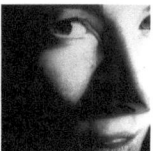
SKIN 2
80 X 100 CMS

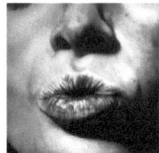
KISS
120 X 120 CMS

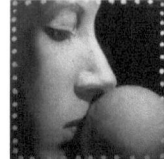
ORANGE
160 X 150 CMS

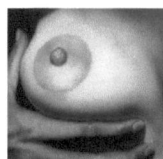
BREAST
120 X 120 CMS

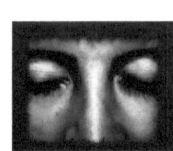
SLUMBER 2
80 X 100 CMS

1994

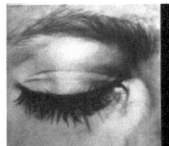
SLUMBER 3
(DIPTYCH, 80 X 80 CMS EACH)

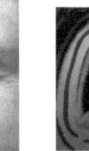
VOICE
120 X 120 CMS

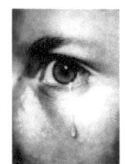
TEAR
90 X 70 CMS

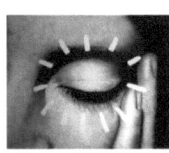
SKIN 3
100 X 120 CMS

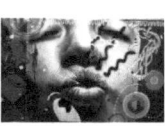
KISS 2
120 X 200 CMS

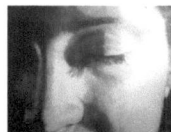
SLUMBER 5
100 X 120 CMS

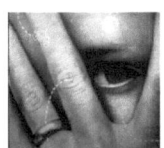
RING
100 X 100 CMS

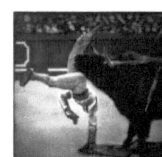
TOROS
150 X 160 CMS

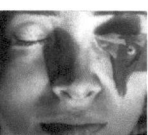
SLUMBER 8
100 X 120 CMS

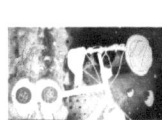
BICYCLE
60 X 100 CMS

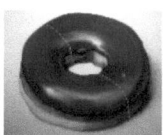
DONUT/ANT
80 X 100 CMS

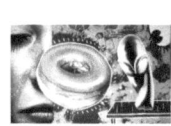
DONUT/BRANCUSI
90 X 140 CMS

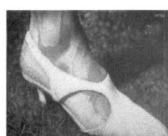
WHITE SHOE
100 X 120 CMS

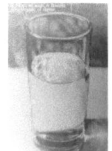
NOVIO
150 X 100 CMS

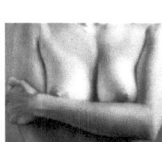
TORSO
100 X 120 CMS

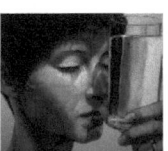
AGUA
150 X 160 CMS

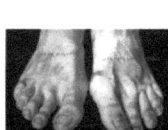
FEET
100 X 150 CMS

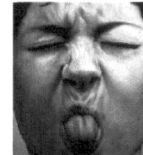
TANTRUM
120 X 100 CMS

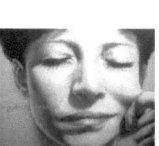
SLUMBER 9
120 X 150 CMS

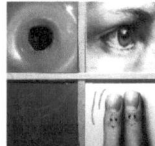
SEX 2
(POLYPTYCH,
50 X 50 CMS EACH)

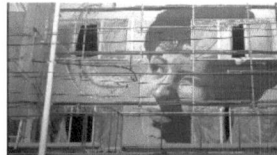
BANANA
MURAL (OSAKA, JAPAN)
10 X 14 MTS

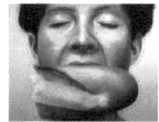
BAGUETTE
120 X 150 CMS

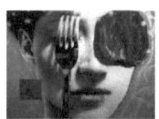
WINTER
120 X 150 CMS

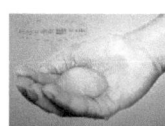
YOLK
120 X 150 CMS

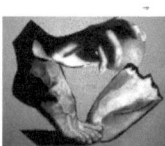
THREE
120 X 150 CMS

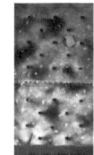
CRACKER
160 X 80 CMS

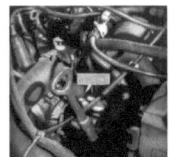
MOTOR
150 X 150 CMS

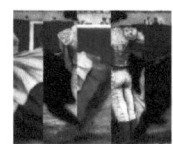
BIG TOROS
200 X 250 CMS

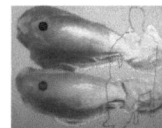
DRUMSTICKS
100 X 120 CMS

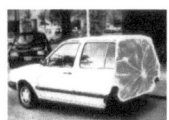
CAR-HAM
120 X 150 CMS

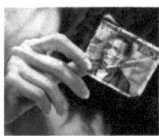
FIFTY
120 X 150 CMS

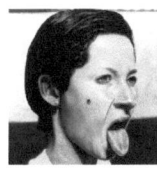
MYSTERIES
BIG HEAD
200 X 200 CMS

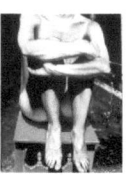
PINK CHAIR
200 X 150 CMS

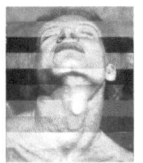
NECK
150 X 120 CMS

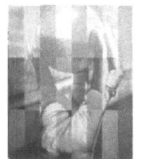
COLOR ATLAS
150 X 120 CMS

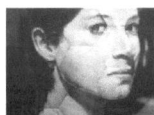
BLACK HEAD
120 X 150 CMS

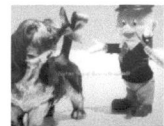
BLUE RIBBON
120 X 150 CMS

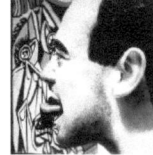
MYSTERIES
WEEPING WOMAN
150 X 150 CMS

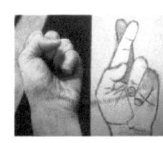
20 MINUTES
120 X 150 CMS

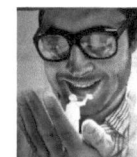
MYSTERIES
NOTIFICATION
150 X 120 CMS

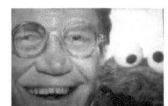
MYSTERIES
DAVE & COOKIE
110 X 160 CMS

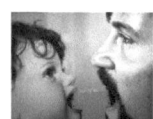
MYSTERIES
TWO MOUTHS
120 X 150 CMS

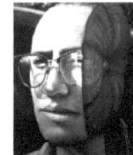
MYSTERIES
CUSHION-MAN
148 X 112 CMS

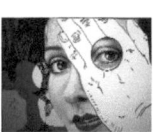
MYSTERIES
WHITE HAND
110 X 145 CMS

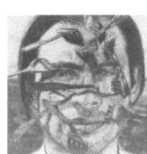
MYSTERIES
FORKS
150 X 150 CMS

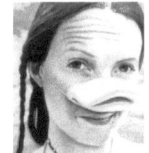
MYSTERIES
BAD DUCK
180 X 150 CMS

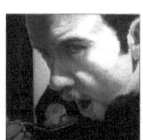
MYSTERIES
MONEY
160 X 160 CMS

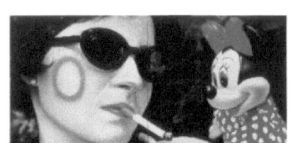
VICTIMS
DIALOGUE 1
(DIPTYCH, 160 X 160 CMS EACH)

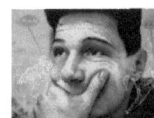
VICTIMS
DILEMMA
150 X 200 CMS

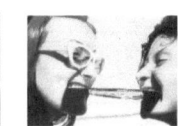
VICTIMS
RECORD
150 X 200 CMS

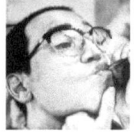
VICTIMS
LIPS
150 X 150 CMS

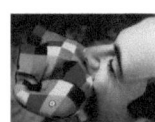
VICTIMS
BITE
130 X 170 CMS

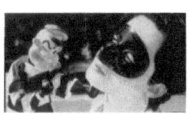
VICTIMS
DIALOGUE 2
150 X 270 CMS

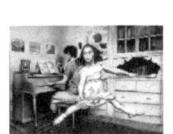
VICTIMS
LA DANCE
150 X 200 CMS

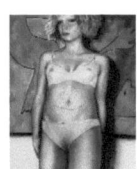
VICTIMS
THE SWIMMER
170 X 130 CMS

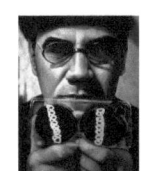
VICTIMS
CUPCAKES
170 X 130 CMS

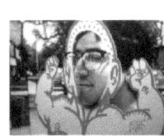
VICTIMS
STRONG MAN
150 X 200 CMS

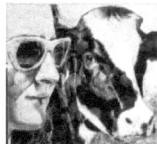
VICTIMS
NOSTALGIA
200 X 200 CMS

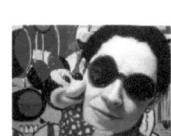
VICTIMS
DIALOGUE 3
150 X 200 CMS

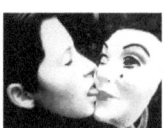
K SERIES
FRENCH KISS
150 X 200 CMS

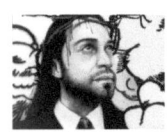
K SERIES
CLOUDS
150 X 200 CMS

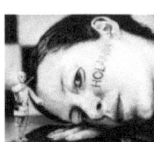
K SERIES
HOLANDA
150 X 150 CMS

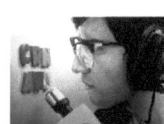
K SERIES
INTERVIEW
150 X 200 CMS

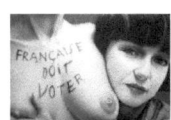
K SERIES
WOMEN
150 X 200 CMS

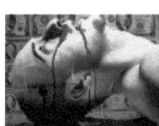
K SERIES
DEAD MAN
150 X 200 CMS

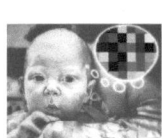
K SERIES
KID
150 X 200 CMS

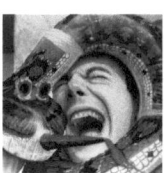
K SERIES
LAOCOÖNTE
200 X 200 CMS

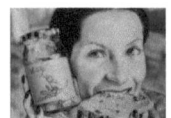
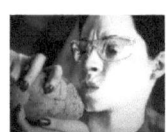
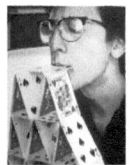
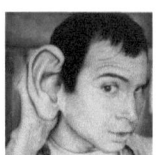
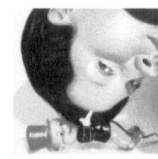
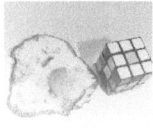
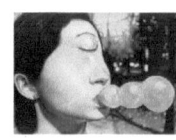

K SERIES
BIRD
150 X 200 CMS

K SERIES
BRAIN
150 X 200 CMS

K SERIES
CARDS
200 X 150 CMS

K SERIES
EAR
150 X 150 CMS

K SERIES
ATLAS
150 X 150 CMS

EGG / RUBIK
214 X 218 CMS

K SERIES
CYCLOPS
150 X 200 CMS

1997

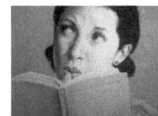
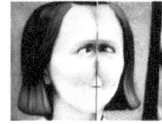
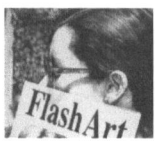
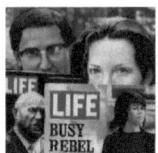
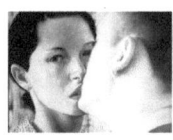
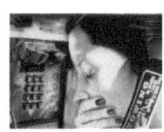
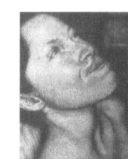

K SERIES
EAT-ME
150 X 200 CMS

K SERIES
MIRROR
150 X 200 CMS

K SERIES
FLASH-ART
150 X 170 CMS

K SERIES
FAMILY
200 X 200 CMS

K SERIES
LOVE
150 X 200 CMS

K SERIES
BAD NEWS
148 X 198 CMS

RED PAINTINGS
TRICK
198 X 148 CMS

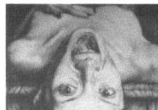
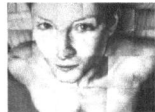
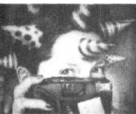
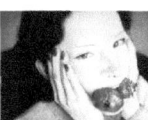
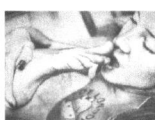
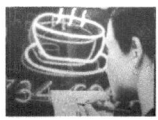
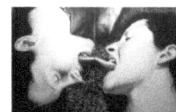

RED PAINTINGS
OPEN MOUTH
148 X 198 CMS

RED PAINTINGS
CLOSED MOUTH
148 X 198 CMS

RED PAINTINGS
YOU SUCK
148 X 198 CMS

K SERIES (PART 2)
STRAWBERRIES
148 X 198 CMS

RED PAINTINGS
FOOT
148 X 198 CMS

RED PAINTINGS
BOWL
148 X 198 CMS

K SERIES (PART 2)
TONGUE
148 X 296 CMS (DIPTYCH,
198 X 148 CMS EACH)

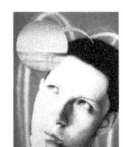
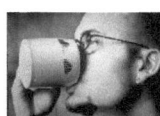
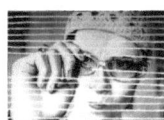
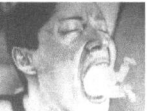
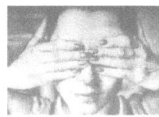
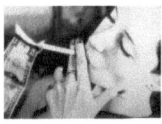
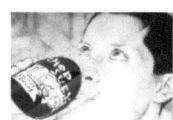

K SERIES (PART 2)
WATER
198 X 148 CMS

K SERIES (PART 2)
DAD
148 X 198 CMS

K SERIES (PART 2)
LINES
148 X 198 CMS

RED PAINTINGS
FAT GUY
148 X 198 CMS

RED PAINTINGS
BLIND
148 X 198 CMS

K SERIES (PART 2)
CIGARETTE
148 X 198 CMS

K SERIES (PART 2)
CHOP-SUEY
148 X 198 CMS

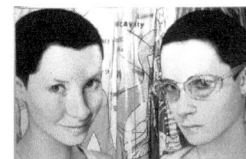
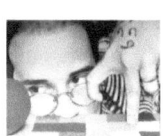
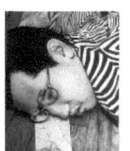
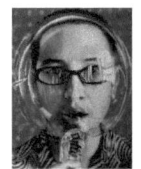
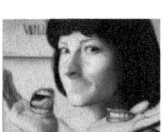
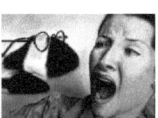

K SERIES (PART 2)
ANATOMY
198 X 296 CMS
(DIPTYCH, 198 X 148 CMS EACH)

K SERIES (PART 2)
ADAM
148 X 198 CMS

K SERIES (PART 2)
LAST DRAWING
198 X 148 CMS

K SERIES (PART 2)
IMPOTENCE
198 X 148 CMS

K SERIES (PART 2)
WILL
148 X 198 CMS

K SERIES (PART 2)
SOCK PUPPET
148 X 198 CMS

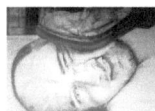
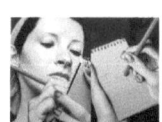
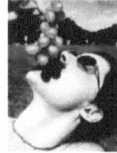
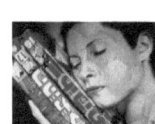
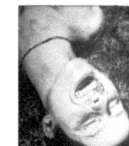
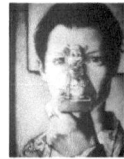
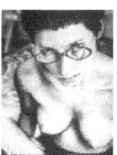

K SERIES (PART 2)
BOOT
148 X 198 CMS

K SERIES (PART 2)
PENCIL
148 X 198 CMS

K SERIES (PART 2)
LITERATURE
198 X 148 CMS

K SERIES (PART 2)
MANGA
148 X 198 CMS

RED PAINTINGS
SUN
198 X 148 CMS

RED PAINTINGS
MONKEY
198 X 148 CMS

RED PAINTINGS
DIARY
198 X 148 CMS

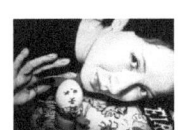
D SERIES
DATE
148 X 198 CMS

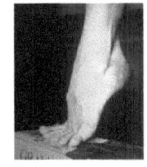
D SERIES
ANATOMY BOOK
180 X 150 CMS

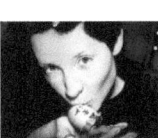
D SERIES
KISS
148 X 198 CMS

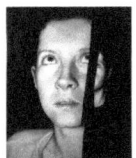
D SERIES
SPLIT
198 X 148 CMS

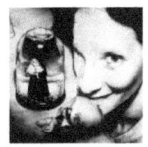
D SERIES
SCHOOL
150 X 150 CMS

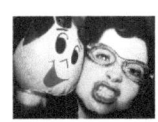
D SERIES
GIRLS
148 X 198 CMS

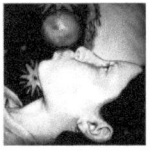
D SERIES
BUBBLE
148 X 148 CMS

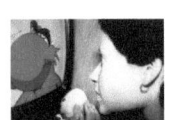
D SERIES
TV 2
148 X 198 CMS

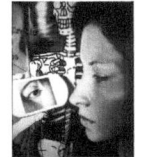
D SERIES
CLAVICLE
198 X 148 CMS

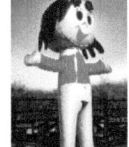
D SERIES
BIG GIRL
198 X 148 CMS

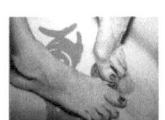
D SERIES
DRAIN
148 X 198 CMS

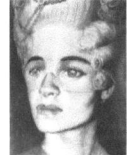
RED PAINTINGS
GRAND DAME
198 X 148 CMS

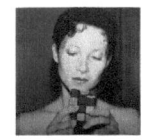
100 WATER
CUBE
228 X 228 CMS

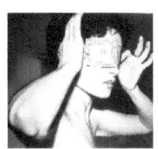
100 WATER
TWENTY
202 X 212 CMS

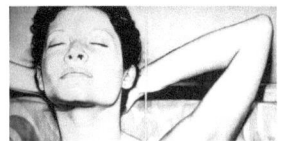
100 WATER
ARM
148 X 296 CMS
(DIPTYCH, 148 X 148 CMS EACH)

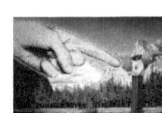
100 WATER
GOD
148 X 198 CMS

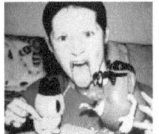
100 WATER
WAR
202 X 212 CMS

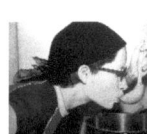
100 WATER
SOUP
172 X 202 CMS

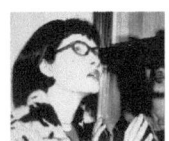
100 WATER
WINDOW
172 X 202 CMS

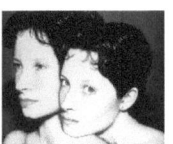
100 WATER
RED/BLUE
172 X 212 CMS

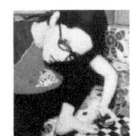
100 WATER
NAIL POLISH
202 X 172 CMS

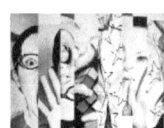
100 WATER
STARS
198 X 172 CMS

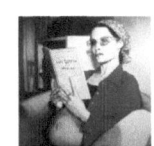
100 WATER
DON QUIJOTE
200 X 200 CMS

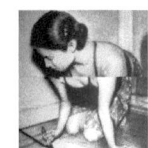
100 WATER
RED STRIPE
150 X 200 CMS

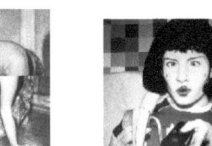
100 WATER
BANANA
172 X 198 CMS

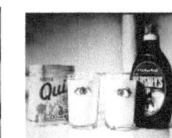
100 WATER
CHOICES
172 X 198 CMS

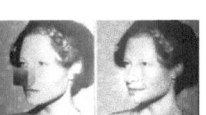
100 WATER
BEFORE/AFTER
150 X 300 CMS (DIPTYCH,
150 X 150 CMS EACH)

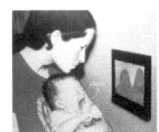
100 WATER
YAWN
198 X 228 CMS

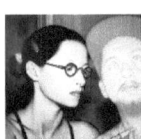
100 WATER
ROBOT
152 X 172 CMS

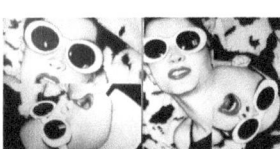
100 WATER
FASHION
148 X 296 CMS (DIPTYCH,
148 X 148 CMS EACH)

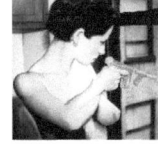
100 WATER
JFK
202 X 212 CMS

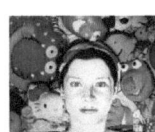
100 WATER
MODERN SEX
172 X 212 CMS

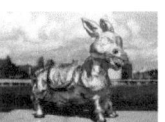
100 WATER
BURRO DE ORO
148 X 198 CMS

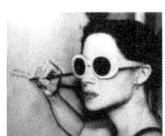
100 WATER
REBEL
152 X 172 CMS

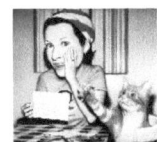
100 WATER
CAT ART
152 X 172 CMS

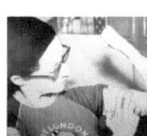
100 WATER
BICEPS
152 X 172 CMS

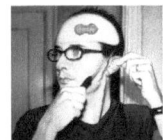
100 WATER
GOOD ARTIST
152 X 172 CMS

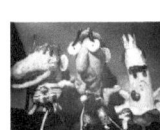
100 WATER
THREE ARTISTS
148 X 198 CMS

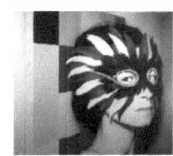
100 WATER
BLUE BIRD
148 X 198 CMS

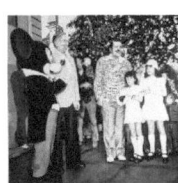
100 WATER
LIC. ALEMAN
198 X 198 CMS

1999

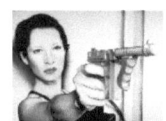
100 WATER
GREEN GUN
172 X 202 CMS

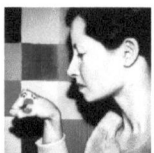
100 WATER
BEST FRIEND
148 X 148 CMS

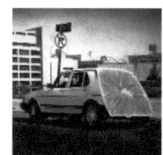
100 WATER
CAR-HAM 2
152 X 152 CMS

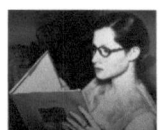
TOILET
ART BOOK
172 X 202 CMS

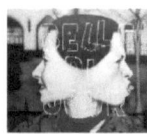
100 WATER
THEATER
172 X 202 CMS

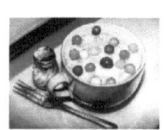
TOILET
COSMIC SOUP
148 X 198 CMS

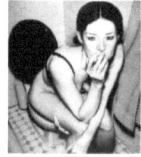
TOILET
TOILET 1
202 X 172 CMS

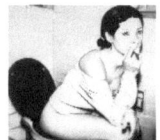
TOILET
TOILET 2
148 X 148 CMS

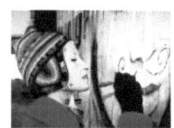
TOILET
VANDAL
148 X 198 CMS

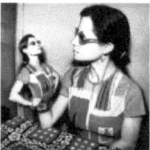
TOILET
DIALOGUE 4
198 X 198 CMS

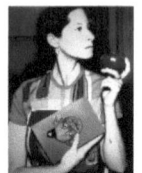
TOILET
CLASSICAL POSE
198 X 148 CMS

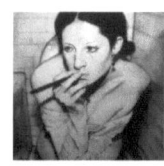
TOILET
TOILET 3
198 X 198 CMS

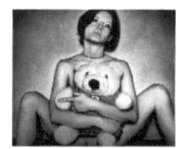
TOILET
CLASSICAL POSE 2
172 X 202 CMS

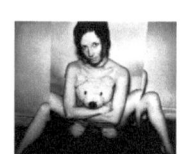
TOILET
CLASSICAL POSE 3
172 X 202 CMS

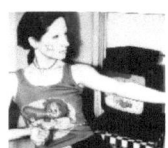
TOILET
KUNG-FU
172 X 202 CMS

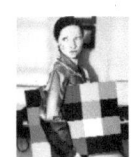
TOILET
ABSTRACT PAINTING
198 X 148 CMS

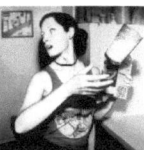
TOILET
ACCIDENT
198 X 198 CMS

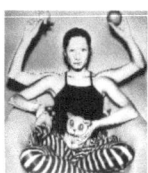
TOILET
FOUR ARMS
202 X 172 CMS

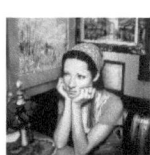
TOILET
CAFÉ
198 X 198 CMS

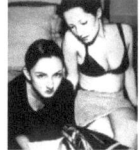
TOILET
TWO GIRLS
202 X 172 CMS

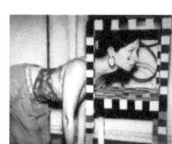
TOILET
CAGED LIONESS
172 X 202 CMS

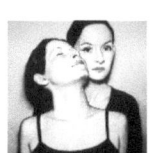
TOILET
TWO GIRLS 2
148 X 148 CMS

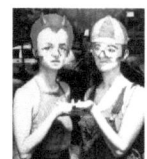
TOILET
DEVIL/BOY
202 X 172 CMS

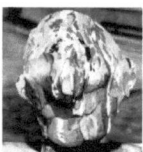
D SERIES (PART 2)
HEAD
148 X 148 CMS

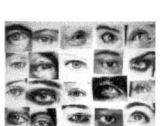
POWDERBOX
20 EYES
148 X 198 CMS

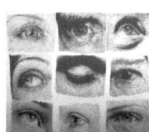
POWDERBOX
9 EYES
148 X 148 CMS

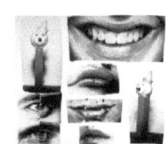
D SERIES (PART 2)
LONELY CLOWN
152 X 172 CMS

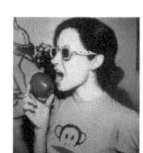
D SERIES (PART 2)
APPLE
202 X 172 CMS

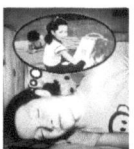
D SERIES (PART 2)
DREAM
202 X 172 CMS

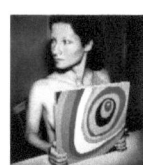
D SERIES (PART 2)
ABSTRACT
PAINTING 2
202 X 172 CMS

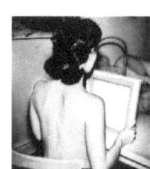
D SERIES (PART 2)
BACK
172 X 162 CMS

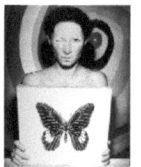
D SERIES (PART 2)
BUTTERFLY
202 X 172 CMS

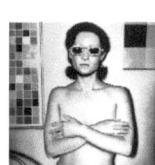
D SERIES (PART 2)
ART LOVER
172 X 162 CMS

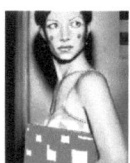
D SERIES (PART 2)
SMALL RED
PAINTING
24 X 18 CMS

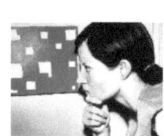
D SERIES (PART 2)
SMALL RED
PAINTING 2
18 X 24 CMS

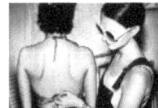
D SERIES (PART 2)
TWO DOLLARS
148 X 198 CMS

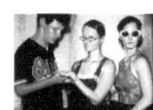
D SERIES (PART 2)
SMALL GYPSIES
45 X 60 CMS

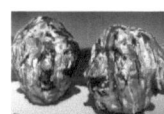
TWO HEADS
148 X 198 CMS

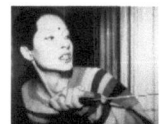
POWDERBOX
CRAZY BUDDHA
172 X 202 CMS

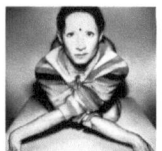
POWDERBOX
KAFKA
198 X 198 CMS

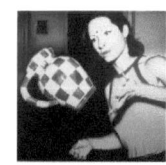
POWDERBOX
ACCIDENT 2
198 X 198 CMS

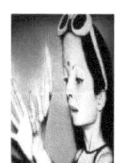
POWDERBOX
CATHEDRAL
228 X 172 CMS

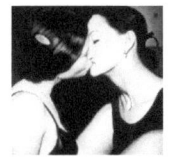

POWDERBOX
GIRL KISS
198 X 198 CMS

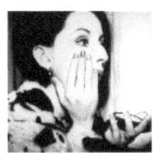

POWDERBOX
POWDERBOX
198 X 198 CMS

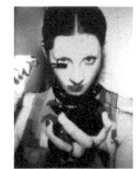

POWDERBOX
POWDERBOX 4
198 X 148 CMS

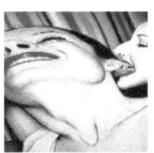

POWDERBOX
RED SMILE
148 X 148 CMS

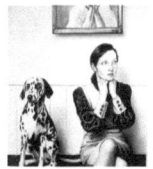

POWDERBOX
GIRL/DOG/
PAINTING
60 X 45 CMS

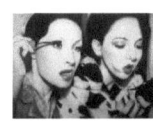

POWDERBOX
POWDERBOX 2
148 X 198 CMS

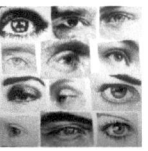

POWDERBOX
12 EYES
172 X 172 CMS

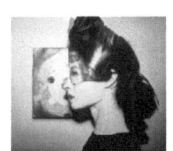

POWDERBOX
GRAND DAME 2
172 X 202 CMS

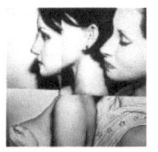

POWDERBOX
TWO GIRLS
148 X 148 CMS

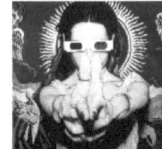

POWDERBOX
TWO METHODS
172 X 172 CMS

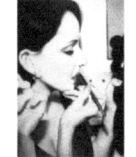

POWDERBOX
POWDERBOX 3
228 X 152 CMS

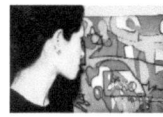

OUTSIDE
100 X 120 CMS

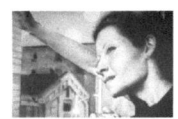

INSIDE
100 X 120 CMS

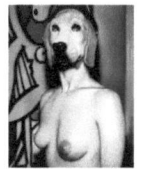

DOG GIRL
202 X 212 CMS

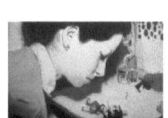

DONATELLO
152 X 228 CMS

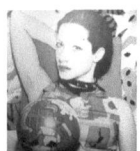

UP
GIRL WITH BALL
202 X 172 CMS

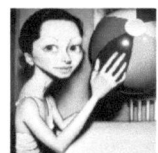

UP
GIRL WITH BALL 2
172 X 172 CMS

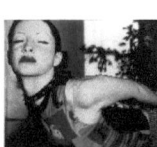

UP
MERMAID
172 X 202 CMS

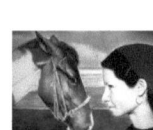

UP
DIALOGUE 5
148 X 198 CMS

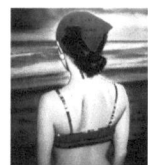

UP
MERMAID 2
172 X 162 CMS

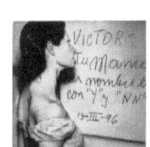

UP
DAD 2
148 X 148 CMS

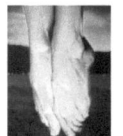

UP
UP
198 X 148 CMS

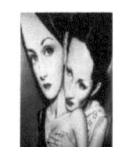

UP
TWO GIRLS 4
228 X 152 CMS

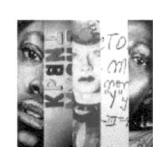

UP
KPBNT
198 X 198 CMS

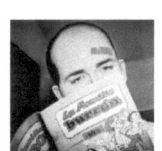

UP
READING
172 X 172 CMS

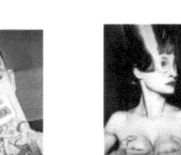

UP
GRAND DAME 3
212 X 148 CMS

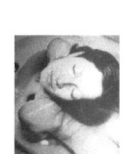

RED MERMAID
198 X 148 CMS

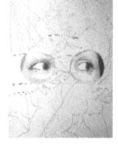

TWO EYES
198 X 148 CMS

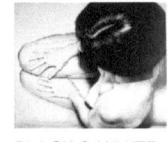

BLACK & WHITE
MERMAID
152 X 162 CMS

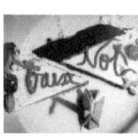

LA TOUR
TRUST NOT
172 X 198 CMS

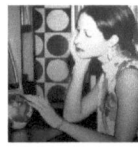

LA TOUR
MAGDALENE
198 X 198 CMS

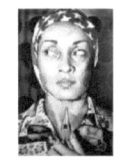

LA TOUR
GYPSY
228 X 148 CMS

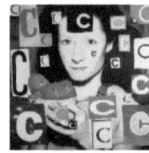

LA TOUR
TOMATOES
198 X 198 CMS

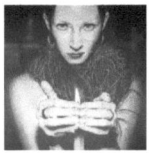

LA TOUR
RED CANDLE
172 X 162 CMS

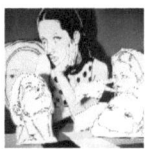

LA TOUR
CUT-OUTS
172 X 172 CMS

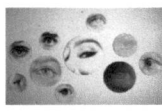

LA TOUR
10 EYES
(POLYPTYCH,
152 X 172 CMS
DIAMETERS 20-70 CMS)

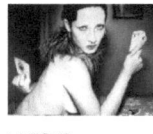

LA TOUR
THE CHEAT
148 X 198 CMS

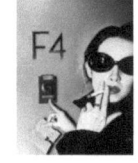

CINEMA NOTEBOOKS
F4
198 X 148 CMS

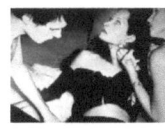

LA TOUR
3 PEOPLE
148 X 198 CMS

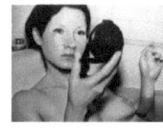

CINEMA NOTEBOOKS
POWDERBOX 5
148 X 198 CMS

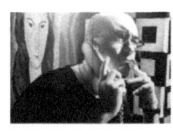

CINEMA NOTEBOOKS
PHONECALL
198 X 294 CMS
(DIPTYCH,
198 X 148 CMS EA)

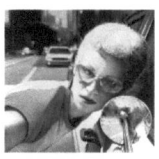

CINEMA NOTEBOOKS
BUBBLEGUM CAR
198 X 198 CMS

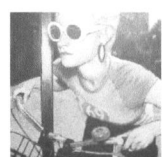

CINEMA NOTEBOOKS
BICYCLE THIEF
198 X 198 CMS

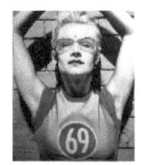

CINEMA NOTEBOOKS
YELLOW BUDDHA
202 X 172 CMS

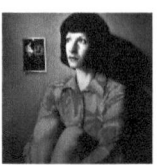

CINEMA NOTEBOOKS
BLUE MAGDALENE
202 X 202 CMS

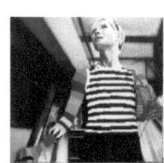

CINEMA NOTEBOOKS
DANTE'S STAIRS
202 X 212 CMS

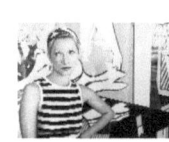

CINEMA NOTEBOOKS
TEN MINUTES
148 X 198 CMS

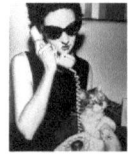

CINEMA NOTEBOOKS
PHONECALL 2
212 X 152 CMS

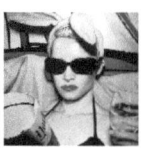

CINEMA NOTEBOOKS
BUNNY
202 X 202 CMS

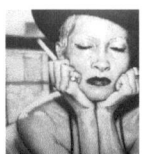

CINEMA NOTEBOOKS
THE OTHERS
172 X 162 CMS

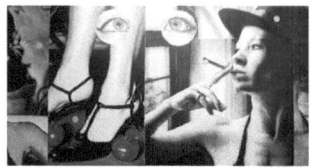

CINEMA NOTEBOOKS
SEPTEMBER
202 X 375 CMS (DIPTYCH,
202 X 202 CMS AND 202 X 172 CMS)

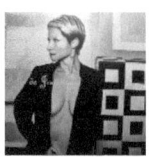

CINEMA NOTEBOOKS
BELLE DE JOUR
198 X 198 CMS

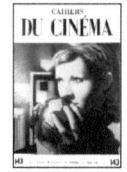

CINEMA
NOTEBOOKS
243 X 152 CMS

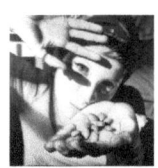

CINEMA NOTEBOOKS
BLUE PILLS
198 X 198 CMS

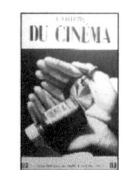

CINEMA
NOTEBOOKS 2
243 X 152 CMS

2002

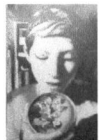

CINEMA NOTEBOOKS
SNOWBOX
243 X 152 CMS

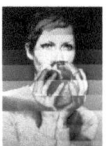

CINEMA NOTEBOOKS
SEPTEMBER 2
198 X 148 CMS

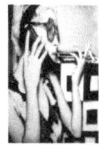

CINEMA NOTEBOOKS
PHONECALL 3
198 X 162 CMS

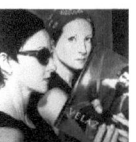

CINEMA NOTEBOOKS
DWARF
198 X 198 CMS

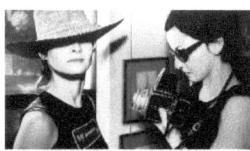

CINEMA NOTEBOOKS
BLOW-UP
198 X 345 CMS (DIPTYCH,
198 X 172 CMS EACH)

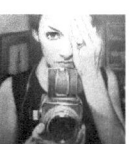

CINEMA NOTEBOOKS
BLUE BLOW-UP
198 X 198 CMS

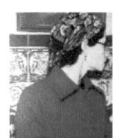

CINEMA NOTEBOOKS
RED BELLE
DE JOUR
198 X 148 CMS

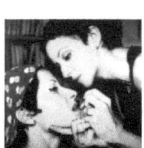

CINEMA NOTEBOOKS
LIPSTICK
202 X 202 CMS

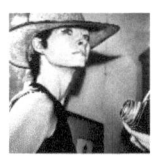

CINEMA NOTEBOOKS
B&W BLOW-UP
170 X 152 CMS

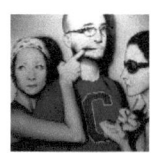

CINEMA NOTEBOOKS
GYPSIES 2
202 X 202 CMS

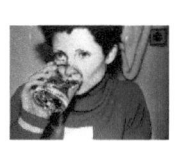

CINEMA NOTEBOOKS
GLASS OF WATER
172 X 202 CMS

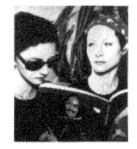

CINEMA NOTEBOOKS
DWARF 2
202 X 172 CMS

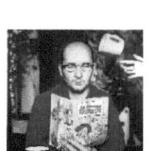

CINEMA NOTEBOOKS
ACCIDENT 3
198 X 198 CMS

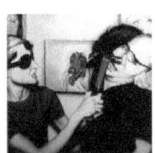

CINEMA NOTEBOOKS
ACCIDENT 4
198 X 198 CMS

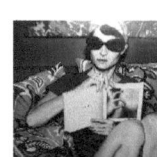

CINEMA NOTEBOOKS
PEZÓN
198 X 198 CMS

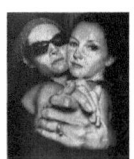

CINEMA NOTEBOOKS
RED TANGO
172 X 162 CMS

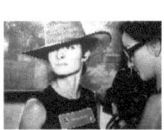

CINEMA NOTEBOOKS
RED BLOW-UP
152 X 214 CMS

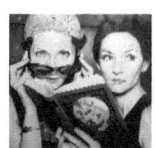

CINEMA NOTEBOOKS
TWO GIRLS 6
198 X 198 CMS

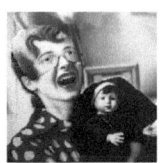

CIRCUSFUNK
CIRCUSFUNK
198 X 198 CMS

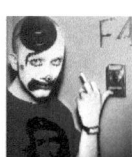

CIRCUSFUNK
F4 2
198 X 148 CMS

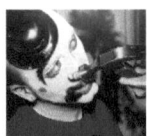

CIRCUSFUNK
SMALL CLOWN
WITH HAMMER
110 X 114 CMS

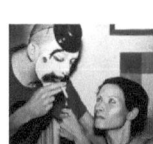

CIRCUSFUNK
GREAT ESCAPE
172 X 198 CMS

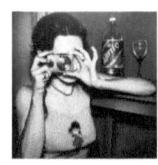

CIRCUSFUNK
TWO LEMONS
172 X 172 CMS

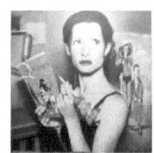

CIRCUSFUNK
WHITE PENCIL
198 X 198 CMS

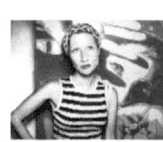

TEN MINUTES 2
148 X 198 CMS

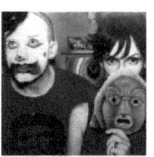

CIRCUSFUNK
CIRCUSFUNK 2
198 X 198 CMS

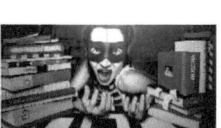

CIRCUSFUNK
BIG CIRCUSFUNK
198 X 396 CMS (DIPTYCH,
198 X 198 CMS EACH)

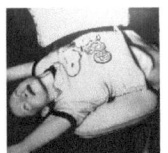

DE RIBERA
ST BARTHOLOMEW
198 X 198 CMS

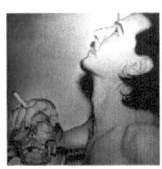

DE RIBERA
JUDAS
198 X 198 CMS

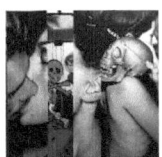

DE RIBERA
MAGDALENE 2
198 X 198 CMS

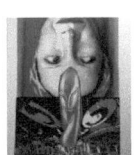

DE RIBERA
CALVARY
202 X 172 CMS

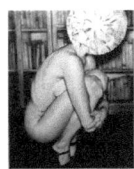

DE RIBERA
DIAMOND GIRL
172 X 162 CMS

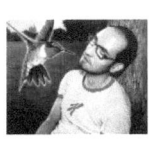

DE RIBERA
JACOB'S DREAM
172 X 202 CMS

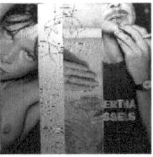

DE RIBERA
JUDAS 2
198 X 198 CMS

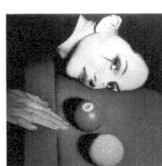

DE RIBERA
MAGDALENE 3
198 X 198 CMS

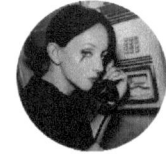

DE RIBERA
ROUND
MAGDALENE
110 CMS DIAMETER

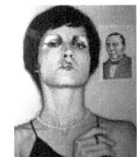

COLOR
BLACK
243 X 198 CMS

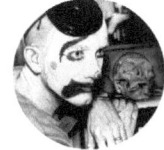

CIRCUSFUNK
ROUND CLOWN
WITH SKULL
110 CMS DIAMETER

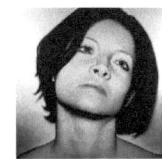

COLOR
SILVER
198 X 198 CMS

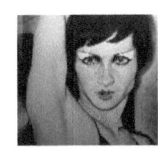

COLOR
GRAY
198 X 198 CMS

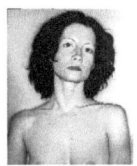

COLOR
WHITE
243 X 198 CMS

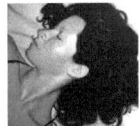

COLOR
GOLD
198 X 198 CMS

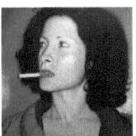

COLOR
PINK
198 X 198 CMS

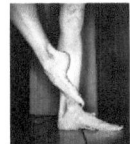

SAMSON
243 X 198 CMS

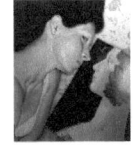

TIME
243 X 198 CMS

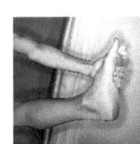

FEAR NOT
198 X 198 CMS

Victor Rodriguez | Mexico City, 1970 | Lives and works in Brooklyn, NY

SOLO EXHIBITIONS

2004 *1541*, Galeria Ramis Barquet, New York, NY USA | 2003 *José de Ribera Series*, Galería Fernando Pradilla, Madrid, Spain | 2002 *Cinema Notebooks*, Galeria Ramis Barquet, New York, NY, USA *Dos Años*, Galería Enrique Guerrero, Mexico City, Mexico *Phone Call*, Klaus Steinmetz Arte Contemporáneo, Escazú, Costa Rica *Glass of Water*, Momus Gallery, Atlanta, GA, USA *Snowbox*, ARCO '02, Madrid, Spain, Galeria Ramis Barquet, New York, NY, USA | 2001 *La Tour Series*, Galeria Mateo Sariel, Panama City, Panama | 2000 *UP*, Galeria Ramis Barquet, Monterrey, N.L., Mexico *Powder Box*, Marella Arte Contemporanea, Milano, Italy *l'Peintres Rouges*, Espace d'Art Yvonamor Palix, Paris, France | 1999 *Victor Rodriguez*, Galería Enrique Guerrero, Mexico City, Mexico *New Work*, David Klein Gallery, Birmingham, MI, USA *Sous La Grisaille de Mexico*, Espace d'Art Yvonamor Palix, Paris, France | 1998 *The D Series*, David Klein Gallery, Birmingham, MI, USA *Series R* Galeria Ramis Barquet, Monterrey, N.L., Mexico | 1997 *Victor Rodriguez*, OK Harris Gallery, New York, NY, USA

2004 *Prodigios de Fin de Siglo*, Museo de Arte Contemporáneo MARCO, Monterrey, Mexico | 2003 *Trans-Figuration*, Palazzo Mediceo, Seravezza, Italy *The Artist and His Model*, Scott White Contemporary Art, La Jolla, CA, USA *Paper Works*, Galeria Ramis Barquet, New York, NY, USA *Dubrow International*, Roger Smith Gallery, Kravets/Wehby, New York, NY, USA | 2002 *XI Bienal de Pintura Rufino Tamayo*, Museo Tamayo, Mexico City; Museo de Arte Contemporáneo de Oaxaca, Oaxaca, Oax., Mexico *Generazionale*, LAMeC, Basilica Palladiana, Vicenza, Italy *Photorealism Revisited*, Tucson Museum of Contemporary Art, Tucson, AZ, USA *MexArtFest*, Midome Art Center, Kyoto, Japan *Anécdotas*, Arte3, León, Gto., Mexico *En Centímteros*, Galeria Fernando Pradilla, Madrid, Spain *Arte de America Latina*, Galeria Lucia de la Puente, Lima, Peru | 2001 *VII Salón Bancomer*, Museo de Arte Moderno, Mexico City, Mexico *Denos una Mano*, Grupo de los 16, Ex Hacienda de los Morales, Mexico City, Mexico *Rotaciones XII*, Muca Roma, Mexico City, Mexico *26-36 Jóvenes Propuestas Contemporáneas*, Museo de la SHCP, Mexico City, Mexico *Ernesto Pujol, Marta María Pérez Bravo, Ray Smith, Victor Rodriguez*, Momus Gallery, Atlanta, GA, USA *Arte Mexicano Actual*, Instituto Cultural Mexicano, Washington D.C., USA *Flor y Canto*, Salt Lake City Museum of Art, Salt Lake City, UT, USA | 2000 *Paisaje Urbano*, Galería Enrique Guerrero, Mexico City, Mexico *El Poder de la Humanidad*, Mexican Cultural Institute, New York, NY, USA | 1999 *Picture This—New Contemporary Figuration*, Associated American Artists, NY, USA *Bajo la Grisalla de Mexico*, Capella de l'Antic Hospital, Barcelona, España *Sous la Grisaille de Mexico II*, Espace d'Art Yvonamor Palix/Passage de Retz, Paris, France *IV Bienal Monterrey*, Museo de Monterrey, Monterrey N.L., Mexico *Group Show*, Galeria Ramis Barquet, New York, NY, USA *Grupo de los 16*, Hacienda de los Morales, Mexico City, Mexico | 1998 *Summer Show*, SOMA Gallery, La Jolla, CA, USA *In the Nineties: A View*

of Contemporary Mexican Art, Instituto Cultural Mexicano, Washington D.C., USA |
1997 *An Assessment in Contemporary Figuration*, David Klein Gallery, Birmingham, MI,
USA *Faces and Figures*, Nassau County Museum, Long Island, NY, USA *New Artists from
the 90's*, Flint Institute of Contemporary Art, Flint, MI, USA *Triunfadores de la Bienal
Monterrey*, Museo de Monterrey, Monterrey, N.L., Mexico *III Bienal de Monterrey*,
Museo de Monterrey, Monterrey, N.L., Mexico *III Salón Bancomer*, Fundación Cultural
Bancomer, Mexico D.F., Mexico *I Concurso BID de Pintura Joven*, CentroCultural SHCP
(Secretaría de Hacienda y Crédito Público), Mexico City, Mexico, Pinacoteca de Nuevo
León, Monterrey, N.L., Mexico | 1996 *VII Osaka Triennale*, Mydone Osaka Museum,
Osaka, Japón *Creación en Movimiento*, Museo de Arte Contemporáneo Carrillo Gil,
Mexico D.F., Mexico *XVI Encuentro Nacional de Arte Joven*, Instituto Cultural de
Aguascalientes, Aguascalientes, Ags.; Pinacoteca de Nuevo León, Monterrey, N.L.;
Museo de Arte Contemporáneo Carrillo Gil, Mexico City, Mexico | 1995 *XV Encuentro
Nacional de Arte Joven*, Instituto Cultural de Aguascalientes, Aguascalientes, Ags.,
Pinacoteca de Nuevo León, Monterrey, N.L.; Museo de Arte Contemporáneo Carrillo
Gil, Mexico D.F., Mexico *Pinturerías, Arte Taurino*, Exposición Itinerante Museo de
Monterrey, Monterrey, N.L.; Instituto Cultural de Aguascalientes, Aguascalientes, Ags.,
Centro Cultural Tijuana, Tijuana, B.C.N.; Instituto Cultural Cabañas, Guadalajara, Jal.;
Museo de Arte de Querétaro, Querétaro, Qro., Mexico | 1994 *II Bienal de Monterrey*,
Museo de Monterrey, Monterrey, N.L., Mexico *Pinturerías*, Arte Taurino, Museo del
Palacio de Bellas Artes, Mexico D.F., Mexico *Japan Paintings*, Zero Gallery, Osaka,
Japón Mural on Abeno St., Abeno Soho Project, Osaka, Japan

2002 *XI Bienal de Pintura Rufino Tamayo*, Acquisition Prize, Museo Tamayo, Mexico City, Mexico | 2000 *Jóvenes Creadores Grant*, FONCA, Fondo Nacional para la cultura y las Artes, Mexico | 1997 *I Concurso BID de Pintura Joven*, Acquisition Prize, Centro Cultural SHCP, Mexico City, Mexico *III Bienal de Monterrey*, Honorific Mention, Museo de Monterrey, Monterrey, N.L., Mexico | 1996 *XIII Encuentro Nacional de Arte Joven*, Acquisition Prize, Mexico City, Mexico | 1994 *Jóvenes Creadores Grant*, FONCA, Fondo Nacional para la cultura y las Artes, Mexico

Victor Rodriguez: Paintings 95 / 05

First published by Jorge Pinto Books Inc. in November
2005 under the title: Victor Rodriguez: VICTOR RODRIGUEZ

All images 2005
©Victor Rodriguez

Text 2005
©Victor Rodriguez
©Ricardo Polhenz

All rights are reserved. This book may not be reproduced
in whole or in part, in any form (beyond copying permitted
by Sections 107 and 108 of the United States Copyright
Law, and except by reviewers for the public press), without
written permission by Jorge Pinto Books Inc. 212 East 57th
Street, New York, NY, USA

Published in 2007 by
Jorge Pinto Books Inc.
www.pintobooks.com

Design and typesetting: Susan Hildebrand
Print ISBN-10: 0-9774724-8-5
Print ISBN-13: 978-0-9774724-8-2

Library of Congress Cataloging –in– Publication Data

Victor Rodriguez
Art book. 10-year collection.

Jorge Pinto Books Inc. would like to thank Galería Ramis
Barquet. www.ramisbarquet.com

www.ingramcontent.com/pod-product-compliance
Lightning Source LLC
Chambersburg PA
CBHW050727180526
45159CB00003B/1149

* 9 7 8 0 9 7 7 4 7 2 4 8 2 *